D1808742

Shakespeare and the Politics of Nostalgia

RELATED TITLES

The Arden Introduction to Reading Shakespeare
Jeremy Lopez
ISBN 9781472581020

Performing Shakespeare's Women: Playing Dead
Paige Martin Reynolds
ISBN 9781350002593

*Playing Indoors: Staging Early Modern Drama in the Sam
Wanamaker Playhouse*
Will Tosh
ISBN 9781350109506

Shakespeare: Actors and Audiences
Fiona Banks
ISBN 9781474257930

Shakespeare and the Gods
Virginia Mason Vaughan
ISBN 9781474284271

Shakespeare's Pictures: Visual Objects in the Drama
Keir Elam
ISBN 9781350106109

Shakespeare and the Politics of Nostalgia

Negotiating the Memory of Elizabeth I on the Jacobean Stage

Yuichi Tsukada

THE ARDEN SHAKESPEARE

LONDON • NEW YORK • OXFORD • NEW DELHI • SYDNEY

THE ARDEN SHAKESPEARE
Bloomsbury Publishing Plc
50 Bedford Square, London, WC1B 3DP, UK
1385 Broadway, New York, NY 10018, USA

BLOOMSBURY, THE ARDEN SHAKESPEARE and the
Arden Shakespeare logo are trademarks of Bloomsbury Publishing Plc

First published in Great Britain 2019

Copyright © Yuichi Tsukada, 2019

Yuichi Tsukada has asserted his right under the Copyright, Designs and
Patents Act, 1988, to be identified as the author of this work.

For legal purposes the Acknowledgements on p. vi constitute
an extension of this copyright page.

Cover design by Stuart Cockburn
Cover image: *Portrait of Queen Elizabeth I* (Armada Portrait) by Marcus
Gheeraerts © Photo Josse/Leemage/Getty

All rights reserved. No part of this publication may be reproduced or
transmitted in any form or by any means, electronic or mechanical,
including photocopying, recording, or any information storage or retrieval
system, without prior permission in writing from the publishers.

Bloomsbury Publishing Plc does not have any control over, or
responsibility for, any third-party websites referred to or in this book.
All internet addresses given in this book were correct at the time of going
to press. The author and publisher regret any inconvenience caused if
addresses have changed or sites have ceased to exist, but can accept
no responsibility for any such changes.

A catalogue record for this book is available from the British Library.

A catalog record for this book is available from the Library of Congress.

ISBN: HB: 978-1-350-06722-6
        ePDF: 978-1-350-06724-0
        eBook: 978-1-350-06723-3

Typeset by Integra Software Services Pvt. Ltd.
Printed and bound in Great Britain

To find out more about our authors and books visit www.bloomsbury.com
and sign up for our newsletters.

CONTENTS

ACKNOWLEDGEMENTS

I would like to thank Gordon McMullan for all his support and encouragement and Martin Butler, Sarah Dustagheer, Helen Hackett, Lucy Munro and Ann Thompson for their invaluable comments on the earlier drafts of this book. Any faults that remain, however, are entirely my own. I am also grateful to Margaret Bartley, Lara Bateman and Mark Dudgeon at The Arden Shakespeare and to the anonymous readers who reviewed and offered insightful comments on my submission to the publisher. Shorter and earlier versions of Chapters 1 and 2 appeared in *Studies in English Literature*; some elements of the discussion in Chapter 3 appeared in my short essay collected in *Shakespeare and Theatre Culture* (Tokyo: Kenkyusha, 2012). I would like to thank the journal and the publisher for giving me the opportunities to test out my initial thoughts on Jacobean Shakespeare and for their permission to use substantially revised versions of my essays.

A NOTE ON TEXTS

Dates of first performance are provided in round brackets after each play is named. They are based on a variety of sources and these sources are discussed in the endnotes. Where no sources are mentioned, dates are taken from Alfred Harbage, *Annals of English Drama, 975–1700*, 3rd ed., rev. Samuel Schoenbaum and Sylvia Stoler Wagonheim (London: Routledge, 1989). Primary works have been quoted as they appear in the editions cited. When quoting directly from early modern texts, however, I have modernized the long *s* (ſ) throughout. All quotations from Shakespeare refer to the Arden Shakespeare Third Series editions.

Introduction

At the climax of William Shakespeare and John Fletcher's *Henry VIII* (1613), trumpets sound and a '*child richly habited in a mantle*' (5.4.0 SD) appears on stage. Under a canopy borne by four noblemen, the infant, who has just been christened, is carried by her godmother the Duchess of Norfolk. The train of noblemen and women '*pass once about the stage*' (5.4.0 SD) as if they intend to display the infant to the audience in the manner of a pageant. When the march is over, Garter delivers a speech, pronouncing, for the first time in the play, the name of the infant who is at the centre of this pageantry:

> GARTER
> Heaven, from thy endless goodness, send prosperous life, long and ever happy, to the high and mighty Princess of England, Elizabeth.
>
> (5.4.1–3)

Henry VIII then appears on stage and, as if to reconfirm the infant's identity for the audience, asks Thomas Cranmer to pronounce her name once again before blessing her:

> KING
>   What is her name?
> CRANMER   Elizabeth.
> KING   Stand up, lord.

> [*to the child*] With this kiss, take my blessing. God
>   protect thee,
> Into whose hand I give thy life.
> CRANMER   Amen.
>
> (5.4.9–11)

This scene has long been seen as a rare instance of Shakespeare's involvement in the commemoration of Elizabeth I, who died in 1603. Many studies in the past attempted to seek evidence of Shakespeare's connection with Elizabeth in those of his plays that were performed during her reign, often citing Oberon's reference to 'a fair vestal, throned by west' (2.1.158) in *A Midsummer Night's Dream* (1596) and the Chorus's address to 'our gracious Empress' (5.0.30) in *Henry V* (1599) as instances. Yet Elizabeth has been markedly absent from studies of Shakespeare's Jacobean plays. This may even be the case at this moment in *Henry VIII* since attribution studies suggest the final scene may have been written not by Shakespeare but by his collaborator Fletcher – but equally it can be argued that, since Shakespeare chose to collaborate on a play about the reign of Henry VIII that leads steadily to the baptism of Elizabeth, the play's political nostalgia can hardly be handed solely to the other half of the collaboration.[1] The Jacobean Shakespeare has been generally regarded as a playwright who, once the queen died, quickly shifted his attention to his new monarch and patron James I, composing plays that satisfied James's interests, for example, in his Scottish ancestry, witchcraft and Britain's Roman origin.

Indeed, Shakespeare did not publicly comment on the death of Elizabeth. Many poets composed elegies upon her death; as Henry Petowe puts it in his collection of elegies for Elizabeth, *Elizabetha Quasi Viuens* (1603), 'each modern Poet that can make a verse / Writes of *Eliza*, euen at their Muses birth'.[2] The public expectation for Shakespeare to react to Elizabeth's death was certainly high; *A Mournful Ditty Entitled Elizabeth's Loss* (1603), a single-sheet ballad, calls for Shakespeare to contribute to this national mourning:

You Poets all braue *Shakspeare, Iohnson, Greene,*
Bestow your time to write for Englands Quéene.
Lament, lament, &c.

Returne your songs and Sonnets and your sayes:
To set foorth swéete *Elizabeths* praise.
Lament, lament, &c.[3]

However, Shakespeare did not publish such an elegy. Henry
Chettle noted his silence and rebuked him in *Englands
Mourning Garment* (1603): 'Nor doth the siluer tongued
Melicert [Shakespeare], / Drop from his honied Muse one
sable teare / To mourne her death that graced his desert'.[4] In
fact, Shakespeare might have made one obscure reference to
Elizabeth in his Sonnet 107, which was published in 1609:

The mortal moon hath her eclipse endured,
And the sad augurs mock their own presage;
Uncertainties now crown themselves assured,
And peace proclaims olives of endless age.

Although it has been argued that the eclipsed moon refers
to the death of Elizabeth, the Jacobean dating of the sonnet
remains debatable.[5] Even if the 'mortal moon' does refer to
Elizabeth, the sonnet does not say anything meaningful about
Elizabeth or her reign. Shakespeare is not actually lamenting
the death of Elizabeth; he is merely referring to the transition
of time by using the language associated with Elizabeth's reign
('mortal moon') and James's ('peace'; 'olives'). Perhaps the fact
that Shakespeare did not eulogize Elizabeth and seemed to
distance himself from the dead queen has discouraged critics
from probing into Shakespeare's interaction with the memory
of Elizabeth and her reign. Shakespeare's Jacobean plays – with
the exception of *Henry VIII* and *Antony and Cleopatra* (as we
will see, Shakespeare's Cleopatra has been read, if uncritically
and inappropriately, as a personation of Elizabeth) – have not
been seen as related to the cultural phenomenon of nostalgia.

Shakespeare and the Politics of Nostalgia is the first book-length study that seeks to illuminate the relationship between Shakespeare's Jacobean drama and the phenomenon of nostalgia for Elizabeth in the specific political contexts of the first decade of the reign of James I. In this book, I will contest the premise that Shakespeare remained silent about Elizabeth in the first decade of James's reign. Although the memory of Elizabeth recurred in other forms of discourse throughout this period, his pre-1613 drama has not been sufficiently examined against this cultural undercurrent. I seek to redress this critical oversight by resituating four Shakespearean plays composed between 1606 and 1610 – *Macbeth*, *Antony and Cleopatra*, *Coriolanus* and *Cymbeline* – within the Jacobean discourse of nostalgia for Elizabeth, illustrating thereby Shakespeare's sustained interest in, and active engagement with, the cultural memory of Elizabeth.

I will argue that Shakespeare actively explored the politics of negotiating the memory of Elizabeth throughout these plays and that by the time Elizabeth appeared on stage in *Henry VIII* in 1613, Shakespeare had already been interacting with the discourse of Elizabeth for several years. Shakespeare probed deeply into the phenomenon of nostalgia for Elizabeth and, far from not involving himself in the phenomenon until his collaboration with Fletcher in 1613, closely examined the complex politics behind this phenomenon during the first decade of the Jacobean period. In fact, the representation of the infant Elizabeth in the final scene of *Henry VIII* should be re-read as the culmination of his continued engagement with the politics of nostalgia for Elizabeth.

The Jacobean politics of commemorating Elizabeth I

According to the traditional account of nostalgia for Elizabeth, when disillusionment and discontent with James and his policies intensified in the 1610s, many Jacobean Englishmen and women began to look back to the reign of his predecessor with a marked degree of wistfulness. Accordingly, the final scene of *Henry VIII* has been cited as the starting point of the revival of interest in Elizabeth on the Jacobean stage; the underlying assumption is that, after eulogizing Elizabeth for a brief nostalgic phase immediately after her death – a phase marked by the performances in 1604–6 of plays by Thomas Heywood and Thomas Dekker which feature Elizabeth as protagonists – Jacobean dramatists began to care less about the dead queen, and that nostalgia for Elizabeth did not significantly reappear on stage until 1613. While my analyses of Shakespeare's plays composed between 1606 and 1610 are aimed at highlighting the understudied history of the interaction between Jacobean theatre and the phenomenon of nostalgia during this period, it is certainly true that Elizabeth had not been personated on stage since the plays of Heywood and Dekker. However, during the first decade of James's reign, the retrospective discourse of Elizabeth assumed highly political significance, and Jacobean writers had to interact with the memory of Elizabeth in a more nuanced way as a result. As I wish to argue in this book, Shakespeare's plays were not so much making topical allusions to Elizabeth as examining the complex politics of commemorating her in the first decade of James's reign. How, then, did the memory of Elizabeth become such a political issue?

In 1603, Elizabeth I died and James VI of Scotland succeeded her as James I of England. A number of poems and pamphlets commemorating the death of Elizabeth were published in the same year. Although they begin on a sombre note, mourning the death of Elizabeth, nearly all of these texts end on a promising note; they praise James as the new king whom God has sent to the grief-stricken English people to make up for the loss of their dear queen. The ways English writers lament Elizabeth differ from writer to writer. Some commemorate Elizabeth as a peace-minded monarch, focusing on peace as her key monarchical achievement, while others commemorate her as a mighty Protestant monarch who courageously defended England from Catholic aggressions. Intriguingly, the ways these writers represent Elizabeth often reveal their expectations for their new sovereign.

In his elegy, *Elizaes Memoriall* (1603), Anthony Nixon commemorates the reign of Elizabeth as that of 'long and quiet peace': 'For such a peace before was neuer seene, / As we enioy'd vnder a Virgin-Queene'.[6] Similarly, the verse entitled 'Upon the Day of Our Queenes Death and Our Kings Proclamation', one of the elegiac verses printed in *Sorrowes Ioy* (1603), hails Elizabeth as 'the Queene of peace':

> Peace did her raigne begin, peace it maintaind,
> Peace gaue her leaue in peace hence to depart,
> Peace shee hath left behind; which no way staind
> With bloody warre reioyceth Englands heart:
> > Though we a king of peace haue in her stead,
> > Yet let vs mourne: The Queene of peace is dead.[7]

These writers were not the first to praise Elizabeth as the monarch who established 'such a peace before was neuer seene'. The revised edition of James's *Basilicon Doron* (1599) circulated in London upon Elizabeth's death. The book provided the English people with a timely opportunity to get to know their new monarch and the fact that several further printings appeared in 1603 indicates that it was widely read.[8] In his preface 'To the Readers', James praises Elizabeth – still living at the time of his writing – and compares her reign to that of Augustus Caesar, the Roman emperor whom James admired for establishing *Pax Romana*: Elizabeth 'hath so long with so great wisedome and felicitie gouerned her kingdomes, as (I must in trew sinceritie confesse) the like hath not been read nor heard of, either in our time, or since the dayes of the Romane Emperour Augustus'.[9] James's representation of Elizabeth as an Augustus-like ruler did not escape the attention of English readers; for example, in his elegiac verse for Elizabeth, John Fenton noted that 'at *Elizaes* prayse he [James] will not grutch, / Whose peacefull regiment (as his owne booke sayes) / Was neuer matched since *Augustus* dayes'.[10] These elegiac verses commemorating Elizabeth as the queen of peace effectively replicate James's view. In this regard, they can be read as panegyrics to their new sovereign – 'a king of peace' – who valued peace and praised Elizabeth's reign from that perspective. By representing Elizabeth as such, these writers were able to express their support for James and his preference for peace.

On the other hand, some writers attempted to provide counsel by praising not only James but also his predecessor, representing the latter as the vanguard of English Protestantism. In a verse printed in *Threno-Thriambeuticon* (1603), Samuel Hawarden asks James to 'break the dragon-like force of the pope', who 'contrive[s] against us poor folk', and to 'drive out the whirlwinds of the papists', emphasizing the constant threat the papists posed to the English people. Hawarden then harks back to James's predecessor, praising her as the 'holy Queen, who wished to banish the pope, / The auspicious Queen, who was able to banish the pope, / The loyal Queen, who was accustomed to banish the pope / From the borders of her realm'.[11] Whether or not Elizabeth was able successfully to eliminate the Pope's influence from England is debatable; in fact, James himself wrote in 1602 that he was surprised at 'the daily increase I hear of popery' in Elizabeth's England: 'so great flocks of Jesuits and priests … so proudly do use their functions through all the parts of England without any controlment or punishment these divers years past'.[12] Yet the historical accuracy of their representations of Elizabeth must have been the least concern for these writers of elegiac verses. In order to encourage James to be tough on the Pope and the papists, Hawarden found it useful to present his idealized image of Elizabeth so that James might see it as his model. Similarly, in *A Souldiers Wish vnto His Soveraigne Lord King Iames* (1603), Robert Pricket implores James to continue to fund the armed forces even in peacetime since England is surrounded by Catholic foes, asking him to maintain Elizabeth's legacy – 'A

fleet of ships, inricht with wars great thunder, / Whose force
hath causde earthes nations all to wonder, / That Nauie Royall,
the terror of Spaynes feare' – in order to defend England.[13] As
if encouraging James to do the same, Pricket commemorates
Elizabeth as the defender whom God had sent to protect
the English people from 'the Pope that Antichristian deuill',
reminding him that, with Elizabeth at the helm, 'no forrayne
foes could once her land inuade, / Proude Spaine to flie by
Englands force was made'.[14]

The memory of Elizabeth thus became a useful vehicle
immediately after her death for Englishmen and women
to express their ideas about Jacobean political issues. By
recalling Elizabeth and her reign as precedents, they were not
only able to lend authority to their thoughts but also able to
express them in public without sounding opposed to James
and his government since James himself respected Elizabeth
as his predecessor. Their representations of Elizabeth did
not necessarily reflect the reality of her reign; the memory of
Elizabeth was often adjusted and rewritten according to the
political messages the writer wished to convey. This practice
of appropriating the memory of Elizabeth did not end with
the elegiac publications of 1603; on the contrary, it began to
feature in various types of text and played an important role in
the formation of Jacobean political discourse.

Upon his accession, James implemented his foreign policy
in the face of opposition both from English aristocrats and
from public opinion. In August 1604, he concluded the
Treaty of London, a peace treaty which finally ended the
hostile relationship between England and Spain; James then
even began the negotiations for a Spanish match for Prince
Henry, a marriage alliance with the Catholic power which
James considered as an essential step in fulfilling his role
as European peacemaker.[15] Already in the first years of his
reign, however, muffled but distinctly dissentious voices
speaking against James's conciliatory stance were beginning
to be heard. One English courtier wrote that 'the Kingdom
generally wishes this peace broken, but *Jacobus Pacificus* I

believe will scarce incline to that side', while the Venetian ambassador similarly reported that James's peace policy 'little pleases many of his subjects'.[16] During the period when direct challenges to James's conciliatory stance were clearly risky, his disaffected English subjects resorted to alternative means to voice their opposition; they harked back to his predecessor as a hard-line Protestant monarch who (they insisted) courageously fought against Spain and the Roman Catholic Church, presenting her as the ideal on which the new king could have modelled himself. This image of Elizabeth, which was already popular during Elizabeth's reign, was significantly revived through the performance and printing of drama. Theatre was one discursive field where the conflicting voices of support for and disapproval of the king's conciliatory stance collided. Playwrights chose to avoid directly challenging the policies of the regime but, at the same time, they needed to provide plays that could appeal to London theatregoers, which included citizen audiences such as tradesmen and apprentices who were known for their anti-Catholic and anti-Spanish sentiments.[17]

The most influential play in this regard was Thomas Heywood's *If You Know Not Me, You Know Nobody, Part I* (1604), a play set in the reign of Mary Tudor.[18] Heywood's play is a dramatization of John Foxe's account of the life of Elizabeth under Mary's rule in his *Acts and Monuments* (1563) – also known as *The Book of Martyrs* – the Elizabethan bestseller whose second edition (1570) was ordered to be installed in every cathedral church in England together with the Bishop's Bible.[19] Just as she does in Foxe's account, Heywood's Princess Elizabeth greatly suffers under Catholic persecution for her Protestant faith; she is portrayed as a powerless and defenceless maid besieged by Mary's Catholic advisors who plot to eliminate her. Their persecution is so persistent and fierce that even her servant protests to her prosecutor: 'why doe you thus begirt, / A poor weake Lady, neere at poynt of death' (TLN 170–71).[20] While Elizabeth's vulnerability, helplessness and physical weakness are emphasized throughout, her faith never wavers and she is determined to die a Protestant martyr rather than submit to her half-sister ('A Virgine and a Martyr both I dy' [TLN 342]), aligning her fate with that of the executed Lady Jane Grey, another victim of Marian persecution. The beleaguered Elizabeth repeatedly declares that her fate is in the hands of God: 'They shalbe welcome; my god in whome I trust, / Will helpe, deliuer, saue, defend the iust' (TLN 357–58). Eventually, her ordeal ends with the death of Mary. Her deliverance from Catholic persecution and her subsequent accession to the English crown are presented as a divine sign that she and England are protected by God. Heywood's dramatization of Foxe's *Acts and Monuments* proved hugely popular and became a bestselling play text which was to be continuously reprinted throughout the Jacobean period.[21]

The Foxean representation of Elizabeth directly played into the debate about contemporary Jacobean politics. James's foreign policy towards Spain was coupled with his tolerant attitude to Catholics.[22] James styled himself a mediator among the religiously divided sects, as evidenced when he hosted the Hampton Court Conference in 1604. Although James publicly expressed his opposition to the Pope, James's religious policy was negatively viewed as too tolerant of Catholics by some of his English subjects. In this context, the Foxean representation of Elizabeth served as a focal point of opposition to James; by glorifying Elizabeth as a symbol of unwavering Protestantism, English writers were able to express dissatisfaction with James's religious stance and to encourage him to follow the example of Elizabeth and protect English Protestantism. In a 1604 foreword to William Perkins's *Hepieíkeia*, for example, William Crashawe represents Elizabeth as a pious Protestant queen and expresses his expectation for her male successor to take an equally firm or even firmer stance against England's Catholic foes:

Shee is dead, but her Heroicall zeale and loue to Religion is aliue; shee bequeathed it with her kingdome to his

Highnesse, who doubtlesse will make both her Religion, and her Kingdome, to flourish as much more, as a man doth excell a woman.[23]

In the theatre once more, Samuel Rowley's *When You See Me, You Know Me* (1604) also imagines Elizabeth as a guiding star of English Protestantism. The play is set in a religiously divided Tudor England under Henry VIII, an England which 'stands wauering in her Faith, / Betwixt the Papists and the Protestants' (TNL 1991–92) in the wake of the Reformation, featuring a range of historical events from the birth of Prince Edward and the death of Jane Seymour, to the failed attempt by Bonner and Gardiner to oust Catherine Parr, to the downfall of Cardinal Wolsey.[24] Although the young Princess Elizabeth does not appear on stage during the play, she assumes a key symbolic role when her letter addressed to her half-brother Prince Edward is read aloud. In her letter to Edward, who has begun to have misgivings about Protestantism, she counsels him to '*shun Idolatrie*' (TLN 2416) and to dedicate his prayers '*to God onely, for tis he alone / Can strengthen thee, and confound thine enimies*' (TLN 2412–13). Elizabeth's letter restores Edward's firm Protestant faith ('Thy lines shalbe my contemplations cures' [TLN 2421]) and inspires him to rescue Catherine Parr, his Protestant mother-in-law, from the persecution of Henry VIII's Catholic advisors. The play thus presents Elizabeth as a beacon for Protestant rulers and evokes contemporaries' expectation that the memory of Elizabeth would inspire James to adopt a firmer Protestant stance.

However uncomfortable James personally might have felt towards the glorification of English Protestantism, he did not treat it as a direct attack on his policy. As Curtis Perry points out, the glorification of Elizabeth as the paragon of a Protestant monarch did not explicitly work against James in the early years of his reign.[25] Although James showed considerable toleration towards Catholics, he also made it clear that Protestantism was the true religion. The representation of Elizabeth as a symbol and beacon of English Protestantism did not therefore contradict James's official self-stylization as Elizabeth's Protestant successor. Representing Elizabeth as the Protestant princess/queen with 'her Heroicall zeale and loue to Religion' was thus an effective means to present one's religious standpoint in opposition to James's conciliatory stance. Given the religious and political implication of the Foxean image of Elizabeth, it is no surprise that Heywood's play was marketed by the London publisher Nathaniel Butter, whose publications of sermons and religious writings between 1603 and 1606, as Teresa Grant puts it, 'show a fascination with anti-Catholic propaganda, including several works claiming to reveal (and revelling in) the "shocking" errors of the Catholic faith'.[26] As we will see, Butter subsequently published two more plays which directly feature Elizabeth; his involvement in the propagation of the representation of Elizabeth reveals the extent to which the image of Elizabeth was used in a political context and demonstrates that the image of Elizabeth played a key role in the articulation and formation of Jacobeans' responses to some of James's controversial policies.

Although idealized representations of Elizabeth did not explicitly challenge James's authority at the beginning of his reign, circumstances began to change when the representation of Elizabeth in a range of textual forms became more overtly anti-Catholic and, more worryingly for James's policies, specifically militant. The turning point was the failed Gunpowder Plot in November 1605, a Catholic plot which targeted James, his royal household and Parliament; the failed plot not only refuelled anti-Catholic sentiments among his people but also significantly influenced the way in which Elizabeth was represented in the nostalgic discourse. The failed Gunpowder Plot was paralleled with the failed invasion of the Spanish Armada in 1588.[27] In fact, as John Watkins's study has convincingly shown, 'the governing elite used the Plot to seal James's identity as a second Elizabeth protected by God against papist intrigue' by emphasizing this parallel.[28] It was not only the governing elite but also poets and dramatists who made the comparison. While James attempted to evoke Elizabeth as God's protected monarch and to align himself with that image, these writers went further; after the Gunpowder Plot, they were apparently less hesitant to represent Elizabeth as the embattled warlike queen who courageously defended England from Catholic Spain, reimagining Elizabeth's reign as the militant age.

The two plays published by Butter after the Plot in 1606–7 specifically associate the image of Elizabeth with the victory over the Armada – Heywood's *If You Know Not Me, You Know Nobody, Part II* (1605) and Dekker's *The Whore of Babylon* (1606). Although the first performance of Heywood's *Part II* took place in 1605, possibly before 5 November, it has been argued that the failed Gunpowder Plot influenced the play text published in 1606.[29] *Part II* is a London city comedy which features Thomas Gresham, a merchant and a benefactor to the city, and his founding of the Royal Exchange; in much of the play, Elizabeth is represented as an accessible and down-to-earth queen, communicating directly with the London citizens. Yet the play abruptly changes gear in the final scene, which could possibly have been added to the main plot after 5 November.[30] In the final scene set in Tilbury, Elizabeth awaits the arrival of the Armada. In the face of the Armada invasion, she is shown to take a military initiative:

QUEEN
    Our Armies royall so be equall our hearts,
    For with the meanest heere ile spend my blood,
    And so to loose it count my onely good.
    A March, lead on: wee'le meet the worst can fall,
    A mayden Queene will be your Generall.
                    (TLN 2635–39)[31]

She is represented as the strong leader of the English troops. This image of Elizabeth as a military leader markedly contrasts with the powerless, victimized Princess Elizabeth in *Part I*, who passively endures Catholic persecution and never fights back, or with the amicable and wise Elizabeth beloved by the London citizens as represented in the earlier scenes of *Part II*.

The Whore of Babylon represents an even more elaborate image of the warlike queen. The Whore of Babylon, an allegorical representation of depraved Catholic Rome, attempts to destroy Fairy Land (England) with the mighty Armada; Dekker personates Elizabeth in the figure of the fairy queen Titania, who readies her countrymen for the attack on her kingdom and confidently styles herself their military leader:

TITANIA
   Trust me, I like the martiall life so well,
   I could change Courts to campes, in fieldes to dwell.
   Tis a braue life: Me thinkes it best becomes
   A Prince to march thus, betweene guns and drummes.
   My fellow souldiers I dare sware youl'e fight,
   To the last man, your Captaine being in sight.
   …
   We come with yours to venture our owne bloud.
   For you and we are fellowes.

                                           $(5.6.8–20)^{32}$

When her subject worryingly asks whether the sound of guns will not offend her, Titania/Elizabeth brushes him aside: 'How? we are tried, / Wh'im'e borne a souldier by the fathers side. / The Cannon (thunders Zany) playes to vs' (5.6.24–26). She even boasts of the masculine spirit she has inherited from her royal father Oberon – glossed by Dekker as Henry VIII. The play ends with Titania/Elizabeth's defeat of the invading Armada, celebrating the victory of English Protestantism over Roman Catholicism.

Nostalgia for the warlike queen was certainly a worrying trend for James, who, though he took a firmer stance on English Catholics in response to the Plot, still pursued his conciliatory foreign policy. Dekker's play, for example, openly expresses the hope that James will follow the course of the militant queen; one of the characters prophesies that, when Titania/Elizabeth dies, an even mightier monarch would inherit her throne and bring destruction to Catholic Rome:

> FIRST CARDINAL
> Say that *Titania* were now drawing short breath,
> (As that's the Cone and Button that together
> Claspes all our hopes) out of her ashes may
> A second Phoenix rise, of larger wing,
> Of stronger talent, of more dreadfull beake,
> Who swooping through the ayre, may with his beating
> So well commaund the winds, that all those trees
> Where sit birds of our hatching (now fled thither)
> Will tremble, and (through feare struck dead) to earth,
> Throw those that sit and sing there, or in flockes
> Driue them from thence, yea and perhaps his talent
> May be so bonie and so large of gripe,
> That it may shake all *Babilon*.
>
> (3.1.232–44)

The representation of the warlike queen was unsettling for James as it could be seen as an unwanted intervention in his foreign policy – what he perceived as his untouchable royal prerogative. In fact, for the aristocracy, a warlike queen was already perceived as an allegory of opposition to James; for example, Queen Anne, who patronized dissentious militant Protestant courtiers, specifically chose to play the role of Pallas Athena, the goddess of war, in *The Vision of the Twelve Goddesses* – the 1604 masque she commissioned Samuel Daniel to write – styling herself the second Elizabeth.[33] The Gunpowder Plot brought the potentially unsettling image of the warlike queen shared within the court into the public arena, unleashing nostalgia for Elizabethan militarism in the public imagination.

After Dekker's play, Elizabeth was not directly personated on the Jacobean stage until 1613. It has been speculated that Heywood's two-part dramatization of Elizabeth's life was so commercially successful, becoming the definitive stage

adaptation of the history of Elizabethan England, that no
other playwright dared to compete with his plays.[34] However,
given that popular characters were repeatedly represented
on stage during the early modern period – Cleopatra, for
example, featured in the plays of Samuel Daniel, Mary Sidney,
Shakespeare and John Fletcher – the success of Heywood's
two-part drama would not explain why Elizabeth no longer
featured in new plays after 1606. In fact, it is more plausible
that the memory of Elizabeth became so immediate to
Jacobean political contexts that playwrights avoided directly
personating her on stage. Indeed, George Chapman's direct
presentation of Elizabeth as a speaking character in *The
Conspiracy and Tragedy of Charles Duke of Byron* (1608)
was censored and removed from the play text; the censored
text indicates that the original scene where the eponymous
protagonist visits Elizabeth's court and converses with the
queen was replaced by the indirect report of the messenger
who recounts Elizabeth's reception of Byron.[35] A brief look
at the practice of censorship shows the extent to which
playwrights needed to be aware that characters and events in
Jacobean drama were vulnerable to interpretation as bearing a
direct relation to contemporary political issues. As Janet Clare
notes, the interventions of the authorities in performances of
Sejanus (1603), *Philotas* (1604), *Eastward Ho* (1605) and *The
Conspiracy and Tragedy of Charles Duke of Byron* illustrate
'the continual difficulty of handling political material which
was vulnerable to factional interpretation'.[36] Ben Jonson
and John Marston were both questioned by the authorities
wishing to know whether or not their allegedly sympathetic
representations of the protagonists, Sejanus and Philotas,
were meant to glorify the memory of the Earl of Essex. As
will be discussed in Chapter 3, glorifying Essex was perceived
by the authorities as politically unsettling under James. Just as
it was dangerous to associate one's work with the late Essex,
then, so too, I would suggest, it became politically risky for
playwrights to directly represent Elizabeth on the Jacobean
stage.

The memory of Elizabeth, however, never exited the Jacobean stage. It was not only through the dramatization of Elizabeth's life that theatre created politically charged representations of female leaders, such as embattled warlike queens. For example, Barnabe Barnes's *The Devil's Charter* (1607), an ostensibly anti-Catholic play which details the corruption of Rome, features the siege of the Amazonian town by Caesar Borgias, the leader of the Roman army. Determined to be killed in battle rather than submit to the Romans, the Amazonian Queen Katherine rallies her tribe and fights against the invaders. Although the Roman army eventually overwhelms her, the embattled warlike queen fights courageously to defend her people. Even Caesar Borgias, her victorious enemy, praises the 'couragious' warlike queen as the 'wonder of thy sex, / The Grace of all *Italian* womanhood'.[37] *The Devil's Charter* has been read as a post-Gunpowder Plot play as it expresses strong anti-Catholic sentiments.[38] However, what aligns this play with other post-Gunpowder Plot plays is not only its anti-Catholic tenor but also its representation of the embattled warlike queen – a symbol of resilience and the ideal model of female leader – which evokes the representation of the warlike Elizabeth, defending her country from the Armada attack. Playwrights were thus able to interact with the discourse of nostalgia for Elizabeth without having to represent her directly on stage. As Catherine Loomis puts it, 'closer examinations of Elizabeth's character were accomplished by creating dramatic substitutes who displayed some but not all of her attributes'.[39] Women who are turned into crowned effigies, warlike female leaders and besieged virgins were all, as I wish to show, part of the ongoing practice of constructing, adjusting and appropriating the memory of Elizabeth. The cultural and political negotiation of the memory of Elizabeth continued on the Jacobean stage. Shakespeare's plays were not exceptions; in the same year as the first performance of *The Devil's Charter*, for example, Shakespeare also presented an image – an equivocal one, admittedly – of a warlike queen in the figure of Cleopatra, who insists on appearing on the battlefield to defend her beleaguered kingdom. As will be discussed in the following chapters, Shakespeare interacts with the discourse of nostalgia for Elizabeth and illuminates the politics of representing Elizabeth.

When Elizabeth reappeared on stage as a character at the end of the first decade of the Jacobean period, what was enacted on stage was not a simple glorification of the memory of Elizabeth and her reign, as one might expect, but a complex politics of cultural negotiation. After the king blesses his child in the final scene of *Henry VIII*, Cranmer delivers a prophetic speech about Elizabeth and her successor James. Cranmer begins his laudatory account of Elizabeth by praising her 'wisdom and fair virtue' (5.4.24) and then shifts his focus to her Protestantism, describing her as the staunch Protestant queen who will be feared by her enemies:

CRANMER
                    Truth shall nurse her;
    Holy and heavenly thoughts still counsel her.
    She shall be loved and feared: her own shall bless her;
    Her foes shake like a field of beaten corn,
    And hang their heads with sorrow.
                                        (5.4.28–32)

Elizabeth is represented as the child of 'Truth' – as Gordon McMullan puts it, 'a distinctly Protestant personification' – and a terror to her foes who, in this context, clearly refer to the Catholic enemies of England.[40] Cranmer's description of Elizabeth closely echoes the hard-line Protestant view of Elizabeth as illustrated, for example, in William Leigh's collection of sermons, *Queene Elizabeth, Paraleld in Her Princely Vertues, with Dauid, Iosua, and Hezekia* (1612), in which Leigh exalts her uncompromising stance towards her Catholic foes, praising her for providing 'a guard of comfort to her neighbour-bordering friendes, and a terror to her frowning enemies'.[41]

If Cranmer had ended his speech at this point, the representation of the infant Elizabeth in *Henry VIII* could be simply seen as part of the common practice of commemorating Elizabeth as the unwavering defender of English Protestantism. In this particular instance, this representation could be associated with the surge of nostalgic sentiment in 1612–13 that attended the marriage of Princess Elizabeth Stuart (James's daughter) with Frederick V, Elector Palatine, a militant prince and leader of the Protestant cause in Europe; writers hailed her as the incarnation of her godmother and namesake Queen Elizabeth, evoking the latter as a guiding spirit of English Protestantism.[42] In *Henry VIII*, however, Cranmer goes on to complicate his account of Elizabeth's reign by representing her as the precursor of Jacobean peace:

CRANMER
In her days, every man shall eat in safety
Under his own vine what he plants, and sing
The merry songs of peace to all his neighbours.

(5.4.33–35)

This image of peace specifically derives from passages in the Bible which were often associated with James's political stance.[43] Cranmer's representation of Elizabeth cannot be simply categorized as a militant Protestant representation of Elizabeth as the terror and scourge of Catholics. Nor can it solely be identified with the pro-James representation of Elizabeth as the queen of peace. Compared to the representations of Elizabeth in early Jacobean drama, the representation of Elizabeth in *Henry VIII* is thus complex and multifaceted.

What made the memory of Elizabeth so complex even while Elizabeth herself was not directly represented on stage? What was the significance of representing Elizabeth by way of a baby doll when playwrights finally decided to bring her back to the theatre? The key to these questions, I wish to argue, lies in the plays Shakespeare authored in the first decade of the Jacobean period.

Shakespeare and the Politics of Nostalgia

Scholars have attempted to illustrate the vibrant interaction between Jacobean theatre and Jacobean politics through examinations of the ways in which political issues are represented in theatrical texts. A limited number of studies of Jacobean drama, however, have taken the discourse of nostalgia for Elizabeth as their main focus, and the majority of these studies feature civic pageants, the masques of Samuel Daniel and Ben Jonson and only a small number of Jacobean plays – in most cases, these are Heywood's two-part drama *If You Know Not Me, You Know Nobody*, Dekker's *The Whore of Babylon* and Shakespeare and Fletcher's *Henry VIII* – a set of texts that was examined in Anne Barton's 'Harking Back to Elizabeth: Ben Jonson and Caroline Nostalgia' (1981), one of the first influential essays on nostalgia for Elizabeth. Although there are a few important precursors to my study of Jacobean theatrical nostalgia for Elizabeth – most notably, Curtis Perry's *The Making of Jacobean Culture: James I and the Renegotiation of Elizabethan Literary Practice* (1997), John Watkins's *Representing Elizabeth in Stuart England: Literature, History, Sovereignty* (2002) and Catherine Loomis's *The Death of Elizabeth I: Remembering and Reconstructing the Virgin Queen* (2010) – these studies of the posthumous representation of Elizabeth mainly focus on non-Shakespearean drama such as the plays of Heywood and Dekker I have listed above, and my approach to, and readings of, the representation of Elizabeth differ from them on many points. While there have been specialized studies of particular plays in relation to the cultural memory of Elizabeth, studies to which I will refer in the course of my analysis, no single book has explored the posthumous representation of Elizabeth in a variety of ways with a sustained interest in Shakespeare's drama. This book, then, attempts to fill this critical vacuum by directly addressing Shakespeare's interaction with the retrospective discourse of Elizabeth in the first decade of James's reign.

The following chapters examine Shakespeare's *Macbeth*, *Antony and Cleopatra*, *Coriolanus* and *Cymbeline*, illustrating their close interactions with the retrospective discourse of Elizabeth in the first decade of James's reign. Each chapter focuses on one play, featuring a specific aspect of the Jacobean representation of Elizabeth. I analyse the politics of representing a diseased body politic (Chapter 1), a warlike queen (Chapter 2), a peace goddess (Chapter 3) and an imperilled princess (Chapter 4), illustrating the ways in which these representations – marked by complex and often contradictory perspectives – engaged with the struggle for control of the memory of Elizabeth and both reflected and informed the complexity of contemporary political culture.

Except for *Antony and Cleopatra*, these plays have not generally been read in the context of nostalgia for Elizabeth. This book, therefore, aims to offer fresh insights into aspects of the plays that can be seen to be particularly Jacobean – for example, the unnoticed political significance of the two contentious prophecies in *Macbeth* or that of the seemingly out-of-place triumphal procession in *Coriolanus*, neither of which has featured adequately in Shakespearean studies. Although Shakespeare's texts are central to my investigation, I will also examine a range of texts that express the discourse of Elizabeth – in particular, poems and plays by Shakespeare's contemporaries – since Jacobean readers and audiences encountered the discourse of Elizabeth not only through Shakespeare's drama but also through bestselling books, including frequently reprinted play texts of his contemporaries. In this book, I will focus on the specific representations of Elizabeth which these sources popularized: the representation of Elizabeth as a besieged, pious princess and the representation of Elizabeth as a commanding mistress/mother to her militant knights and defender of her besieged kingdom. These images were popularized by hugely influential bestsellers such as Foxe's *Acts and Monuments* and Heywood's two-part drama *If You Know Not Me, You Know Nobody*, both of which were widely available during the Jacobean period. This popular discourse of Elizabeth is crucial to understanding Shakespeare's engagement with the phenomenon of nostalgia since Shakespeare interacted with the ongoing cultural negotiation of her memory by variously responding to these popularized images of Elizabeth.

The two images are seemingly poles apart; one is passive and weak, while the other is authoritative and militant. However, they are in fact closely connected by and built upon the most common perception of Elizabeth as England's body politic. The Elizabethans cast their vision of the well-defended state in Elizabeth's image by identifying England with her impregnable body, and the Jacobeans continued to do so even under the rule of a male monarch. Both versions of Elizabeth – the vulnerable, pious princess and the commanding mother – evoked the recent memory of Elizabethan England threatened by Catholic powers. The Elizabethan trope identifying Elizabeth's body natural with England's body politic is at the heart of a variety of posthumous images of Elizabeth. For this reason, I begin this book by analysing the way in which Shakespeare explores Jacobeans' deployment of the Elizabethan trope of the queen's two bodies in Chapter 1 and then probe into the ways in which Shakespeare engages with the popularized representations of Elizabeth in the subsequent three chapters.

Shakespeare's Jacobean plays from *Macbeth* to *Cymbeline* dramatically illustrate the ways in which the memory of Elizabeth played a key part in the formation of Jacobean discourse and in which attempts to appropriate the memory of Elizabeth often created competition over the authoring of her images among the Jacobeans. These chapters illustrate both the sustained textual and dramatic culture of nostalgia for Elizabeth and the extent to which that culture of nostalgia remained a focus for ideological negotiation and competition throughout the first decade of James's reign. Theatrical memorialization of Elizabeth, I wish to show, was a contested ideological field under James and offers an ideal test case for rethinking Shakespeare's interaction with contemporary political culture.

Notes

1 For Fletcher's authorship of Cranmer's speech, see esp. Jonathan Hope, *The Authorship of Shakespeare's Plays: A Socio-Linguistic Study* (Cambridge: Cambridge University Press, 1994), 67–83, 150 and Brian Vickers, *Shakespeare, Co-Author: A Historical Study of Five Collaborative Plays* (Oxford: Oxford University Press, 2004), 333–402 (esp. 384), 480–91 (esp. 489).

2 Henry Petowe, *Elizabetha Quasi Viuens* (London, 1603), A3v.

3 *A Mournefull Dittie, Entituled Elizabeths Losse* (London, 1603), 1.

4 Henry Chettle, *Englands Mourning Garment* (London, 1603), D2r. See also Helen Hackett, *Shakespeare and Elizabeth: The Meeting of Two Myths* (Princeton, NJ: Princeton University Press, 2009), 13–14.

5 For the Jacobean dating of Sonnet 107, see, for example, Katherine Duncan-Jones, introduction to *Shakespeare's Sonnets*, ed. Katherine Duncan-Jones (London: Arden Shakespeare, 2010), 21–24 and John Kerrigan, commentary to *The Sonnets and A Lover's Complaint*, ed. John Kerrigan (London: Penguin Books, 1986), 313–19.

6 Anthony Nixon, *Elizaes Memoriall* (London, 1603), B1r.

7 *Sorrowes Ioy*, in John Nichols, *John Nichols's The Progresses and Public Processions of Queen Elizabeth I: A New Edition of the Early Modern Sources*, ed. Elizabeth Goldring, Faith Eales, Elizabeth Clarke and Jayne Elisabeth Archer, vol. 4 (Oxford: Oxford University Press, 2014), 748.

8 See Johann P. Sommerville, ed., *Political Writings*, by James VI and I (Cambridge: Cambridge University Press, 1994), 268n1.

9 James VI and I, *Political Writings*, 11.

10 John Fenton, *King Iames His Welcome to London* (London, 1603), B1v.

11 *Threno-Thriambeuticon*, in Nichols, *Progresses of Elizabeth*, 4: 334–35.

12 James VI and I, *Letters of King James VI & I*, ed. G. P. V. Akrigg (Berkeley: University of California Press, 1984), 201.

13   Robert Pricket, *A Souldiers Wish vnto His Soveraigne Lord King Iames* (London, 1603), B4r.

14   Pricket, *A Souldiers Wish*, A4v.

15   For James's foreign policy, see esp. Simon Adams, 'Spain or the Netherlands? The Dilemmas of Early Stuart Foreign Policy', in *Before the English Civil War: Essays on Early Stuart Politics and Government*, ed. Howard Tomlinson (London: Macmillan, 1983), 79–101 and Maurice Lee Jr., *James I and Henri IV: An Essay in English Foreign Policy, 1603–1610* (Urbana: University of Illinois Press, 1970), 17–40.

16   John Nichols, *The Progresses, Processions, and Magnificent Festivities of King James the First, His Royal Consort, Family, and Court*, vol. 2 (London: J. B. Nichols, 1828), 50. Great Britain. Public Record Office, *Calendar of State Papers and Manuscripts, Relating to English Affairs, Existing in the Archives and Collections of Venice*, ed. Horatio F. Brown, vol. 10 (London: Her Majesty's Stationery Office, 1900), 513.

17   For the audience in the London public playhouses, see, for example, Alexander Leggatt, *Jacobean Public Theatre* (London: Routledge, 1992), 28–45 (esp. 36–40). For the anti-Catholic and anti-Spanish disposition of the citizen audience, see Mark Bayer, *Theatre, Community, and Civic Engagement in Jacobean London* (Iowa City: University of Iowa Press, 2011), 116–47.

18   For attempts to read Heywood's two-part drama in relation to the phenomenon of nostalgia for Elizabeth, see esp. Michael Dobson and Nicola J. Watson, *England's Elizabeth: An Afterlife in Fame and Fantasy* (Oxford: Oxford University Press, 2002), 52–61; Curtis Perry, *The Making of Jacobean Culture: James I and the Renegotiation of Elizabethan Literary Practice* (Cambridge: Cambridge University Press, 1997), 172–87; and John Watkins, *Representing Elizabeth in Stuart England: Literature, History, Sovereignty* (Cambridge: Cambridge University Press, 2002), 25–27, 36–55.

19   For Foxe's representation of Elizabeth, see esp. Ramona Garcia, '"Most Wicked Superstition and Idolatry": John Foxe, His Predecessors and the Development of an Anti-Catholic Polemic in the Sixteenth-Century Accounts of the Reign of Mary I', in *John Foxe at Home and Abroad*, ed. David Loades (Aldershot: Ashgate, 2004), 79–87 (esp. 79–80) and Thomas S. Freeman,

'Providence and Prescription: The Account of Elizabeth in Foxe's "Book of Martyrs"', in *The Myth of Elizabeth*, ed. Susan Doran and Thomas S. Freeman (Basingstoke: Palgrave Macmillan, 2003), 27–55. As Garcia puts it, Foxe's *Acts and Monuments* 'became part of an Elizabethan ecclesiastical policy for fostering anti-Catholicism among ordinary Englishmen and Englishwomen' (80).

20 Thomas Heywood, *If You Know Not Me, You Know Nobody, Part I*, ed. Madeleine Doran (London: Malone Society; Oxford: Oxford University Press, 1935).

21 For the popularity of Heywood's drama, see esp. Dieter Mehl, 'The Late Queen on the Public Stage: Thomas Heywood's *If You Know Not Me You Know Nobody, Parts I and II*', in *Queen Elizabeth I: Past and Present*, ed. Christa Jansohn (Münster: LIT, 2004), 153–71 (esp. 154).

22 For James's religious policy, see esp. W. B. Patterson, *King James VI and I and the Reunion of Christendom* (Cambridge: Cambridge University Press, 1997), 31–74.

23 William Crashawe, foreword to *Hepieíkeia*, by William Perkins (Cambridge, 1604), 2.

24 Samuel Rowley, *When You See Me, You Know Me*, ed. F. P. Wilson (London: Malone Society; Oxford: Oxford University Press, 1952).

25 See Perry, *The Making of Jacobean Culture*, 153–87.

26 Teresa Grant, 'History in the Making: The Case of Samuel Rowley's *When You See Me You Know Me* (1604/5)', in *English Historical Drama, 1500–1660: Forms outside the Canon*, ed. Barbara Ravelhofer (Basingstoke: Palgrave Macmillan, 2008), 143.

27 On this point, see David Cressy, *Bonfires and Bells: National Memory and the Protestant Calendar in Elizabethan and Stuart England* (London: Weidenfeld and Nicolson, 1989), 124–25.

28 Watkins, *Representing Elizabeth*, 26.

29 For the dramatization of the Armada attack in Heywood's *Part II* as a response to the Gunpowder Plot, see, for example, Teresa Grant, '"Thus like a Nun, Not like a Princess Born": Dramatic Representations of Mary Tudor in the Early Years of the Seventeenth Century', in *Mary Tudor: Old and New Perspectives*, ed. Susan Doran and Thomas S. Freeman (Basingstoke: Palgrave Macmillan, 2011), 62–77 (esp. 75–76).

30 For critical debates on the nature of the Tilbury scene in *If You Know Not Me, You Know Nobody, Part II*, see esp. Madeleine Doran, introduction to *If You Know Not Me, You Know Nobody, Part II*, ed. Madeleine Doran (London: Malone Society; Oxford: Oxford University Press, 1935), v–xix.

31 Thomas Heywood, *If You Know Not Me, You Know Nobody, Part II*, ed. Madeleine Doran. Quotations are from the 1606 text. The 1633 reprint contains an expanded final scene which offers an even more militant image of Elizabeth, who compares herself to the warlike queen Zenobia. On this point, see, for example, Watkins, *Representing Elizabeth*, 53–54.

32 *The Whore of Babylon*, in *The Dramatic Works of Thomas Dekker*, ed. Fredson Bowers, vol. 2 (Cambridge: Cambridge University Press, 1955).

33 See, for example, Clare McManus, *Women on the Renaissance Stage: Anna of Denmark and Female Masquing in the Stuart Court (1590–1619)* (Manchester: Manchester University Press, 2002), 106–11.

34 See Catherine Loomis, *The Death of Elizabeth I: Remembering and Reconstructing the Virgin Queen* (New York: Palgrave Macmillan, 2010), 127.

35 John Margeson, introduction to *The Conspiracy and Tragedy of Charles Duke of Byron*, ed. John Margeson (Manchester: Manchester University Press, 1988), 36–37.

36 Janet Clare, '*Art Made Tongue-Tied by Authority*': *Elizabethan and Jacobean Dramatic Censorship* (Manchester: Manchester University Press, 1990), 144.

37 Barnabe Barnes, *The Diuils Charter* (London, 1607), I1v.

38 See, for example, Garry Wills, *Witches and Jesuits: Shakespeare's 'Macbeth'* (Oxford: Oxford University Press, 1996), 24–26.

39 Loomis, *The Death of Elizabeth I*, 128.

40 Gordon McMullan, ed., *King Henry VIII* (London: Arden Shakespeare, 2000), 430n.

41 William Leigh, *Queene Elizabeth, Paraleld in Her Princely Vertues, with Dauid, Iosua, and Hezekia* (London, 1612), E4v. Leigh's sermons were delivered in the last three years of Elizabeth's reign, yet they were re-introduced to Jacobean readers in 1612.

42 For the marriage of Princess Elizabeth Stuart and its possible impact on *Henry VIII*, see, for example, McMullan, ed., *Henry VIII*, 63–65. For the representation of Princess Elizabeth as Elizabeth I's incarnate, see Barbara Kiefer Lewalski, *Writing Women in Jacobean England* (Cambridge, MA: Harvard University Press, 1993), 50–51 and Georgianna Ziegler, 'A Second Phoenix: The Rebirth of Elizabeth I in Elizabeth Stuart', in *Resurrecting Elizabeth I in Seventeenth-Century England*, ed. Elizabeth H. Hageman and Katherine Conway (Madison, WI: Fairleigh Dickinson University Press, 2007), 111–31.

43 On this point, see esp. McMullan, ed., *Henry VIII*, 430n.

1

Macbeth: Performing a Caesarean Section on the Mother Country

James I's accession and British union

James I's accession to the English throne in 1603 marked significant governmental and monarchical changes. His succession to Elizabeth I effectively achieved the Union of the Crowns, yet James had no intention to stop there; he proclaimed that the two kingdoms, Scotland and England, should be fully united as one nation.[1] As a symbolic step towards full union, James declared:

> Wee have thought good to discontinue the divided names of England and Scotland out of our Regall Stile, and doe intend and resolve to take and assume unto Us is maner and forme hereafter expressed, The Name and Stile of KING OF GREAT BRITTAINE, including therein according to the trueth, the whole Island.[2]

The image of James as the king of Great Britain was publicized throughout the realm; an accession medal of 1603 portrayed James's bust with an inscription that says, 'James I, Emperor of the whole island of Britain and King of France and Ireland', and the common coinage that circulated from 1604 similarly presented him with the title of 'king of Great Britain'.[3] At the end of 1604, a parliamentary commission composed a proposal for full union, and thereafter James's vision of Great Britain was debated across the realm.

As Kevin Curran puts it, 'one of the first steps James took in his project to unite England and Scotland was performed at the linguistic level', and the language of union 'played a crucial role in the early stages of James's new British policy'.[4] Many writers took part in creating this language of union; the political discourse of those who supported James's project can be characterized by their use of ancient myths and prophecies. They compared James to key historical and legendary figures, such as Augustus Caesar, the Roman emperor who united different regions into one majestic empire, David, the king who governed both Israel and Judah, King Arthur, the defender of the ancient British kingdom, and Aeneas, the forefather of the Roman Empire.[5] The association of James with such figures served to represent him as the founder of the British empire. In this light, another significant figure with whom James was often associated is Brutus, the legendary Trojan founder of ancient Britain. In *A Prophesie of Cadwallader* (1604), William Herbert praises James as the 'second *Brute*', who 'with peace and ioy' came to unite Britain, implying that the union by the second Brute would be even more promising than the short-lived union by '*Britaines* first Monarch warlike *Brute*', who first united the British Isles 'with fire and sword'.[6] In *Poly-Olbion* (1612), Michael Drayton writes that '*the Isle shall be stiled with* Brutes *name, and the name of strangers shall perish*: as it is in *Merlins* prophecies'.[7] These passages exemplify pro-unionist discourse since they establish a relationship for James not only with ancient legend but also with the political prophecies that were widely popular in the early Jacobean period.

Ancient prophecies were often used to legitimize the authority and policy of the monarch in early modern England; Henry VIII and Elizabeth I both capitalized on such prophecies during their reigns.[8] Such prophecies were usually re-edited and interpreted according to political exigencies. Sharon L. Jansen Jaech observes that 'although these so-called prophecies pretended to be ancient predictions made by reputed prophets, they were, in truth, potent political propaganda circulated to influence popular opinion'.[9] In other words, ancient prophecies often functioned as an ideological device to propagate the policy of the sovereign. James and his encomiasts attempted to present his project for Great Britain as the culmination of ancient British prophecies.[10] A notable example is *The Whole Prophesie of Scotland, England, and Somepart of France, and Denmark* (1603), which was published upon James's accession by James's printer Robert Waldegrave. *The Whole Prophesie*, a collection of so-called ancient prophecies, not only attempts to justify James's accession to the English throne but also embellishes his notion of Great Britain; for example, a prophecy which is attributed to Thomas the Rymer, the thirteenth-century Scottish prophet, foretells the foundation of the British empire by Bruce's descendant, James I: 'a French wife shall beare the Son, / Shall rule all Britaine to the sea, / that of the Bruces blood shall come'.[11] This type of prophetic representation of James's empire was not unusual in the pageants and court masques in the early years of James's reign. Keith Thomas points out that 'political prophecies tended to be invoked at a time of crisis, usually to demonstrate that some drastic change, either desired or already accomplished, had been foreseen by the sages of the past'.[12] The re-editing and reinterpretation of ancient prophecies in Jacobean discourse played a vital part in propagating and legitimizing the grand political transition from Tudor England to Stuart Great Britain.

Political prophecies equally played an essential role in theatre, particularly in Shakespeare's plays; Shakespeare's knowledge of the significance of prophecies is vividly demonstrated, for example, in the opening scene of *Richard III* (1592) where Gloucester forges and circulates a prophecy about the treason against King Edward IV in an attempt to remove his brother Clarence from the line of succession (1.1.32–61). As we will see, however, it is in his Jacobean drama that Shakespeare most fully included political prophecies. Given the surge of interest in prophecies at the time of James's accession, it is not surprising that *Macbeth* (1606), a play which specifically features James's Scottish ancestry, places prophecy at the centre of its dramaturgy.[13] *Macbeth* was written soon after the grand dynastic transition from the Tudors to the Stuarts, and had specific ties with James, whose interests in witchcraft and the theory of divine kingship were well known through his publications. Many critics have attempted to link the play with this historical and political context by demonstrating, for example, how Shakespeare might have satisfied his patron's interests by featuring witches and their witchcraft and by staging the procession of the eight Stuart kings in Act 4 Scene 1.[14] It is hardly surprising that *Macbeth* has been singled out as a key play in many studies that examine Shakespeare's commitment to Jacobean political issues. Especially since new historicists have established the close interactive link between theatre and politics, scholars generally agree that any studies of the play must acknowledge its historical and political context. However famous they might be, though, the play's two enigmatic and contentious prophecies – the main focus of this chapter – have not been sufficiently examined in this Jacobean context; their relationship to contemporary political prophecies has not received sufficient attention. Yet the two prophecies are crucial to re-assessing Shakespeare's engagement with the Jacobean contexts not least because it is through these prophecies, I wish to show, that Shakespeare began his exploration into Jacobeans' political appropriation of the memory of Elizabeth and her England.

The prophecies about 'none of woman born' and Birnam Wood

Malcolm, the legitimate heir to the Scottish throne, advances his army into Scotland to avenge his father's death and to claim back the crown from Macbeth, the increasingly deranged usurper. Yet Macbeth remains undaunted by the approaching army; the three witches have given him two prophecies which assure him that he is not to be defeated until a man who is not born from a woman confronts him and the trees of Birnam Wood march towards his castle. The first prophecy, 'none of woman born / Shall harm Macbeth' (4.1.79–80), seems to promise Macbeth that he is virtually invincible since every man is born from a mother's womb, including, Macbeth optimistically concludes, his revengeful opponent Macduff, whose family Macbeth has savagely slaughtered. Macbeth, however, realizes that his interpretation of the prophecy is false when Macduff, before overpowering Macbeth, declares that 'Macduff was from his mother's womb / Untimely ripped' (5.8.15–16). For the episode of Macduff's birth, Shakespeare follows the account in the second edition of Raphael Holinshed's *Chronicles* (1587), a main source for *Macbeth*.[15] In Holinshed's account, Macduff announces that 'I am even he that thy wizzards have told thee of, who was never borne of my mother, but ripped out of her wombe'.[16] Both in *Macbeth* and in Holinshed's *Chronicles*, the Caesarean-born Macduff is entitled to be called what the witches term 'none of woman born'. Indeed, the prophecy plays on the 'double sense' (5.8.20) of the phrase 'none of woman born', a phrase which, along with terms such as 'the Fortunate' and 'the Unborn', signified Caesarean birth in medieval and early modern Europe.[17] The 'double sense' of the witches' phrase – its literal meaning of a man not born of a woman, and its idiomatic meaning of a man born by Caesarean section – tricks Macbeth into falsely believing that he would not be defeated by any man on earth.

The significance of the Caesarean birth in this prophecy was first highlighted by feminist critics, such as Janet Adelman and Coppélia Kahn, who approached the play by way of object-relations psychoanalysis.[18] Adelman, for example, in her influential reading of Shakespeare's plays, *Suffocating Mothers*, analyses the representation of gender in *Macbeth* in the light of Freudian psychoanalytical theory and illustrates the way in which a symptom of cultural anxieties about a singular masculinity and a male fantasy of autonomous patriarchal reproduction – a male dream of escaping the matrix of suffocating maternity – underlies the play, including the first prophecy. These critics highlight the significance of Caesarean birth by drawing on the findings of early modern cultural studies. A Caesarean operation was performed only when pregnant mothers were dying or already dead; in most cases, it was a post-mortem operation aimed at saving an infant from the mother's enclosing body.[19] Even when the mother was still alive at the time of the operation, she eventually lost her life due to the loss of blood or post-surgical infection.

Furthermore, while vaginal births were always overseen by women, only male physicians were allowed to perform Caesarean operations; the Caesarean operation was a male prerogative and considered as a manly way to deliver an infant since the Caesarean section violently severed the link, both physical and symbolic, between a mother and her infant.[20] Infants rescued by male physicians by Caesarean section were not seen as born of their mothers but rather as ripped from receptacles, and, in a symbolic sense, produced by male hands. Caesarean-born male infants were therefore seen as truly masculine since their masculine identity was not 'contaminated' by potentially degrading female influences.[21] The Caesarean section thus embodies the male fantasy of nullifying female sway over the process of birth. The cultural significance of the Caesarean section is crucial to reading the play as Shakespeare develops a notably male-centred logic of the Caesarean section – a fatal operation on a dying woman can be justified if it is aimed at rescuing an infant from her confining body – and bases his drama on this premise. In fact, it is the male fantasy of Caesarean section, I would suggest, that is essential to understanding the significance of the second prophecy about Birnam Wood.

Besides the 'none of woman born' prophecy, Macbeth has the other defensive charm:

THIRD APPARITION
    Macbeth shall never vanquished be, until
    Great Birnam Wood to high Dunsinane Hill
    Shall come against him.

                                            (4.1.91–93)

Macbeth is overjoyed, crying out, 'Who can impress the forest, bid the tree / Unfix his earth-bound root?' (4.1.94–95). Malcolm, however, unwittingly answers Macbeth's rhetorical question. Before marching towards Dunsinane, Macbeth's stronghold, Malcolm orders his soldiers to cut the leafy boughs of Birnam Wood and hold them as they march so that he could 'shadow / The numbers' of his army (5.4.5–6). Malcolm's military tactic has an unexpected consequence; it shatters the confidence of Macbeth, who perceives the march of Malcolm's men bearing 'leafy screens' (5.6.1) as 'a moving grove' (5.5.37) itself, and believes that one of his protective spells has been broken.

Unlike the 'none of woman born' prophecy, critics have been reluctant to analyse the Birnam Wood prophecy from a new perspective, holding on to the most influential interpretation, which associates the passage with the May Day festival, where celebrants march wearing sprigs and green branches.[22] Their parade signified the revival of fertility and the purge of the hibernal giant, thereby bringing a new order into the world. According to this interpretation, the abundance of Birnam Wood significantly contrasts with the underlying theme of Macbeth's lack of an heir, as evidenced when he laments his 'fruitless crown' (3.1.60) and 'barren sceptre' (3.1.61) or when he compares himself meaningfully to 'the yellow leaf' (5.3.23). Nevertheless, while the May Day reading thus links the prophecy with the play's botanical imagery of fertility and barrenness, it fails to frame it within the entire context of the play. How does Malcolm's ostentatious performance of seemingly moving the trees correspond with the play's main political theme, that is, the foundation of Malcolm's new kingdom? Should the two prophecies be read separately – the word play and the optical illusion – as they have always been? These questions remain unanswered in earlier studies. I would suggest, however, that not only are the two prophecies closely linked but they together inform the key context in which Malcolm's rise as a new ruler of Scotland assumes an important Jacobean immediacy.

As Malcolm's army approaches, Scottish nobles begin to flee and those who remain in Scotland live in fear. Curiously, Macbeth compares his crumbling kingdom to a sick woman when he speaks to the doctor attending to Lady Macbeth:

MACBETH
                    If thou couldst, doctor, cast
        The water of my land, find her disease,
        And purge it to a sound and pristine health.

                                                (5.3.50–52)

The idea that Scotland is in ill health has been lurking in the play for some time. When Macbeth commits regicide and unlawfully and forcibly takes the Scottish crown from King Duncan, it is reported that 'the earth / Was feverous and did shake' (2.3.60–61). Scotland under the stifling rule of Macbeth is also described as suffering 'the fits o'th' season' (4.2.17). Interestingly, the desperate condition of Macbeth's Scotland corresponds with the condition of his wife Lady Macbeth, whose health deteriorates as Macbeth begins to act tyrannically, as exemplified when he mercilessly slaughters Macduff's wife and children. In this play, Scotland is imagined as the wife of the monarch as well as the mother country of the people, reminiscent of the way in which James I famously identified his kingdom as his 'lawfull Wife': 'I am the Husband, and all the whole Isle is my lawfull Wife'.[23] Both the desperate state of his kingdom and the sickness of Lady Macbeth signal Macbeth's failure as the ruler of Scotland; his kingdom and his wife are in ill health, yet Macbeth cannot restore either of them by his own power.

The sick Lady Macbeth is described as planted with 'a rooted sorrow' – that is, the memory of the brutal regicide she has committed with her husband – that needs to be 'pluck[ed]' for her recovery (5.3.41). Similarly, Macbeth's Scotland is planted with pestering 'weeds' that Malcolm's men find it necessary to 'drown' in order to revitalize Scotland (5.2.30). Interestingly, this pestered, barren Scotland – 'our suffering country, / Under a hand accursed' (3.6.49–50) – is no longer called 'our mother' by her people, but rather 'our grave':

ROSSE

                                        It cannot
    Be called our mother, but our grave. Where nothing,
    But who knows nothing, is once seen to smile;
    Where sighs, and groans, and shrieks that rend the air,
    Are made, not marked; where violent sorrow seems
    A modern ecstasy. The deadman's knell
    Is there scarce asked for who, and good men's lives
    Expire before the flowers in their caps,
    Dying or ere they sicken.

                                        (4.3.165–73)

We might recall that, early in the play, Lady Macbeth calls on the spirits to 'unsex' her and fill her body with 'direst cruelty' to carry out the murder of King Duncan (1.5.41–43). In this invocation scene, Lady Macbeth desires to 'stop up th'access and passage to remorse' so that 'no compunctious visitings of nature' should check her murderous plot (1.5.44–45). As Jenijoy La Belle points out, the early modern medical knowledge about the female body identifies 'th'access and passage to remorse' with the neck of the womb; therefore, her reference to 'no compunctious visitings of nature' suggests the stopping of menstruation.[24] In this sense, Lady Macbeth's unsexing is physical as well as spiritual. She also asks the spirits to 'come to my woman's breasts, / And take my milk for gall' (1.5.47–48), thereby dissociating herself from the notion of child-rearing. Significantly, reminiscent of the way in which Lady Macbeth is thus presented as a barren, murderous mother who would not hesitate to dash 'the brains out' of 'the babe that milks [her]' (1.7.55–58), Macbeth's Scotland is envisaged as a maternal ground that no longer nourishes her children, but rather takes away their lives. Flowers are dying in their caps before they bloom, and so are the people of Scotland, who are entrapped in their dying motherland. Macbeth's rule has changed the nourishing womb of the people to their enclosed tomb.

Macbeth demands the doctor 'cleanse the stuffed bosom' of Lady Macbeth 'with some sweet oblivious antidote' (5.3.43–44). The doctor, however, concludes that Lady Macbeth's 'disease is beyond my practice' (5.1.59), and that 'more needs she the divine than the physician' (5.1.74). Scotland is also beyond the doctor's practice; Macbeth sarcastically asks the doctor to prescribe a 'purgative drug' (5.3.55) to cure his kingdom, yet Scotland is also shown to be incurable by any earthly medical practice, as evidenced when, symbolically enough, the doctor deserts and flees from Macbeth's crumbling kingdom immediately after this exchange (5.3.61–62). The mother country the doctor has forsaken is evidently in a terminal condition and, like Lady Macbeth, she will respond to nothing but divine intervention. Significantly, it is this divine role which Malcolm effectively assumes in his attempt to reclaim Scotland. Before marching into Scotland, one of Malcolm's loyal followers makes it clear that what the suffering Scotland needs is not the 'purgative drug' that Macbeth demands from the doctor, but Malcolm, 'the medicine of the sickly weal':

CAITHNESS
Meet we the medicine of the sickly weal,
And with him pour we in our country's purge,
Each drop of us.

$$(5.2.27–29)^{25}$$

Earlier in the play, when Macduff joins Malcolm in England, trying to persuade him to raise an army against Macbeth, the English doctor abruptly appears on stage and reports to them the 'most miraculous work' (4.3.147) of Edward the Confessor, describing how Edward heals patients of scrofula, a disease that is 'called the Evil' (4.3.146). In fact, the doctor's description of King Edward as a divine medical practitioner is timely and crucial, as it associates kingship with a divine healing power and gives a pretext to Malcolm's subsequent self-stylization as such; before marching into Scotland, Malcolm proclaims, 'Let's make us medicines of our great revenge, / To cure this deadly grief' (4.3.217–18), fashioning himself as a divine 'medicine' – that is, a divine physician – who can restore the dying motherland and bring her 'wholesome days' (4.3.105) back to her people.

In early modern England, the medical model of the public weal was commonplace and frequently used as a justification for various forms of violence, including rebellion against the corrupt state and elimination of individual members who were seen as destabilizing the social order.[26] Shakespeare dramatized the rhetoric of medical justification in several of his earlier plays. In *Julius Caesar* (1599), Brutus explains the assassination of Caesar as 'a piece of work that will make sick men whole' (2.1.326), and presents himself and his conspirators as 'purgers, not murderers' (2.1.179) of Rome, while, in *Henry IV, Part II* (1597), the Archbishop of York attempts to justify the rebellion against Henry IV by comparing England under the usurper Bolingbroke to a diseased body ('Wherefore do I this? So the question stands. / Briefly, to this end: we are all diseased' [4.1.53–54]) and the role of the rebel's military commander to that of a 'physician' (4.1.60), stressing that the aim of the rebellion is to 'purge th'obstructions which begin to stop / Our very veins of life' (4.1.65–66). In *Macbeth*, Shakespeare revisits the rhetoric of medical justification, presenting Malcolm's invasion of Macbeth's crumbling Scotland as a necessary medical operation on the dying mother country.

It is at this point that the Birnam Wood prophecy begins to merge significantly with the 'none of woman born' prophecy. The self-styled physician Malcolm marches into the usurper's diseased kingdom in an attempt to rescue the people who are entrapped in the decaying body politic in much the same way as male physicians free trapped infants from their dying mothers. Symbolically, in the course of his rescue operation, Malcolm 'unfix[es]' the Scottish trees from the barren ground. Malcolm's unfixing of the 'earth-bound root[s]' of Birnam Wood from the maternal ground, I would suggest, vividly conjures up the very image of a premature baby being untimely ripped from his/her mother's womb. Malcolm plucks the roots of the Scottish trees as if he were simultaneously severing the umbilical cord that has been binding the people to their collapsing regime, a symbolic Caesarean operation which saves the lives of the endangered children of mother Scotland. Macduff's declaration – 'Hold fast the mortal sword, and like good men / Bestride our downfall birthdom' (4.3.3–4) – reinforces this medical symbolism. Malcolm attends to the 'downfall birthdom', and helps rescue her children with 'the mortal sword' as a surgical instrument for Caesarean section, just as his conquest delivers his people from tyrannical rule in the devastated mother country.

In reality, Malcolm does not actually unfix or move the forest – he merely cuts the boughs of the trees – and, as we will see further, such unfixing occurs only in the imagination of Macbeth, who interprets Malcolm's action as 'bid[ding] the tree / Unfix his earth-bound root'. Yet it is not only Macbeth who invites us to envisage this strikingly vivid and powerful analogy between the two prophecies; the play itself sets up the context before Act 4 by introducing the language of vegetation that reinforces this analogy. In his first encounter with the witches in Act 1 Scene 3, Banquo demands that they prophesy 'which grain will grow, and which will not'

(1.3.59), and Macbeth later repeats Banquo's trope when he resents the fact that, according to the prophecy given to Banquo, his actions will inevitably serve to make 'the seeds of Banquo kings' (3.1.69). King Duncan too uses the same language of vegetation when he praises Macbeth and Banquo for defending his kingdom against foreign invasion:

> DUNCAN
> I have begun to plant thee, and will labour
> To make thee full of growing.
> …
> BANQUO   There if I grow
> The harvest is your own.
>
> (1.4.28–33)

The king is presented as a gardener who nourishes his trees and makes them 'full of growing'. The trees of his kingdom are the people of Scotland who are, in the same scene, also compared to children craving the love of their father-king (1.4.24–27). Shakespeare thus introduces the association of children and trees early in the play, an association which will activate the link between the seemingly disparate prophecies about a child and a forest in Holinshed's account. It is not surprising, therefore, that Malcolm repeats the language of vegetation when he declares victory at the end of the play: 'What's more to do, / Which would be planted newly with the time' (5.9.30–31). Malcolm unfixes/liberates the trees/children from the tyrant's suffocating motherland, and replants them in his own restored kingdom as their new gardener and father-king.

As will be discussed further, Jacobean theatregoers were not unfamiliar with the anthropomorphic analogy between earth and mother; Shakespeare was certainly not alone when he appropriated this conventional analogy in *Macbeth*. Thomas Heywood's *The Rape of Lucrece* (1607) similarly featured an enigmatic word game which plays on the earth-mother trope. Brutus Junior and the two sons of Tarquin – Aruns and Sextus – visit Apollo's priests in order to discover who will triumph after Tarquin's death:

PRIEST
   sacred *Phoebus* we entreat,
  Which of these three shall be great
  Which largest power and state repleat by the heauens
    doome.
Phoebus thy thoughts no longer smother.
ORACLE He that first shall kisse his mother
  Shall be powerfull and no other
  Of you three in Rome.[27]

Upon hearing the oracle, Aruns and Sextus vie to get to their mother Tullia to 'gaine a kingdome by a mothers kisse', while Brutus immediately falls down and kisses the ground. Although Aruns and Sextus take no notice of his seemingly antic behaviour, Brutus knows what he is doing. Brutus decides not to interpret Apollo's words in a literal sense since 'their phrases are mysticall, they speake still in cloudes' and 'had he meant a naturall mother he would ha spoke it by circumference' and concludes that the earth-mother trope is used in the oracle: 'Earth I acknowledge no mother but thee, accept me as thy sonne, and I shall shine as bright in Rome as *Apollo* himselfe in his temple at *Delphos*'.[28] Indeed, Aruns, the first to kiss his natural mother, is the first to die in the battle between the Tarquins and the rebels led by Brutus. Although he also dies at the end of the battle, it is Brutus who is commemorated as one 'that first gouern'd Rome, / And swaid the people by a consuls name'.[29] *The Rape of Lucrece* shows that Jacobean theatregoers knew enough about the earth-mother trope to enjoy the play. It seems highly likely that the audience of *Macbeth* also understood the earth-mother trope and were thereby equipped to see the symbolic crossover between the two prophecies about a baby ripped from his natural mother and Scottish trees ripped from the mother earth.

In *Macbeth*, the march of Birnam Wood does not necessarily represent the natural order or universal forces linked to the pattern of the seasons, as critics traditionally argue. The trees are 'untimely ripped' from the barren ground, just as Macduff was 'untimely ripped' from his mother; here, male hands change the course of time and the order of nature so as to rescue the lives of children/subjects. Birnam Wood and Macduff are born in the same way: untimely, unnaturally and in a completely masculine way. Birnam Wood is not just a military tool for disguise, but is itself a symbol of 'none of woman born'. The prophecy of Birnam Wood, together with that of Macduff's Caesarean birth, complements the play's one grand design of a fantasy of nullifying female sway over the process of birth by violently detaching children from degrading femininity in a manly way – a symbolic operation which results in the death of the mother, Macbeth's Scotland, and the birth of the new masculine regime.

Macbeth and the body of Elizabethan England

The analogical view of the dysfunctional state as a diseased body was common throughout the early modern period.[30] A notable publication which articulates the anthropomorphic understanding of the English polity is Edward Forset's *A Comparative Discourse of the Bodies Naturall and Politique* (1606), in which Forset compares the disorder of the state to bodily dysfunction: 'Diseases arise as in the body naturall by distemper of humours; so in the politicall, by disorder of manners'.[31] Forset argues that, in order to save the diseased body politic, the people should recognize their sovereign as 'the principall Phisicion' and entrust him with the task of 'redressing or remedying the maladies of the bodie politique' and 'cleansing the verie fountaynes of euill', an important task of the monarch which Macbeth evidently fails to carry out.[32] The identification of the monarch as the medical practitioner was already commonplace during Elizabeth's reign. Ireland, for example, was often seen as a diseased, uncultivated land that needed to be cured and sowed by the queen, as when

Francis Bacon wrote in 1598, 'I think her Majesty shall do well to cure the root of the disease ... and to plant a stronger and surer government than heretofore, for the ease and protection of the subject'.[33] In English imperial discourse, the anthropomorphic understanding of the state and the identification of the monarch as its principal physician were effectively used as a justification for the ongoing attempts to colonize Ireland.[34] Towards the end of her reign, however, this medical – also botanical – rhetoric was used to address the ongoing crisis in England: the weakening of the body natural of England's mother.

As scholars have noted, Elizabeth was often represented as the mother of the English people during her lifetime.[35] She styled herself such in her first parliamentary speech in 1559, when she declared, 'reproach me so no more that I have no children: for every one of you, and as many as are English, are my children and kinsfolks'.[36] Accordingly, Elizabeth was praised as the caring mother of the English people; for example, in *A Meruailous Combat of Contrarieties* (1588), William Averell extols Elizabeth as 'a louing mother vnto you in her carefulnesse, and a diligent nurse in continuall painfulnesse'.[37] For the English people, she remained throughout her reign, as Josias Nichols puts it in the 1602 religious pamphlet, the 'most louing and kind mother Queene *Elizabeth*'.[38] Even after her death, Elizabeth remained the mother of England. An elegy included in *Sorrowes Ioy* (1603) mourns the death of the 'virgin sceptre-swaying mother', while, in *Three Treatises Religiously Handled* (1603), Radford Mavericke similarly laments the loss of 'the Mother of our Countrey', writing that 'though her Maiestie were a Virgin and a mayden Queene, yet was she the mother of as many loyall and obedient children and subiectes, as euer was any Prince in Christendome'.[39] In his account of Elizabeth's funeral in *The Wonderfull Yeare* (1603), Thomas Dekker also eulogizes her as 'the Citizens mother'.[40] In 1607, she was still called in a sermon 'our late most noble Queene *Elizabeth*, worthy of al our memories, vnder whom you haue beene bred, nursed and brought vp'.[41]

From the last years of her reign through the early years of James's reign, however, this nourishing mother of England was not always seen or recalled favourably. Elizabeth suffered from disease while the kingdom suffered inflation, poor harvests, heavy war taxation, religious contention and the threat of Spanish invasion.[42] Indeed, as Leonard Tennenhouse puts it, 'the features of Elizabeth's body natural were always already components of a political figure which made the physical vigor and autonomy of the monarch one and the same thing as the condition of England'.[43] Symbolically, it was during these last years of her reign that the plague raged in England, especially in its heart, the city of London.[44] Besides the social strain on her kingdom, Elizabeth also failed to assuage the anxiety of her people about the uncertainty of the regal succession. Public despair about and resentment towards the barren queen loomed large towards the end of the century, and anti-women rhetoric began to appear in political pamphlets and theatres.[45] Shakespeare's representation of Scotland under a king with 'a barren sceptre', a kingdom that cannot 'be called our mother, but our grave', evokes the desperation of England under the ageing, childless queen. Forset describes the discontent among the people as the most pernicious symptom of a diseased state.[46] In this regard, Elizabeth's England was as diseased as Macbeth's Scotland; in both kingdoms, people awaited the coming of a kingly, divine physician to cure the diseased body politic.

Indeed, James and his supporters made full use of the image of England as the decaying body by styling James its sovereign physician. When James, as James VI of Scotland, finally rode south from Edinburgh to London to ascend to the throne of the deceased queen, petitioners flocked to see their new king, and some of them asked him to cure 'diseases' in England; for example, the petition condemning popish ceremonies in the *Prayer Book* and asking James to institute religious reform in the English church says, 'God, we trust, hath appointed your highness our physician to heal these diseases'.[47] In his 1603 eulogy for Elizabeth, Henry Howgrave praised the new king for reviving the dead body politic of England:

As you [Elizabeth] languished, England languished,
Doomed to death, and lay dead as you lay.
The same day is the last of your life,
    And of the fatherland.
But life returns as you return, James,
And flourishes as long as you flourish.[48]

In *The Wonderfull Yeare*, Dekker also uses the medical trope to mark the accession of James, writing that 'as first, to begin with the Quéenes death, then the Kingdomes falling into an Ague vpon that. Next followes the curing of that feauer by the holesome receipt of a proclaymed King'.[49] The arrival of James, Dekker's account seems to imply, had cured the fever of the England of the dead queen. By giving James the role of the state physician for the sick country and endowing him with a miraculous healing power – a power that helps to represent Edward the Confessor as the divine king in *Macbeth* – his supporters were able to present James as God's anointed, legitimate king.

Elizabeth did not officially recognize James as her successor during her lifetime. There were also constitutional issues; the English statute of 1351 dictated that no foreigners should inherit English lands, while Henry VIII's will specifically ruled out the Scottish line of his sister Margaret, who married James IV.[50] Even after his successful succession to Elizabeth's throne, therefore, James and his supporters remained worried that James's regal union appeared, particularly to those who were dissatisfied with the influx of the Scots into the English court, to be the 'conquest' of England by the Scottish king. As Brian P. Levack writes, 'the possibility that Scotland would absorb England or at least make England accessory to it generated a fear of *de facto* conquest and a loss of sovereignty'.[51] It is hardly surprising, therefore, that, in 1603, Samuel Walsall found it necessary to stress in his panegyric commemorating James's succession that 'James, you are James not by force: / And whether the sixth of Scotland, or the First / Of England hardly matters, if only you are an unparalleled Brit'.[52] In this context, fashioning James as the saintly king whom God had sent to rescue England helped to divert the public's attention from matters of James's legitimacy.

Like Elizabeth, James also knew how important it was for a monarch to act well in front of his people, and which roles he particularly needed to play; he once wrote that 'a King is as one set on a stage, whose smallest actions and gestures, all the people gazingly doe behold'.[53] He therefore continued to style himself England's state physician. In *Counterblast to Tabacco* (1604), James defines his role as 'the proper Phisician of his Politicke-bodie' who strives to 'maintaine the Publicke quietnesse, and prevent all occasions of Commotion' in order to maintain the health of 'their mother the Common-wealth'.[54] In the proclamation of 1607, James again compared himself to the state physician, describing rebellious rioting in some parts of the state as a symptom of a dangerous disease of the body politic, a disease that needs to be cured for the whole state:

> We are bound (as the head of the politike body of our Realme) to follow the course which the best Phisitians use in dangerous diseases, which is, by a sharpe remedy applyed to a small and infected part, to save the whole from dissolution and destruction.[55]

By 1610, his subjects became so familiar with his vaunted self-styled role that parliamentarians attempted to encourage James to institute political reform by ingratiatingly referring to James's self-stylization: 'May it therefore please your most excellent Maiestie, who is the great, and soveraigne physition of this estate, to apply such a remedie as this disease may be presently cured, and all diseases for tyme to come, of like nature, prevented'.[56] In this context, the rhetoric of medical justification and the representation of Malcolm as a kingly physician for the diseased mother country in *Macbeth* would have struck a chord among the Jacobean audience who were familiar with James's much publicized self-styled role. Indeed, confronted by the persistent scepticism expressed towards the legitimacy of his regal union, what James needed was this medical trope; just as Malcolm saves the Scottish people from the smothering body politic, so too did James desire to present himself as the rescuer of the English people in their sick mother country, renewing the narrative of his orderly succession not as conquest but as the succession awaited and welcomed by the suffering people.[57]

In this context, equally important is James's other famous self-stylization. Elizabeth had not left an heir to assume her role as parent for England and, apparently, the vulnerable people needed parental protection; as one elegiac verse by an anonymous writer printed in *Sorrowes Ioy* puts it, 'Our common parent from vs all thus taken, / We all may weepe, all orphans left forsaken'.[58] James and his supporters, then, styled him the father of the English people, a father whom God had sent to make up for the loss of the mother. In one of his verses also printed in *Sorrowes Ioy*, Thomas Byng first conjures up a bleak picture of England, where the people wail the death of their mother:

> Great god in dreadfull iudgement reft away
> The aged mother of these orphane lands;
> The children wayled for their dames decay,
> Lifting to highest heauen their folded hands;
> Deare god, they sayd, rue on our heauie case.

His verse then introduces James as God's anointed father of these orphaned children; in answer to their plea, God proclaims, 'Him will I giue, he shall you rule aright. / Your mother gon, he shall your father hight', turning their sorrow into joy.[59] The anonymous pamphlet entitled *Weepe with Ioy* (1603) compares James to 'Nurce-father' who came to replace England's 'Nurce-mother':

> though God hath taken away Queene *Elizabeth* our late and louing Nurce-mother, yet the succeeding of that mightie and godly Prince, King *Iames,* our new and renowned Nurce-father, doeth giue vs exceeding cause of ioy.[60]

One of the pageants welcoming the new king to London also paid tribute to James by proclaiming that 'the *Love*, which wee once dedicated to her (as a Mother) doubly doe wee vow it to you, our Soueraigne, and Father; intreating wee may be sheltred vnder your winges now, as then vnder hers', while Richard Mulcaster welcomed James's entry into England as the arrival of a new father:

> How sore had mournfull death shaked th'english soyle,
> If God had not afforded present helpe?
> Who though he tooke our Queene, a King he gaue
> To play the fathers part in mothers losse.[61]

James willingly played 'the fathers part', continuously presenting himself to his subjects not only as state physician but also as '*Parens patriae*, the politique father of his people' and 'a louing nourish-father'.[62] James also writes:

> By the Law of Nature the King becomes a naturall Father to all his lieges at his Coronation: And as the Father of his fatherly duty is bound to care for the nourishing, education, and virtuous gouernment of his children; euen so is the king bound to care for all his subiects.[63]

James thus compared himself to a father and his people to his children, his favourite comparison which, as we have seen, also applies to the relationship between a king and the Scottish people in *Macbeth*. By assuming the role of father-king as well as that of state physician, James appropriated Elizabeth's self-stylization as England's mother and reframed his succession to her throne in a style that was acceptable to his English subjects.

The spectacle of Malcolm's conquest of the dying mother country in *Macbeth* curiously interacts with the way in which James publicized his succession to Elizabeth and attempted to assert superiority over his once powerful 'mother'. Malcolm proves his masculine and monarchical strength as the new king of Scotland through his rescue operation of the Scottish subjects from the dying motherland. In this regard, Shakespeare's play evokes the way in which, at a time when his English subjects constantly harked back to Elizabeth, James attempted to stage his mature independent kingship by presenting himself as the manly state physician for England and as the new father-king of the English people. His succession, however, was not the only political issue that occupied the minds of James and his subjects; at the time of first performances of *Macbeth*, there was a more imminent political project for which James needed to demonstrate his fatherly authority: that is, his ongoing project of creating Jacobean Britain out of Elizabethan England.

'A perfect Child': A vision of Britain

By revitalizing the memory of the last years of Elizabethan England and effectively making use of the early modern four-part trope of the body politic, the medical model, the comparison of monarch to parent and the metaphor of vegetation, *Macbeth*'s two Caesarean prophecies dramatically stage the replacement of the diseased, barren mother with the fertile father in a way that recalls James's political vision of launching Jacobean England from Elizabeth's barren body politic. Yet, as I noted at the beginning of this chapter, James's ambition did not stop there; what he aspired to create from Elizabethan England was, in fact, not Jacobean England but Great Britain.

Early in the play, Macbeth describes the witches' predictions that have come true as 'happy prologues to the swelling act / Of the imperial theme' (1.3.130–31), though the 'imperial theme' in *Macbeth*, Macbeth later comes to realize, does not culminate in Macbeth's acquisition of the Scottish crown but in Malcolm's. The word 'imperial' is anachronistic and is not in the original sources of *Macbeth*. As Arthur F. Kinney points out, the word 'imperial', as a matter of fact, was known as an adjective for James's British project.[64] James continuously referred to his God-given task as 'the blessed Union, or rather Reuniting of these two mightie, famous, and ancient Kingdomes of England and Scotland, under one Imperiall Crowne'.[65] In his pro-unionist *A Panegyrike Congratulatorie to the Kings Maiestie* (1603), Samuel Daniel also hailed James as 'one imperiall Prince' of both English and Scottish subjects.[66] In this regard, the 'imperial theme' of *Macbeth* evokes James's imperial design for Great Britain. Indeed, as several critics have shown, *Macbeth* can be variously linked to the discourse of the British union.[67] Notably, the play's presentation of the eight Stuart monarchs, which will be examined later, has often been seen as an encomiastic reference not only to James's Scottish ancestry but also to James's vision of Great Britain, for one of the Stuart kings carries 'twofold balls and treble sceptres' (4.1.120); 'twofold balls' can be taken to signify double orbs of England and Scotland, while 'treble sceptres' can be read either as reference to the three regions, England, Wales and Scotland, or to the three countries, Britain, France and Ireland.[68] Both readings agree that these symbols serve to represent James, the ninth king of the Stuart lineage, as the legitimate ruler of the united Britain.

Another important link between the play and the British union project that has been highlighted by critics is Malcolm. As David Norbrook points out, George Buc in *Daphnis Polystephanos* (1605) traces James's English ancestry to Edward the Confessor and sees the alliance of Malcolm (James's ancestor on the Scottish side) and Edward (James's ancestor on the English side) as prefiguring James's union of England and Scotland.[69] In his dramatization of Malcolm's victory over Macbeth, Shakespeare similarly stresses the alliance between Malcolm and Edward, describing the ways in which Edward supports Malcolm's attempt to reclaim the Scottish crown; as one lord puts it, Malcolm 'lives in the English court, and is received / Of the most pious Edward with such grace / That the malevolence of fortune nothing / Takes from his high respect' (3.6.26–29). Supplied with English soldiers and flanked by the English lord, 'warlike Siward' (3.6.31), Malcolm launches the war against Macbeth. Furthermore, as I have argued, Malcolm and Edward are rhetorically aligned as state medical healer. In this context, Malcolm's victory at the end of the play signifies more than the restoration of Duncan's Scotland. It is the victory of the friendly alliance between Scotland and England; what Malcolm establishes is the new anglophile Scotland, which contrasts with the Scotland under Macbeth, for whom England only means the country of despicable epicureans ('fly, false thanes, / And mingle with the English epicures' [5.3.7–8]).

Although several studies have attempted to situate the play in the context of the British union, none of them focuses on the two prophecies in *Macbeth*. I would suggest, however, that the two prophecies and the majestic image of the Caesarean plucking that they represent – the plucking of an infant from its mother's womb and the plucking of Birnam Wood from the motherland – highlight a new mode of representing the mythical birth of James's new state, a mode which Shakespeare's contemporary writers were variously exploring in their union-related discourse. Malcolm does not simply restore or inherit his father's kingdom but creates the anglophile Scotland from the dying mother country. Similarly, what James aspired to create from the collapsing Elizabethan England was not the England of his own but a much larger political entity. In this context, the two prophecies can be closely linked to James's grand vision of launching the fully united Britain after Elizabeth's death. As Andrew Escobedo puts it, the nationhood 'emerges ... from the severing of roots, which defines that nationhood in distinction of the past'.[70] Malcolm uproots the Scottish trees from the motherland in order to create the new Scotland, reminiscent of the way in which James attempted to symbolically sever the roots between his people and their recently deceased mother. The first step James took after unveiling his vision to create Great Britain was to proclaim that all children born after his accession were admissible to the privileges of both kingdoms and were to be recognized neither as English nor Scottish but as children of Great Britain; as he proclaimed, 'the *Post nati* were Naturalized (*Ipso facto*) by my Accession to this Crowne'.[71] James attempted to pluck the roots of newborn children from English soil and replant them in his ideological construct, detaching them from mother England and fashioning them as the citizens of Great Britain – a symbolic operation of giving birth to his own people through severing of English roots.

In a speech he delivered to Parliament in 1607, James, after showing his medical knowledge by noting that a foetus in the mother's womb 'hath all the Lineaments and Parts of a Body' and 'when it is born … it then be a perfect Child', likened his vision of Great Britain to this 'perfect Child':

> Upon the late Queen's Death, the Child was first brought to Light; but to make it a perfect Man, to bring it to an accomplished Union, it must have Time and Means; and if it be not at the first, blame not me; blame Time; blame the Order of Nature.[72]

James claimed that the 'Child' was born upon the death of Elizabeth, reconstructing his succession to the dead queen as the act of giving birth to the child – that is, the notion of the perfect union of the two kingdoms.[73] The child was conceived in ancient times. Yet the child, though already 'perfect' and ready to be delivered, had been confined within the notion of Englishness since the end of Brutus's reign. James, the self-styled second Brutus, attempted to free this 'perfect Child' from the confines of England and bring the child to light as his own, seeing the death of Elizabeth/England as the ideal opportunity. Malcolm's Caesarean operation that results in the creation of the Scotland allied with England interacts with James's vision of restoring the fully united Britain from the dead mother England.

However, although James believed that his child already had a perfect body, he also knew that his project would need more 'Time and Means' to be 'a perfect Man'. James was highly conscious that his project was not well received by his subjects and that, in order to bring his child into maturity, he needed their support. Yet James also believed that his people would eventually back the full union; now that the child was born, 'Time must ripen and work'.[74] In describing the status of his union project, James also used the trope of vegetation that I have examined in *Macbeth*. James was aware that he needed to wait patiently until the seed he had planted as the sovereign gardener would eventually grow into a tree; as James put it in regard to his union scheme, a man 'may plant, *Apollo* may water, but it is GOD onely that must giue the increase'.[75] James was right to assume that his plan for Great Britain needed more time to be realized. 'Upon the late Queen's Death', a 'perfect Child' was 'brought to Light'. Yet his ideal child was not likely to grow and become a complete man as the opposition to his project was far stronger than he had initially anticipated.

Cross-currents: Unease and scepticism

Although James had certainly planted the seed for the future, fuller Anglo-Scottish Union in 1707, his 'perfect Child' never grew up during his reign.[76] His ambitious project for full union failed to win support. In fact, many of his subjects already began to see it as a failed project by the time of first performances of *Macbeth* and, as was clear to his audience, James's political vision was not expected to be accomplished so easily – in stark contrast to the way in which the Caesarean prophecies in *Macbeth* seem to be spectacularly fulfilled. Worse still, James's union project fuelled anxiety among his English subjects about the growing prominence of the Scots in England, an anxiety which James had to address and assuage. James showed his understanding of their fear that the completed union would be 'the *Crisis* to the ouerthrow of England, and setting vp of Scotland', as well as their antagonism towards 'the Scots, who if the Vnion were effected, would raigne and rule all'.[77] In the

Parliament of 1607, then, James meaningfully responded to the widespread fear about the influx of Scots into England:

> Some thinke that I will draw the Scottish Nation hither, talking idlely of transporting of Trees out of a barren ground into a better, and of leane cattell out of bad pasture into a more fertile soile. Can any man displant you, vnlesse you will? or can any man thinke that Scotland is so strong to pull you out of your houses? or doe you not thinke I know England hath more people, Scotland more wast ground?[78]

Significantly, James employs the trope of vegetation in his defence of the British project and claims that he was unjustly accused of unfixing the roots of barren Scotland and 'transporting' them to the fertile ground of England. This use of the trope of vegetation reinforces my case for situating the Birnam Wood scenes in the context of the Jacobean union debate. More importantly, however, this exchange between James and his English subjects suggests an alternative reading of the Birnam Wood scenes. For some English people, the Scots appeared to be the sole beneficiary when the complete union would be effected; as Nicholas Fuller, MP for London, warned his countrymen in 1607, 'there is Benefitt say some by this Union; it is true, but the whole Benefitt is to the other Side; for I doe not heare of any English preferred there; therefore the Profitt is theirs'.[79] Macbeth's barren Scotland, from which Malcolm creates his fertile kingdom, might not have been associated with Elizabeth's England by some in the audience but rather with James's Scotland, from which James plucked his fellow Scots to replant them into England, an unpopular union scheme, which was condemned as enriching destitute Scotland by incorporating it into relatively rich England – a rescue operation of the Scots at the sacrifice of England.

Anglo-Scottish tensions had continuously featured on the London stage; in particular, the representation of Scotland as a barren land and that of its inhabitants as uncivil, destitute people constantly attempting to invade England were commonplace in

Elizabethan plays. In *Edward III* (1590), in which Shakespeare possibly had a hand, the Countess of Salisbury, whose town is besieged by the invading Scottish King David, taunts the 'rough insulting barbarism' (2.9) of the Scottish people and despises them for living 'in the barren, bleak and fruitless air' (2.14). In Shakespeare's *Henry V* (1599), Henry V reminds his subjects of the external threat from 'pilfering borderers', that is, 'the Scot, / Who hath been still a giddy neighbour to us' (1.2.142–45):

HENRY V
For you shall read that my great-grandfather
Never went with his forces into France
But that the Scot on his unfurnished kingdom
Came pouring like the tide into a breach.

(1.2.146–49)

In these Elizabethan history plays, the Scots are often represented as needy, aggressive people attempting to break into England's rich soil at any given moment. Even in comedies, Scotland is often associated with barrenness. In Shakespeare's *The Comedy of Errors* (1594), for example, Doromio of Syracuse playfully compares the body of Nell, a kitchen wench, to a terrestrial globe; when asked in which part of her body Scotland can be located, Doromio says, 'I found it by the barrenness, hard in the palm of her hand' (3.2.123–24), articulating the conventional derogatory perception of Scotland as unfruitful.

Even after James's accession and his proclamation of the union of the two kingdoms, playwrights continued to express the discomfort of the English people with the Scots, particularly with those who began to populate London. In *Eastward Ho* (1605), a popular city comedy by George Chapman, Ben Jonson and John Marston, Captain Seagull boasts of his knowledge of Virginia, to which he plans to sail – a topical issue for the Jacobean audience as the English resumed their expeditions to Virginia when the war with Spain formally ended in 1604 – and talks about the Scots who are already there:

SEAGULL
> And then you shall live freely there, without sergeants, or courtiers, or lawyers, or intelligencers – only a few industrious Scots, perhaps, who, indeed, are dispersed over the face of the whole earth. But as for them, there are no greater friends to Englishmen and England, when they are out on 't, in the world, than they are. And for my part, I would a hundred thousand of 'em were there, for we are all one countrymen now, ye know; and we should find ten times more comfort of them there than we do here.
>
> (3.3.42–52)[80]

The English captain is well aware of James's proclamation of the union of the two kingdoms: 'we are all one country men, ye know'. However, although he tries to sound positive about the Scots, his discomfort with the Scots residing in England is also evident in his remark ('we should find ten times more comfort of them there than we do here'). The play thus deftly addresses the negative sentiments towards the Scots among the English citizens without sounding explicitly anti-Scottish.

Situated in this theatrical context of negative representations of Scotland and its people, it is not surprising if the English audience saw the moving of the forest by the Scottish Malcolm and his achievements of Anglo-Scottish alliance in a sceptical light. In fact, Shakespeare's play allows such an anti-Scottish interpretation of Malcolm on the part of the English audience. First, the play allows us to question the validity of the Birnam Wood spectacle. While Macbeth, upon hearing the report of his credulous messenger, firmly believes that Birnam Wood has unfixed its roots and begun to march towards him, the audience know well that the march of the forest, orchestrated by Malcolm, is a mere disguise for his invasion of Macbeth's kingdom as fully explained in the preceding scene: 'Let every soldier hew him down a bough, / And bear't before him; thereby shall we shadow / The numbers of our host, and make discovery / Err in report of us' (5.4.4–7). Indeed, Birnam Wood moves only in the mind of Macbeth, the distracted tyrant; Malcolm merely cuts the boughs of the trees and stages a spectacle which only superficially fulfils the witches' prophecy. The spectacle of unfixing and moving the forest is not genuine but just an illusion. Neither the witches nor Malcolm achieve the potentially majestic project of moving the forest, but they merely deceive Macbeth into believing that the forest has actually moved.

Indeed, Malcolm's role in producing this false spectacle is problematic. On the one hand, Malcolm styles himself a legitimate sovereign/rescuer of his suffering Scottish people, establishing harmony and alliance between Scotland and England, a consequence which could possibly have evoked James's union project in many audience members. On the other hand, however, he is actually a tactful strategist who, like the witches, uses deception as a means to accomplish his invasion. In fact, the Birnam Wood spectacle not only masks the size of Malcolm's army but also deflects our attention from the contentious nature of Malcolm's enterprise, that is, the invasion of Scotland with foreign soldiers. In this respect, Malcolm's conduct eerily evokes English dissident voices against James, who was anxious to divert the attention of his English subjects from one contentious implication of his succession and his union scheme – the 'conquest' of England by the Scottish king – by flaunting an olive branch, a symbol of peace and harmony. In Gervase Markham's *Honour in His Perfection* (1624), James was retrospectively described as succeeding to the English throne 'not with an Oliue Branch in his hand, but with an whole Forrest of *Oliues* round about him; for he brought not Peace to this Kingdome alone, but almost to all the Christian Kingdomes in Europe'.[81] Just as Malcolm hides his army under the branches of Birnam Wood, James too was able to use the forest of olives symbolically, performing the self-styled role of peacemaker as well as those of state physician and father-king, in order to effectively tone down the implication of his takeover of the English throne.

Equally problematic is that Malcolm is not an independent, masculine monarch as he would wish himself to appear; he is dependent not only on the English monarch and lords but also, like Macbeth, on the demonic power of the witches. The Birnam Wood scenes show that, whether knowingly or not, Malcolm is complicit with the witches in deceiving Macbeth, practically acting as their minister by helping to create the witches' illusion. Indeed, it is not Malcolm but rather the witches who have the controlling power; they are the main authors of the fate of Scotland. The implication of this is significant. The supposedly majestic prophecies about the birth of the new regime are provided by the witches – 'the instruments of darkness' (1.3.126) – who are constantly portrayed in the play as unreliable and beguiling orators. In this respect, the other powerful spectacle in *Macbeth* – which has even more apparent links with James himself – also needs re-examination. In Act 4 Scene 1, the witches not only give Macbeth the prophecies about Macduff and Birnam Wood but also unveil the grandiose vision of Banquo's kingly descendants – that is, the ancestors of James, who was known as Banquo's descendant:

A show of eight kings, the last with a glass in his hand; and BANQUO.

MACBETH
Thou art too like the spirit of Banquo; down:
Thy crown does sear mine eyeballs. And thy hair,
Thou other gold-bound brow, is like the first.
A third is like the former. Filthy hags,
Why do you show me this? – A fourth? Start, eyes!
What, will the line stretch out to th' crack of doom?
Another yet? A seventh? I'll see no more;
And yet the eighth appears, who bears a glass
Which shows me many more; and some I see
That twofold balls and treble sceptres carry.
                                        (4.1.111–20)

As I noted earlier, this spectacle can be seen as an encomiastic reference to James's vision of the British union. However, just like the Birnam Wood spectacle, this spectacle of James's ancestors is equally elusive; the march is conjured up by the beguiling witches and is witnessed only by the increasingly deranged Macbeth.

Early in the play, Banquo himself warns that, by trusting the witches, one would suffer terrible consequences: 'oftentimes, to win us to our harm, / The instruments of darkness tell us truths, / Win us with honest trifles, to betray's / In deepest consequence' (1.3.125–28). At the end of the play, the tragic protagonist finally comes to the same conclusion that 'the words of the witches should not be believed as they 'keep the word of promise to our ear, / And break it to our hope' (5.8.21–22). To what extent, then, can the audience believe the two prophecies about the creation of a new regime or the prophetic vision of the Stuart lineage which would 'stretch out to th' crack of doom'? Even if one chooses to believe that the witches are unveiling the truth, one is still left to wonder what would be the consequence of believing so, as Macbeth does to his tragic end. Given that, in *Macbeth*, prophecy is always presented as beguiling and delivered with hidden malicious intents, the links between the play and James's political vision are not necessarily encomiastic but rather unsettling. By re-editing and reinterpreting ancient prophecies, James attempted to present his succession as the fulfilment of ancient prophecies and his British project as the next to be fulfilled. Yet some of his English subjects doubted the authenticity of these ancient prophecies, which were in some ways as dubious as the witches' prophecies, and, as we have seen, also expressed concern over James's British project, doubting his real motive behind the union scheme which was likely to benefit the Scottish people alone.[82] The play addresses this unease with James; it allows the audience to question the validity of the prophetic visions of the witches, highlighting the fact that prophecies can often mask the true intention of those who pronounce them. The play leaves the audience to wonder what would be the consequence of believing James's political vision based on prophecies. By doing so, I would suggest that the play lays bare the ideological and iconographical tactics of James through which he staged his succession and his union scheme, shedding light on the precariousness and dubiousness of the ways in which James's political vision was informed and publicized.

Macbeth does not passively reflect James's political vision. While directing our attention to his political fantasy, the play simultaneously allows the audience to variously question the ways in which this fantasy is staged. Shakespeare illustrates the ways in which James used rhetorical strategies – prophecies, the tropes of medical operation and the anthropomorphic image of the state – and effectively appropriated the memory of Elizabeth. Yet, by doing so, he incorporates the voices of Jacobeans who felt uneasy and remained sceptical about the idealistic vision of their new monarch. In this respect, *Macbeth* is not a univocal play. *Macbeth* invites the audience to interpret the vision it presents, yet it does not articulate or impose its own political judgement on the audience. In *Macbeth*, what particularly informs this interpretative multifariousness is the effective use of prophecies. By staging James's much publicized political vision through this problematic vehicle, Shakespeare addresses the conflicting emotions felt by the Jacobeans towards that vision, highlighting both the hope and the unease James's reign aroused.

Macbeth reveals the ideological and rhetorical strategies through which James attempted to legitimize his succession and his union scheme, highlighting, in particular, the way in which James negotiated and appropriated both prophecies and the discourse of Elizabeth for informing and publicizing his political vision. In the following three chapters, I will continue to illustrate the ways in which Shakespeare examines Jacobeans' negotiation of the memory of the late Tudor queen, shifting my focus from a moribund state mother in *Macbeth* to the equally political representations of a commanding mistress to chivalric knights, a mother of peace and an imperilled, suffering heroine.

Notes

1 For James's project for full union, see Bruce Galloway, *The Union of England and Scotland, 1603–1608* (Edinburgh: Donald, 1986), 15–78 and Brian P. Levack, *The Formation of the British State: England, Scotland, and the Union, 1603–1707* (Oxford: Clarendon Press, 1987), 1–9.

2 *Stuart Royal Proclamations: Royal Proclamations of King James I, 1603–1625*, ed. James F. Larkin and Paul L. Hughes, vol. 1 (Oxford: Clarendon Press, 1973), 96.

3 For the iconography of James as the emperor of Great Britain, see, for example, Roberta Florence Brinkley, *Arthurian Legend in the Seventeenth Century* (New York: Octagon, 1967), 20–22 and Jonathan Goldberg, *James I and the Politics of Literature: Jonson, Shakespeare, Donne, and Their Contemporaries* (Baltimore, MD: Johns Hopkins University Press, 1983). For the coinage, see esp. Galloway, *The Union of England and Scotland*, 59–60, 82–88.

4 Kevin Curran, *Marriage, Performance, and Politics at the Jacobean Court* (Farnham: Ashgate, 2009), 20.

5 See Brinkley, *Arthurian Legend*, 20–22; Goldberg, *James I and the Politics of Literature*, 43; John Kerrigan, *Archipelagic English: Literature, History, and Politics, 1603–1707* (Oxford: Oxford University Press, 2008), 13; and Graham Parry, *The Golden Age Restor'd: The Culture of the Stuart Court, 1603–42* (Manchester: Manchester University Press, 1981), 1–39.

6 William Herbert, *A Prophesie of Cadwallader* (London, 1604), G4v.

7 *The Works of Michael Drayton*, ed. J. William Hebel, vol. 4 (Oxford: Blackwell, 1961), 107.

8 For an overview of political prophecy and its function, see Rupert Taylor, *The Political Prophecy in England* (New York: Columbia University Press, 1911), 1–24.

9 Sharon L. Jansen Jaech, 'Political Prophecy and Macbeth's "Sweet Bodements"', *Shakespeare Quarterly* 34, no. 3 (1983): 291.

10 For the appropriation of political prophecy by James and his supporters at the time of his accession, see esp. Brinkley,

Arthurian Legend, 4–22; Robin Headlam Wells, *Shakespeare on Masculinity* (Cambridge: Cambridge University Press, 2000), 125–30; and Keith Thomas, *Religion and the Decline of Magic* (New York: Scribner, 1971), 494–96.

11 *The Whole Prophesie of Scotland, England, and Somepart of France, and Denmark* (London, 1603), B5r.

12 Thomas, *Religion and the Decline of Magic*, 493.

13 For the date of *Macbeth*, see esp. Leeds Barroll, *Politics, Plague, and Shakespeare's Theater: The Stuart Years* (Ithaca, NY: Cornell University Press, 1991), 133–52; A. R. Braunmuller, introduction to *Macbeth*, ed. A. R. Braunmuller (Cambridge: Cambridge University Press, 2008), 6–8; and Stanley Wells and Gary Taylor, *William Shakespeare: A Textual Companion* (Oxford: Clarendon Press, 1987), 128–29.

14 See esp. Henry Neill Paul, *The Royal Play of 'Macbeth': When, Why, and How It Was Written by Shakespeare* (New York: Macmillan, 1950), 90–161.

15 For the possible sources of *Macbeth*, see M. C. Bradbrook, 'The Sources of *Macbeth*', *Shakespeare Survey* 4 (1951): 35–48 and Geoffrey Bullough, ed., *Narrative and Dramatic Sources of Shakespeare*, vol. 7 (London: Routledge; New York: Columbia University Press, 1973), 470–527.

16 Holinshed, *Chronicles*, in Bullough, ed., *Sources*, 7:505.

17 See esp. Renate Blumenfeld-Kosinski, *Not of Woman Born: Representations of Caesarean Birth in Medieval and Renaissance Culture* (Ithaca, NY: Cornell University Press, 1990), 1.

18 See esp. Janet Adelman, *Suffocating Mothers: Fantasies of Maternal Origin in Shakespeare's Plays, 'Hamlet' to 'The Tempest'* (London: Routledge, 1992), 130–46 and Coppélia Kahn, *Man's Estate: Masculine Identity in Shakespeare* (Berkeley: University of California Press, 1981), 151–92.

19 See esp. Michael J. O'Dowd and Elliot E. Philipp, *The History of Obstetrics and Gynaecology* (London: Parthenon, 1994), 159.

20 See Blumenfeld-Kosinski, *Not of Woman Born*, 91; Stephanie Chamberlain, 'Fantasizing Infanticide: Lady Macbeth and the Murdering Mother in Early Modern England', *College*

Literature 32 (2005): 72–91; and Barbara Ehrenreich and Deirdre English, *Witches, Midwives and Nurses: A History of Women Healers* (New York: Feminist Press, 1973), 19–20.

21 See also Stephen Orgel, 'Macbeth and the Antic Round', *Shakespeare Survey* 52 (1999): 143–53 (esp. 150) and Robert N. Watson, *Shakespeare and the Hazards of Ambition* (Cambridge, MA: Harvard University Press, 1984), 3–5.

22 For the May Day reading of Birnam Wood, see esp. Norman Holland, 'Macbeth as Hibernal Giant', *Literature and Psychology* 10 (1960): 37–38 and John Holloway, *The Story of the Night: Studies in Shakespeare's Major Tragedies* (London: Routledge, 1961), 63–66.

23 James VI and I, *Political Writings*, 136.

24 Jenijoy La Belle, '"A Strange Infirmity": Lady Macbeth's Amenorrhea', *Shakespeare Quarterly* 31, no. 3 (1980): 381–86 (esp. 382–83).

25 The word 'medicine' signifies physician or medical practitioner. See, for example, Braunmuller, ed., *Macbeth*, 238n. For the identification of 'the medicine of the sickly weal' with Malcolm, see also David Norbrook, '*Macbeth* and the Politics of Historiography', in *The Politics of Discourse: The Literature and History of Seventeenth-Century England*, ed. Kevin Sharpe and Steven Zwicker (Berkeley: University of California Press, 1987), 114 and Caroline F. E. Spurgeon, *Shakespeare's Imagery and What It Tells Us* (Cambridge: Cambridge University Press, 1935), 332.

26 See, for example, William Spates, 'Shakespeare and the Irony of Early Modern Disease Metaphor and Metonymy', in *Rhetorics of Bodily Disease and Health in Medieval and Early Modern England*, ed. Jennifer C. Vaught (Farnham: Ashgate, 2010), 155–70.

27 Thomas Heywood, *The Rape of Lucrece* (London, 1608), C4r.

28 Heywood, *The Rape of Lucrece*, C4r–C4v.

29 Heywood, *The Rape of Lucrece*, K1r.

30 For example, Leonard Barkan writes that 'Renaissance England represents in a way the hey day of the anthropomorphic image of the commonwealth' (*Nature's Work of Art: The Human Body as Image of the World* [New Haven, CT: Yale University Press,

1975], 75). For the early modern analogical view on the body politic and the body natural, see also Marie Axton, *The Queen's Two Bodies: Drama and the Elizabethan Succession* (London: Royal Historical Society, 1977), 11–15; David George Hale, *The Body Politic: A Political Metaphor in Renaissance English Literature* (The Hague: Mouton, 1971), 52–107; Jonathan Gil Harris, *Foreign Bodies and the Body Politic: Discourses of Social Pathology in Early Modern England* (Cambridge: Cambridge University Press, 1998), 1–16; and Ernst H. Kantorowicz, *The King's Two Bodies: A Study in Mediaeval Political Theology* (Princeton, NJ: Princeton University Press, 1957), 372–83.

31 Edward Forset, *A Comparative Discourse of the Bodies Natural and Politique* (New York: Da Capo Press, 1973), 73. For the possibility of Shakespeare's knowledge of Forset's book, see Kenneth Muir, 'The Background of *Coriolanus*', *Shakespeare Quarterly* 10, no. 2 (1959): 137–45 (esp. 141–44).

32 Forset, *A Comparative Discourse*, 73–76.

33 *The Works of Francis Bacon*, ed. James Spedding, Robert Leslie Ellis and Douglas Denon Heath, vol. 9 (1862; Cambridge: Cambridge University Press, 2011), 100.

34 For the representation of Ireland in the early modern imperial discourse, see, for example, Tristan Marshall, *Theatre and Empire: Great Britain on the London Stages under James VI and I* (Manchester: Manchester University Press, 2000), 19–20 and Jennifer Munroe, *Gender and the Garden in Early Modern English Literature* (Aldershot: Ashgate, 2008), 47–74.

35 For the representation of Elizabeth as the mother of the English people, see Christine Coch, '"Mother of My Contreye": Elizabeth I and Tudor Constructions of Motherhood', *English Literary Renaissance* 26, no. 3 (1996): 423–50 and Cowen Lena Orlin, 'The Fictional Families of Elizabeth I', in *Political Rhetoric, Power, and Renaissance Women*, ed. Carole Levin and Patricia A. Sullivan (Albany: State University of New York Press, 1995), 85–110.

36 *Elizabeth I: Collected Works*, ed. Leah S. Marcus, Janel Mueller and Mary Beth Rose (Chicago: University of Chicago Press, 2000), 59.

37 William Averell, *A Meruailous Combat of Contrarieties* (London, 1588), C3r.

38 Josias Nichols, *The Plea of the Innocent* (London, 1602), 67.

39 *Sorrowes Ioy*, in Nichols, *Progresses of Elizabeth*, 4:737. Radford Mavericke, *Three Treatises Religiously Handled* (London, 1603), C4r, E2r.

40 Thomas Dekker, *The Wonderfull Yeare* (London, 1603), B2r.

41 John Milward, *Iacobs Great Day of Trouble, and Deliuerance* (London, 1610), K2r.

42 For the social strain in the final years of Elizabeth's reign, see esp. Jim Sharpe, 'Social Strain and Social Dislocation, 1585–1603', in *The Reign of Elizabeth I: Court and Culture in the Last Decade*, ed. John Guy (Cambridge: Cambridge University Press, 1995), 192–211.

43 Leonard Tennenhouse, *Power on Display: The Politics of Shakespeare's Genres* (London: Methuen, 1986), 103–4. For the identification of Elizabeth's body with the English body politic, see also Axton, *The Queen's Two Bodies*, 12 and Harris, *Foreign Bodies*, 45–47.

44 For the outbreak of plague in 1603, see F. P. Wilson, *The Plague in Shakespeare's London* (Oxford: Clarendon Press, 1927), 85–113.

45 For the emergence of misogynistic discourse and the negative representation of Elizabeth around the turn of the century, see esp. Steven Mullaney, 'Mourning and Misogyny: *Hamlet, The Revenger's Tragedy*, and the Final Progress of Elizabeth I, 1600–1607', *Shakespeare Quarterly* 45, no. 2 (1994): 139–62 (esp. 139–45).

46 Forset, *A Comparative Discourse*, 69.

47 *The Humble Petition of the Ministers of the Church of England*, in Thomas Fuller, *The Church History of Britain, from the Birth of Jesus Christ until the Year M.DC.XLVIII*, vol. 5 (Oxford: Oxford University Press, 1845), 308.

48 I quote the English translation of Howgrave's Latin verse from *Threno-Thriambeuticon*, in Nichols, *Progresses of Elizabeth*, 4:320.

49 Dekker, *The Wonderfull Yeare*, C1r.

50 For issues concerning James's succession, see, for example, Pauline Croft, *King James* (Basingstoke: Palgrave Macmillan, 2003), 43–44 and Susan Doran, 'James VI and the English

Succession', in *James VI and I: Ideas, Authority, and Government*, ed. Ralph Houlbrooke (Aldershot: Ashgate, 2006), 25–42.

51 Levack, *The Formation of the British State*, 36. Indeed, James's union plan for England was criticized in this term; as one anti-union pamphlet puts it, 'the change of style will be, as it were, the erecting of a new kingdom, and so it shall be, as it were, a kingdom conquered' (quoted in Levack, *The Formation of the British State*, 38 and Roger Lockyer, *James VI and I* [London: Longman, 1998], 56).

52 I quote the English translation of Walsall's Latin verse from *Threno-Thriambeuticon*, in Nichols, *Progresses of Elizabeth*, 4:324. For James's foreign birth and his attempts to present himself as a non-foreigner, see also Susan Doran, 'Polemic and Prejudice: A Scottish King for an English Throne', in *Doubtful and Dangerous: The Question of Succession in Late Elizabethan England*, ed. Susan Doran and Paulina Kewes (Manchester: Manchester University Press, 2016), 215–35.

53 James VI and I, *Political Writings*, 49 (see also 4, 251). For the familiar metaphor of the monarch as actor, see also Goldberg, *James I and the Politics of Literature*, 113.

54 *King James VI and I: Selected Writings*, ed. Neil Rhodes, Jennifer Richards and Joseph Marshall (Aldershot: Ashgate, 2003), 281.

55 James VI and I, *Stuart Royal Proclamations*, 1:156.

56 England and Wales. Parliament. House of Commons, *A Record of Some Worthy Proceedings in the Honourable, Wise, and Faithfull Howse of Commons in the Late Parliament* (Amsterdam, 1611), 47–48.

57 For attempts to honour James as England's new protector instead of conqueror, see also Martin Butler, *The Stuart Court Masque and Political Culture* (Cambridge: Cambridge University Press, 2008), 102 and Watkins, *Representing Elizabeth*, 14–15.

58 *Sorrowes Ioy*, in Nichols, *Progresses of Elizabeth*, 4:737.

59 *Sorrowes Ioy*, in Nichols, *Progresses of Elizabeth*, 4:745.

60 *Weepe with Ioy* (London, 1603), 1.

61 Dekker, *The Magnificent Entertainment Given to King James*, in *The Dramatic Works*, 2:274. Richard Mulcaster, *The Translation of Certaine Latine Verses Written uppon Her Majesties Death, Called 'A Comforting Complaint'* (London, 1603), A2r.

62 James VI and I, *Political Writings*, 181, 27. Unsurprisingly, James condemned the failed Gunpowder Plot in 1605 as 'so vnnaturall a Parricide' (*Political Writings*, 154). For further analysis of the father-king in relation to James's political views, see Perry, *The Making of Jacobean Culture*, 250 and Debora Kuller Shuger, *Habits of Thought in the English Renaissance: Religion, Politics, and the Dominant Culture* (Berkeley: University of California Press, 1990), 218–49.

63 James VI and I, *Political Writings*, 65.

64 Arthur F. Kinney, 'Scottish History, the Union of the Crowns and the Issue of Right Rule: Shakespeare's *Macbeth*', in *Renaissance Culture in Context: Theory and Practice*, ed. Jean R. Brink and William F. Gentrup (Aldershot: Scolar Press, 1993), 27–28.

65 James VI and I, *Stuart Royal Proclamations*, 1:95.

66 Samuel Daniel, *A Panegyrike Congratulatorie to the Kings Maiestie* (London, 1603), A1r.

67 For earlier studies of *Macbeth* from the perspective of the union debate, see esp. Sharon Alker and Holly Faith Nelson, '*Macbeth*, the Jacobean Scot, and the Politics of the Union', *Studies in English Literature, 1500–1900* 47, no. 2 (2007): 379–401; Kerrigan, *Archipelagic English*, 91–114; Kinney, 'Scottish History', 18–53; and Marshall, *Theatre and Empire*, 60–64.

68 For an overview of critical reception of 'twofold balls and treble sceptres', see esp. Emily B. Lyle, 'The "Twofold Balls and Treble Scepters" in *Macbeth*', *Shakespeare Quarterly* 28, no. 4 (1977): 516–19.

69 Norbrook, '*Macbeth* and the Politics of Historiography', 96.

70 Andrew Escobedo, 'From Britannia to England: *Cymbeline* and the Beginning of Nations', *Shakespeare Quarterly* 59, no. 1 (2008): 86.

71 James VI and I, *Political Writings*, 167.

72 *The Parliamentary or Constitutional History of England: From the Earliest Times, to the Restoration of King Charles II*, 2nd ed., vol. 5 (London: Tonson, 1751), 210.

73 In the Whitehall Banqueting House ceiling, *King James Perfecting the Union of England and Scotland* (1635) by Peter Paul Rubens, James is presented as a father pointing at a crowned babe, which can be taken as an allegorical representation of his political child, Great Britain. See also Butler, *The Stuart Court Masque*, 93 and D. J. Gordon, 'Rubens and the Whitehall Ceiling', in *The Renaissance Imagination*, ed. Stephen Orgel (Berkeley: University of California Press, 1975), 24–50 (esp. 38–41).

74 *The Parliamentary or Constitutional History of England*, 5:210.

75 James VI and I, *Political Writings*, 160.

76 For the failure of James's perfect union, see esp. Jenny Wormald, 'O Brave New World? The Union of England and Scotland in 1603', in *Anglo-Scottish Relations from 1603 to 1900*, ed. T. C. Smout (Oxford: Oxford University Press, 2005), 13–35 (esp. 24–26).

77 James VI and I, *Political Writings*, 162. For anti-Scottish sentiment in England in the early years of James's reign, see esp. Levack, *The Formation of the British State*, 195–97. For analysis of *Macbeth* as the reflection of anti-Scottish sentiment, see, for example, Alker and Nelson, '*Macbeth*, the Jacobean Scot, and the Politics of the Union', 382–90.

78 James VI and I, *Political Writings*, 165.

79 *The Parliamentary Diary of Robert Bowyer, 1606–1607*, ed. David Harris Willson (Minneapolis: University of Minnesota Press, 1931), 265.

80 George Chapman, Ben Jonson and John Marston, *Eastward Ho*, ed. R. W. Van Fossen (Manchester: Manchester University Press, 1979).

81 Gervase Markham, *Honour in His Perfection* (London, 1624), D4v.

82 For the contemporary scepticism towards political prophecy, see esp. Howard Dobin, *Merlin's Disciples: Prophecy, Poetry, and Power in Renaissance England* (Stanford, CA: Stanford University Press, 1990), 105–33, 189–206.

2

Antony and Cleopatra: The Competition for Representing the Queen

Funeral for the queen

At the end of *Macbeth*, Malcolm leads the English army and attempts to restore 'universal peace' to the tyrannized mother country, Scotland, and secure 'all unity on earth' (4.3.99–100). His victory over Macbeth and his wife, who goaded on her husband to regicide, not only brings peace to Scotland but also marks the friendly alliance between Scotland and England. In Shakespeare's next play, *Antony and Cleopatra*, Malcolm's role seems to be taken over by Octavius Caesar, who, before the decisive battle against his enemies, Antony and Cleopatra, proclaims his aim to bring peace and unity to the divided Roman world:

CAESAR
    The time of universal peace is near.
    Prove this a prosp'rous day, the three-nooked world
    Shall bear the olive freely.

                           (4.6.5–7)

As in *Macbeth*, the closing speech of this play is given to the victor. Yet, in sharp contrast to Malcolm's derogatory reference in his closing speech to his enemies, the dead Macbeths – 'this dead butcher, and his fiend-like queen' (5.9.35) – the victorious Caesar pays homage to the defeated, expressing his intention to host a public funeral for Cleopatra:

CAESAR
                    Take up her bed,
And bear her women from the monument.
She shall be buried by her Antony.
No grave upon the earth shall clip in it
A pair so famous. High events as these
Strike those that make them, and their story is
No less pity than his glory which
Brought them to be lamented. Our army shall
In solemn show attend this funeral,
And then to Rome.

                              (5.2.355–64)

Julia M. Walker has offered an influential reading of this scene; she interprets Caesar's order, which is not mentioned in Shakespeare's sources, as a direct reference to a specific historical event of 1606 – James I's order to relocate the tomb of Elizabeth I.[1] Although this episodic parallel is suggestive in its narrow court context, it is highly likely that, as Walker herself admits, the majority of the audience in 1606–7 did not recognize this rigid comparison.[2] Furthermore, Walker argues that, by mirroring James's political action in Caesar's, the play actively supports James.[3] Walker's reading uses the episodic similarities between Caesar's final speech and James's order for Elizabeth's reburial in a way that simplifies the play's complex interaction with Jacobean political contexts. In this chapter, I will offer an alternative interpretation of the final scene and illuminate its complexity by resituating the play in a much broader Jacobean context – that of growing nostalgia for militant aspects of Elizabeth's reign among the audience both courtly and public.

Before situating Shakespeare's play in this context, we should
first note that Cleopatra had already frequently featured in late
Elizabethan and Jacobean writings even before Shakespeare
chose to dramatize her life and that her representation carried
political significance in these writings. As Paulina Kewes has
suggested, Mary Sidney's *Antonius* (1592), a translation of
Robert Garnier's work, and Samuel Daniel's *The Tragedie of
Cleopatra* (1594) both conspicuously evoke parallels between
Caesar's Rome and Philip II's Spain, and between Egypt and
late Elizabethan England, states which were both threatened
by the growing powers of their aggressive rivals.[4] Cleopatra, in
these closet dramas – both are possible sources of Shakespeare's
play – resembles the politically charged representation
of Elizabeth as the staunch Protestant queen besieged by
her Catholic foes, as illustrated in John Foxe's account of
Elizabeth.[5] No other text, however, more vividly illustrates the
extent to which writers were aware of the connotative range
of the representation of Cleopatra and made use of it than
A Dedication to Sir Philip Sidney, a work written by Fulke
Greville during the first decade of James's reign. In a passage
which has attracted little critical attention, Greville recalls
the European political landscape during Elizabeth's reign by
closely paralleling it to that of ancient Rome:

> the undertaking of this Antony single – I mean France –
> would prove a begetting of brave occasions jointly to disturb
> this Spanish Octavian in all his ways of crafty or forcible
> conquests, especially since Queen Elizabeth, the standard of
> this conjunction, would infallibly incline to unite with the
> better part.[6]

Greville compares France to Antony, the isolated Roman
hero, and Hapsburg Spain to Octavius, the crafty leader of
the fledgling Roman Empire. The political implication of
this metaphor is not difficult to conceive; Elizabeth, who
considered the alliance with France as an effective means of
protecting England from rising Spanish power, is identified
with Cleopatra, who united with Antony to defy Roman

domination.[7] Cleopatra was thus perceived by some writers as an appropriate figure to symbolize Elizabeth and her England.[8]

By dramatizing the life of the historical Cleopatra, therefore, Shakespeare inevitably involved himself in the politics of representing Elizabeth. In fact, instead of distancing himself from it, Shakespeare adds another politically charged aspect to his delineation of Cleopatra, tying his protagonist even closer to contemporary discourse of Elizabeth. When Caesar declares war on Egypt and comes to conquer her kingdom, the queen delivers a defiant speech, expressing her 'manly' determination to defend her beleaguered kingdom:

CLEOPATRA
               A charge we bear i'th' war,
     And, as the president of my kingdom, will
     Appear there for a man. Speak not against it!
     I will not stay behind.
                                                (3.7.16–19)

Although Cleopatra's enthusiasm for joining Antony's fleets is noted in Plutarch's *The Lives of the Noble Grecians and Romans* (translated by Thomas North and first published in 1579), the warlike image of Cleopatra is Shakespeare's own invention.[9] Shakespeare's elaboration on the brief account in Plutarch – in particular, his stress on Cleopatra's 'manliness' ('the best of men' [3.7.26]) – activates the latent significance of the image of the warlike queen in the post-Gunpowder Plot discourse, in which, as I discussed in the Introduction, the representation of Elizabeth became specifically militant. Shakespeare's representation of the queen overseeing the sea battle connects the play with this politically charged representation of Elizabeth.

Reflections of the Elizabethan period in *Antony and Cleopatra* have received much critical attention; in particular, possible links between Elizabeth and Shakespeare's Cleopatra have been noted in many studies in the past.[10] However, these earlier studies share a methodological problem; by drawing on loose biographical similarities between Elizabeth and Cleopatra, these studies proposed links that are at best superficial. The representation of Cleopatra should be examined in the context of the representation of Elizabeth not because of some minor biographical similarities between the two queens – obviously, there are more dissimilarities than similarities – but because of the ways in which Shakespeare effectively evokes the nostalgic discourse of Elizabeth by clothing Cleopatra and his general Antony in popular Elizabethan symbolism. Shakespeare connects the play with the nostalgic discourse of Elizabeth not only through the belligerent speech the embattled Cleopatra delivers before the battle but, as I wish to show, also through the language of chivalric romance and oceanic imagery, both of which were essential elements in the contemporary phenomenon of nostalgia for Elizabeth. By examining the various ways in which the play interacted with the discourse of Elizabeth – including the way in which the nostalgic discourse is challenged and critiqued within the play – I will illuminate the complex Jacobean significance of Shakespeare's Egyptian queen and that of the final scene of the play.

The Elizabethan past: The fairy queen and her knight

When Antony temporarily leaves the Egyptian court for Rome, he styles himself Cleopatra's faithful 'soldier' and 'servant' (1.3.71), defining his departure as the trial of his love for Cleopatra:

ANTONY
                    My precious queen, forbear,
And give true evidence to his love, which stands
An honourable trial.

(1.3.74–76)

The unforeseen events in Rome leave Antony no choice but to depart Egypt: the death of his Roman wife Fulvia and Pompey's armed rebellion against the Roman state, for which the letters of his supporters in Rome urge him to return home. In his message to Cleopatra from abroad, however, Antony describes his journey from Egypt to Rome as if he is conducting his grand military expedition into the East:

ALEXAS
                    'Good friend,' quoth he,
'Say the firm Roman to great Egypt sends
This treasure of an oyster, at whose foot,
To mend this petty present, I will piece
Her opulent throne with kingdoms. All the East,
Say thou, shall call her mistress.' So he nodded
And soberly did mount an arm-gaunt steed
Who neighed so high that what I would have spoke
Was beastly dumbed by him.
                                        (1.5.44–52)

As if to find a 'new heaven, new earth' (1.1.17) to encompass his unbounded love for Cleopatra, Antony styles himself Cleopatra's conquering hero who ventures into the eastern kingdoms, even though, as is apparent to the audience, he is merely heading back to Rome to negotiate as much as to fight.

Antony's self-posturing is particularly meaningful as it shows us glimpses into the fruitful relationship Antony had with Cleopatra in his former glorious days when love for his mistress was the driving force of his military actions. Interestingly, Antony replicates the language of chivalric romance, styling himself a knight who ventures into the outside world to test his love for his mistress.[11] As Cleopatra's knight, Antony demands that foreign kings acknowledge Cleopatra as their supreme governor/mistress ('All the East, / Say thou, shall call her mistress'), similarly to the way in which a knight in chivalric romance challenges his opponents and, by defeating them, forces them to acknowledge the virtue of his mistress. Antony is resolved to bestow the fruits of his military ventures on his mistress as a token of his love, with the oriental pearl as its earnest; in fact, this relationship between Antony and

Cleopatra is what infuriates his Roman partner Octavius Caesar: 'Unto her / He gave the stablishment of Egypt; made her / Of lower Syria, Cyprus, Lydia, / Absolute Queen' (3.6.8–11). Antony is her devoted knight who executes the will of his mistress who has 'full supremacy' over him (3.11.59). For Antony, his Egyptian 'empress' (3.11.33) is the 'armourer of' his 'heart' (4.4.7) 'whose eye becked forth my wars and called them home, / Whose bosom was my crownet, my chief end' (4.12.26–27), in other words, the driving force as well as the beneficiary of his military ventures.

Cleopatra's relationship to Antony evokes the framework of chivalric romance, a framework which was widely used to define Elizabeth's relationship to her courtiers during her reign. The Earl of Leicester, for example, appropriated chivalric romance in the entertainments he held at Kenilworth in 1575, in which he presented gifts as 'tokens of true love' to Elizabeth, expressing his knightly devotion to his supreme mistress.[12] Walter Ralegh constantly hailed Elizabeth as his unattainable mistress and called her 'dear Empress of my heart' and 'my true fantasy's mistress', presenting himself as her enamoured knight.[13] Unsurprisingly, these Elizabethan courtiers were represented as the glorious knights in the court of Gloriana/Elizabeth in Edmund Spenser's *The Faerie Queene* (1590/96). The Earl of Essex then styled himself the heir to the chivalric role of these courtiers, as when he performed the role of Erophilus, Elizabeth's knight of love, in the Accession Day Tilts in 1595.[14] Even in the Jacobean period, Essex was commemorated as such; Henry Raymonde hailed Essex in *The Maiden Queene* (1607) as 'that braue Mars of men' who 'dar'd ... proudest spanish knight'.[15]

Furthermore, Shakespeare reinforces this association between the play and the chivalric discourse of Elizabeth by adding another distinctly nostalgic element to the representation of Cleopatra and Antony; he replicates the oceanic imagery deployed in Elizabethan imperial discourse and later reproduced in the Jacobean nostalgia for Elizabeth. Departing from Plutarch's *Lives*, Shakespeare clothes the

couple with the imagery of maritime warfare, representing
Cleopatra as the empress of the sea and Antony as her admiral.
When Antony begins to prepare for a military confrontation
with Caesar, his navy is first mentioned ('Our great navy's
rigged' [3.5.19]), and at Cleopatra's request Antony insists
on fighting Caesar at sea despite their obvious disadvantage.
Later in the play, Antony is nostalgically recalled as the general
who, with his sword, 'quartered the world and o'er green
Neptune's back / With ships made cities' (4.14.59–60), an
emphasis on Antony's ambitious oceanic activities which are
not mentioned in Plutarch's text. We might recall that, during
the late Elizabethan period, not only the aristocracy at court
but, as R. Malcolm Smuts puts it, 'the whole population was ...
encouraged to share vicariously in the romance of marine
warfare'.[16] For example, Richard Hakluyt's publications in the
1580s – *Divers Voyages Touching the Discoverie of America*
(1582) and *The Principal Navigations, Voiages, Traffiques
and Discoueries of the English Nation* (1589–1600) – revived
medieval styles and the themes of chivalric romance to illustrate
England's maritime achievements, popularizing the imperial
image of Elizabethan England as the seat of courageous English
sailors.[17] Military generals who led English fleets against
Catholic Spain or those who argued for colonial ventures
into 'new lands' were similarly represented as Elizabeth's sea-
knights who were inspired by the sea goddess to missions of
empire.[18] Unsurprisingly, what defined the nostalgic view of
Elizabeth's reign was the glorious memory of the late 1580s
and early 1590s – the victory over the Armada, privateering
against Spanish treasure on the high seas and colonial ventures
conducted under Elizabeth – a memory which centred on the
oceans. In *Nova Britannia* (1609), Robert Johnson harks back
to Elizabeth's reign and praises her by singling out England's
maritime activities both military and mercantile:

> to let passe the particular praises, as impertinent to my
> purpose, I doe onely call to minde our Royall Fleetes and
> Marchants Shippes, (the Iewels of our land) our excellent

Nauigators, and admirable voyages, as into all parts and round about the Globe with good successe, to the high fame and glorie of our Nation.[19]

Nostalgia for Elizabeth's militant courtiers was also closely associated with their maritime achievements. In particular, nostalgia for militant aspects of Elizabeth's reign centred on the memory of the Earl of Essex, who was often recalled in the early Jacobean period as Elizabeth's conquering hero; in *Troia Britanica* (1609), for example, Thomas Heywood evokes him as the general of the expeditionary English fleets: 'Renowned *Essex*', Heywood writes, 'martiald our great Fleete, / as that bold *Greeke* that sought the fleece of Gold, / hoping by sea an enemy to meete'.[20]

Before their departure for the battlefield at Actium, Antony calls out, 'We'll to our ship. / Away, my Thetis!' (3.7.59–60), identifying Cleopatra with the sea goddess and mother of Achilles. This identification is highly symbolic given that Elizabeth was often praised as the divine empress of the seas by her seafaring courtiers and those who argued for England's maritime expansion. Many scholars have noted that Elizabeth was often praised by her poets, such as Ralegh and Spenser, as '*Cynthia* the Ladie of the sea'.[21] However, less known is the fact that she was also represented as Thetis, Cynthia's sister. For example, Raphael Holinshed records that the verses presented to the Earl of Leicester in 1586 hailed Elizabeth as 'English Thetis', while praising Leicester as England's Achilles:

Like as the sea goddess Thetis had ingendred,
The valiant Achilles to the Greeks defence,
So hath now this English Thetis, who all praise deserved,
Sent us this Achilles to our Assistance,
Wherefore we yeeld him all due reuerence.[22]

Jacobean writers continued to represent Elizabeth as this sea goddess; William Browne's Book II of *Britannia's Pastorals* (1616) harks back to Elizabeth's iconographical role as the empress of the seas by recalling her as 'faire *Thetis*' of '*English Shepherds*', while Samuel Daniel's *The Vision of the Twelve Goddesses* (1604) similarly refers to Thetis in order to evoke Elizabeth's 'power by sea'.[23] In the context of this cultural symbolism, the representation of Cleopatra as the sea goddess of the maritime general Antony strikes a chord with this nostalgic image of Elizabeth.

It is therefore all the more significant that, in their sea battle against Caesar, Cleopatra and Antony ostentatiously style themselves the fairy queen and her knight – roles specifically tied to the chivalric context of Elizabeth's court. In Act 4 Scene 4, in which Cleopatra and Eros, Antony's soldier, arm Antony before the battle, Antony treats Eros as his squire (4.4.14–15) and Cleopatra as his dame: 'Fare thee well, dame. Whate'er becomes of me, / This is a solder's kiss' (4.4.29–30). Accordingly, when Antony gallantly departs to the battlefield, Cleopatra fantasizes that Antony will enter into single combat with his rival knight: 'He goes forth gallantly. That he and Caesar might / Determine this great war in single fight!' (4.4.36–37). Then, after winning the skirmish against Caesar, Antony triumphantly returns to his mistress to report his 'gests' (4.8.2), referring to her as his 'great fairy' (4.8.12).[24] The fairy queen blesses Antony and his soldier Scarus with her thanks, welcoming her knights who return from their dangerous mission to her court, 'smiling from / The world's great snare uncaught' (4.8.17–18). Shakespeare's Cleopatra and Antony thus take roles which derive from the Elizabethan version of medieval chivalric romance, in which the figure of the fairy queen – a divine, unattainable mistress – was introduced so as to adapt the potentially sexual undertone in chivalric romance to the chaste context of Elizabeth's court, from which, as Francis Bacon retrospectively put it in 1608, 'none was debarred that used fair accostment, and no lasciviousness in love'.[25] Elizabeth had been praised as the fairy queen during her lifetime and continued to be represented as such after her death; for example, an elegy published in 1603 commemorated her as 'Eliza Queene of Fayry lond'.[26] Furthermore, the theme of the fairy queen and her knights was a specifically timely one as it had been made widely known to Shakespeare's audience not only through Spenser's *The Faerie Queene*, a bestselling publication repeatedly reprinted throughout the Jacobean period, but also through Thomas Dekker's *The Whore of Babylon* (1606), a theatrical adaptation of Spenser's allegory. Shakespeare's identification of Cleopatra with the fairy queen evokes these contemporary fairy queens, who were strongly linked by the Jacobeans to the memory of Elizabeth and her court. Resituated in this way in the historicized linguistic and iconographical field of the late Elizabethan and early Jacobean periods, Shakespeare's representation of Cleopatra and Antony has a striking resonance with the nostalgic representation of Elizabeth and her militant courtiers, as he replicates the rhetoric of courtship and chivalry which shaped the relationship between Elizabeth and her courtiers.

My argument so far has illustrated the way in which the idealized view of Cleopatra and Antony links the play with the certain discourse of Elizabeth. However, the play does not, as has often been assumed, uncritically reconstruct or glorify the memory of Elizabeth's reign; on the contrary, *Antony and Cleopatra* simultaneously demonstrates its wry awareness of the limitations of these associations. In this regard, George Chapman's history play might be helpful to illustrate the cultural cross-current against the straightforward glorification of Elizabeth, as it also shows some reservation about the excessively idealized account of Elizabeth's reign. In *Bussy D'Ambois* (1604), Henry III, the king of France, extols Elizabeth – his contemporary in the play – and her court:

HENRY
    Not mixt with Rudeness vs'd in common houses;
    But, as Courts should be th'abstracts of their kingdomes,
    In all the Beautie, State, and Worth they hold;
    So is hers, amplie, and by her inform'd.
    The world is not contracted in a man,
    With more proportion and expression

> Than in her Court, her Kingdome: Our French Court
> Is a meere mirror of confusion to it.[27]

Although the memory of Elizabeth seems to be idealized in this scene, the play also offers a playful account of her court. The Guise, for example, ridicules the way in which Elizabeth and her courtiers are glorified in her court as the 'most immortal Goddess' and her 'semi-gods':

GUISE
> I like not their Court forme, it is too crestfalne,
> In all obseruance; making Semi-gods
> Of their great Nobles; and of their old Queene
> An euer-yoong, and most immortall Goddesse.[28]

The Guise expresses unease with the factitious nature of the court rhetoric, with which, he suggests, Elizabeth and her courtiers fashioned themselves as something that they were apparently not, representing, for example, 'their old Queene' as 'euer-yoong'. Montsurry further mocks Elizabeth's court, claiming that her courtiers are obsessed with French fashion, 'which becomes them / Like Apes, disfigur'd with the attires of men'.[29] Chapman's play attests to the abiding interest of the Jacobeans in Elizabeth and her court.[30] Yet nostalgia for Elizabeth and her courtiers in Chapman's drama is not straightforward; the play evokes idealized memories of Elizabeth and her courtiers but it simultaneously deflates them, articulating in the process that the idealized image of Elizabeth is wilfully one-sided. The process of commemorating Elizabeth and her courtiers, I wish to suggest, is similarly questioned within *Antony and Cleopatra*; the idealized view of Cleopatra and Antony as the symbol of the glorious Elizabethan past should be read more sceptically.

In order to discredit the chivalric fantasy Cleopatra and Antony play out and to justify his action against them, Octavius Caesar not only dismisses Cleopatra, Antony's fairy queen, as the emasculating enchantress who has corrupted the

Roman soldier but also castigates her as the source of strife and discord – a hindrance to his vision of peace and unity. The clear contrast between Caesar and Cleopatra, who, together with her knight Antony, variously evokes the memory of Elizabethan England, bears important Jacobean implications not least because James, who famously compared himself to Caesar, publicized policies which were markedly at odds with Elizabethan militarism.

The Augustan/Jacobean present

Departing from his historical sources, Shakespeare illustrates the way in which heroic militarism and the notion of chivalric honour have lost their lustre. The play marks this with a symbolic episode which receives little attention in Plutarch's account but on which Shakespeare specifically elaborates: Ventidius's victory over the Parthians in Act 3 Scene 1. The brief scene of the Ventidius-led expeditionary force fighting in Antony's name in a far-away location, possibly a plain in Syria, seems irrelevant to the play's central plot, which is mostly set in Rome and Alexandria; unsurprisingly, many stage productions in the past omitted this scene entirely.[31] However, Act 3 Scene 1 is, in fact, crucial to the play; as Paul A. Cantor, one of a few critics to have commented on the scene, rightly points out, it highlights the elimination of the last external threat to Rome.[32] By defeating the Parthians, its longstanding enemy, Rome is no longer threatened by external power. Upon removing the external menace, Ventidius decides to head back rather than to pursue the retreating Parthians. He flatly dismisses Silius's timely suggestion that they 'spur though Media, / Mesopotamia' (3.1.7–8) to extend Roman territory; consequently, Syria, where Ventidius ends Antony's military operations in the East, becomes the easternmost edge of Rome. Act 3 Scene 1 thus spells the end of the era of militaristic expansionism. Furthermore, Ventidius's political decision to end his enterprise so as to court Antony's favour demonstrates that heroism is no longer viewed as virtue but rather as reckless folly (3.1.12–27). Ventidius suggests that military men can no longer flourish solely by the sword, a claim which is confirmed when Antony is slighted as 'a sworder' 'staged to th' show' (3.13.30–31) later in the play. In other words, they are entering a new phase of Roman history, an era of scheme and manoeuvring 'without the which a soldier and his sword / Grants scarce distinction' (3.1.29–30).

The play opens with a nostalgic reference to Antony's heroic persona; one of his soldiers looks back at a time when Antony courageously commanded his army with his eyes glowing 'like plated Mars' (1.1.4). Enobarbus similarly associates Antony with the war god Mars ('Let Antony look over Caesar's head / And speak as loud as Mars' [2.2.5–6]) and, even his rival, Octavius Caesar, who 'no practice had / In the brave squares of war' (3.11.39–40), openly praises Antony's illustrious days of martial expeditions in Modena and the Alps, nostalgically reimagining him as the ideal of the Roman soldier (1.4.57–72). While the Romans lament the degeneracy of their erstwhile hero, Cleopatra continues to address her lover as 'the greatest soldier of the world' (1.3.39), the 'Herculean Roman' (1.3.85) and 'the arm / And burgonet of men' (1.5.24–25). With the disastrous defeat at Actium, however, the glorious image of the couple as the conquering knight and his supportive sea goddess proves to be merely fantastical; their military defeat confirms that their idealistic self-styled roles are, after all, objects of nostalgia, objects with no power to alter the course of history. Caesar thus demonstrates that the 'old' story which Antony and Cleopatra attempt to re-live and embody is, to use Cleopatra's own self-deprecating phrase, nothing but 'their dreams' which 'boys or women tell' only to be laughed at (5.2.73). Before the second and final battle at sea, Hercules, another symbol of military prowess – not Bacchus as in Plutarch's account – is heard to desert Antony's camp: 'Peace! What noise? / ... 'Tis the god Hercules whom Antony loved / Now leaves him' (4.3.13–22). The departure of the archetypal hero from the earth marks the demise of heroic militarism. After his fleets surrender to Caesar, Antony, believing that Cleopatra has taken her own life, stabs himself and eventually dies in Cleopatra's arms:

CLEOPATRA
    The crown o'th' earth doth melt. My lord!
        [ANTONY *dies.*]
    O withered is the garland of the war,
    The soldier's pole is fallen.

                      (4.15.65–67)

Cleopatra thus announces that Antony's death spells the end of the glorious, militant era through which, she wishes to believe, they have been living.

Antony's death draws a similarly emotional response from his rival Caesar. After shedding tears, he acknowledges Antony's contribution to Rome as the ideal soldier, seeing Antony's death as the loss of his own arm ('The arm of mine own body' [5.1.45]). Importantly, however, Caesar emphasizes that they 'could not stall together / In the whole world' (5.1.39–40) and their 'stars' are 'unreconciliable' (5.1.46–47), distancing himself from the erstwhile Roman hero. Caesar also tactfully attempts to justify his campaign against Antony by likening his opponent to a diseased body part, which, left unattended, would ultimately spread throughout the entire body, claiming that he had no choice but to remove 'diseases in our bodies' (5.1.37) in order to save Rome. Antony's outmoded role of romantic conqueror, Caesar also seems to be indicating, though it may appear attractive, is nothing but an infectious, dangerous idea which would frustrate his vision of peace and stability. Caesar thus fashions himself as the state physician in order to justify his action against Antony as an attempt to restore order in the Roman world, a rhetorical strategy which is reminiscent of that of Malcolm in *Macbeth*. Caesar's eulogy for Antony is cut short by the arrival of an Egyptian messenger but, before he exits the stage, Caesar does not forget to emphasize to his supporters that Antony was the cause of war and that he has evidence to support this case:

> CAESAR
> Go with me to my tent, where you shall see
> How hardly I was drawn into this war,
> How calm and gentle I proceeded still
> In all my writings. Go with me and see
> What I can show in this.
>
> (5.1.73–77)

Although the play remains ambiguous about which man started the war, Caesar casts all the blame on Antony and presents himself as 'calm and gentle', replacing his role as vanquisher of his rival with that of restorer of peace and stability. Indeed, we might recall that, even during the war, Caesar takes pains to stage Antony's defeat not as his own military victory but rather as Antony's self-destruction – 'Plant those that have revolted in the van / That Antony may seem to spend his fury / Upon himself' (4.6.9–11) – as if to indicate that he will have no blood on his hands. While showing his sympathy and respect for his rival, Caesar capitalizes on the fall and death of Antony to bolster his status as a new leader of peace and unity, a tactic which, as will be discussed further, he also uses in his dealings with Cleopatra. Caesar seeks to overpower the Roman warrior and his enchanting queen, excising the unsettling militarism in the name of peace and unity.

Furthermore, not only militarism but also the notion of chivalric honour is presented as an increasingly outmoded mind-set for political magnates. Earlier in the play, Shakespeare conspicuously associates Pompey with the notion of chivalric honour, representing him as a man who, for the sake of his honour, refuses to assassinate the triumvirs in his galley: 'Thou must know / 'Tis not my profit that does lead mine honour; / Mine honour, it' (2.7.76–78). By sticking to the notion of honour, Pompey casts away his chance to 'be lord of all the world' (2.7.62) and is eventually defeated by Caesar.

Antony repeatedly echoes Pompey, presenting himself as the man of honour: 'The honour is sacred which he talks on now' (2.2.91); 'If I lose mine honour, / I lose myself' (3.4.22–23). Respecting honour and attempting to play a fair game, Antony even suggests that he and Pompey should fight at sea since the Roman army outnumbers Pompey's on land (2.6.24–26). In Simon Goulart's 'The Life of Octavius Caesar Augustus' (included in the 1603 edition of Plutarch's *Lives*), one of Shakespeare's historical sources, Antony's lieutenant puts Pompey to death 'by *Antonius* commandment: for which fact he was so hated of the people of Rome'.[33] In Shakespeare's play, however, Antony 'threats the throat of that his officer / That murdered Pompey' (3.5.18–19); by obscuring Antony's complicity in the murder of Pompey, Shakespeare preserves the image of Antony as a man who acts honourably, at least, in the Roman political world. Caesar, on the other hand, not only breaks the armistice treaty with Pompey and destroys him but also arrests his own partner Lepidus after 'having made use of him in the wars 'gainst Pompey' (3.5.6–7). Yet it is Caesar who triumphs in the end. The chivalric knight Antony – the 'barked' pine that once 'overtopped them all' – has no place in this new world of politics and is brought down by 'blossoming Caesar' (4.12.23–24) in much the same way as the honourable Pompey, who once boasted of his navy (2.6.20) and his pirates (2.6.36) – an emphasis on his sea power which also associates him with the Elizabethan theme of the play – is overthrown by Caesar.

Significantly, the grand shift in *Antony and Cleopatra* from chivalric past to pragmatic present, from conquering knight to self-styled peacemaker and from war-torn Roman regions to a united Roman Empire is highly relevant to the political context of the early Jacobean period. It is a critical commonplace to associate Shakespeare's Caesar with James, who publicly compared himself to the historical Roman ruler.[34] Shakespeare's representation of Caesar is crucial not because it seemingly mirrors some personal traits of James, as has sometimes been argued.[35] It is because Shakespeare's

Caesar effectively expresses a set of values which James had been attempting to promote since succeeding Elizabeth: most notably, the pacific and unionist policy which James adopted as a new national principle, one perceived by many of his contemporaries as distinctly different from that of Elizabethan England.

On his accession, James styled himself the British Augustus. The Latin inscription on the coronation medal that represents James with a laurel wreath proclaims 'James I, Caesar Augustus of Britain, Caesar the heir of the Caesars', while panegyrics composed for James's coronation entry hailed him as the second Caesar.[36] The aim of James and his panegyrists was to align James with the first Roman emperor who united the three warring regions, Asia, Africa and Europe, into one empire, thereby casting James in the role of the first British emperor who would establish the unity of the British Isles. His self-identification with Augustus had another crucial political implication. Following the example of Augustus's *Pax Romana*, James set himself the task of securing European peace and regarded himself as *Rex Pacificus*, adopting *beati pacifici* as his motto, proclaiming not only the 'inward Peace', that is, 'the Vnion of two ancient and famous Kingdomes [of England and Scotland]' but also the 'outward Peace: that is, peace abroad with all forreine neighbours', signalling a dramatic shift in England's foreign policy.[37] Most notably, James's government chose to defend England from Spain not by armed force but by diplomacy. In order to conclude the peace treaty with Spain, James ordered the cessation of England's naval activities and also penalized the activities of English pirates, who had been key players in England's colonial enterprises and also in England's defence against Spain's maritime activities. As the Venetian ambassador reported in 1607,

The navy has fallen off greatly from the days of Henry VII. and Henry VIII., when it consisted of upwards of a hundred ships fully manned and found, with officers on full pay, ready to put to sea in force at a moment's notice. Now it numbers only thirty-seven ships, many of them old and rotten, and barely fit for service.[38]

By drastically downsizing its own maritime activities, James's government symbolically put an end to the Elizabethan legacy of a flourishing maritime culture and the theme of chivalric romance that informed that culture.

Furthermore, as Mervyn James points out, virtues traditionally associated with chivalric honour, such as wilfulness, assertiveness and idealism, during the Elizabethan period – which saw the revival of a chivalric code as the mind-set of ideal courtiers – were replaced by wisdom, temperance and godliness under James's rule; the ideal role for English courtiers changed from a Christian knight to a godly magistrate.[39] In this context, it is meaningful that, while Antony presents himself as a chivalric knight, Caesar, by contrast, styles himself God's instrument to administer justice: 'You are abused / Beyond the mark of thought, and the high gods, / To do you justice, makes his ministers / Of us and those that love you' (3.6.88–91). Unsurprisingly, King Arthur, to whom James was often compared, was given a new symbolic role under James.[40] As Smuts rightly points out:

> King Arthur was converted from a symbol of chivalric prowess into one of British unity. The imperial theme was now associated almost exclusively with the internal peace and prosperity of the British Isles and the dynastic union of England and Scotland, rather than with dreams of overseas dominions.[41]

Similarly, the imperial theme of the play shifts from the chivalric romance of the fairy queen and her conquering knight to a new story of Augustan peace and unity.

The emerging political phase of Shakespeare's Roman world can thus be aligned with the new political atmosphere under James. It is not surprising, then, that Cleopatra's praise for the illustrious bygone days of the conqueror closely echoes the language used to glorify Elizabethan militarism. In her eulogy for Antony, Cleopatra evokes the image of Antony as a colonial conqueror ('His legs bestrid the ocean; his reared arm / Crested the world' [5.2.81–82]), similarly to the way in which, for example, Michael Drayton, in 'Rowlands Song in Praise of the Fairest Beta' (1600), extols Elizabethan militarism, writing, '*thy large Empire stretch her armes from East vnto the West: / And* Albion *on the* Appenines *aduaunce her conquering crest*'.[42] In this context, the death of Antony closely evokes the demise of Elizabethan militarism which was generally attributed to James's assumption of monarchical power.

Some members of the first audiences might have associated Caesar's victory over Antony with the way in which Jacobean values and principles now prevailed over Elizabethan ones. While this is certainly one of the more plausible interpretations of Shakespeare's dramatization of the war, we should, however, question the assumption that Caesar is so straightforwardly represented as the victor in this play. Military victory is not Caesar's ultimate goal, as he makes it clear that his intention is to keep Cleopatra alive, not to annihilate her, 'for her life in Rome / Would be eternal in our triumph' (5.1.65–66). As Caesar is keenly aware, Antony and Cleopatra are 'a pair so famous' (5.2.359) – the powerful symbol of the values he opposes. In order to justify his action against the couple and to pronounce the arrival of a new era, Caesar attempts to defeat them not only militarily but also ideologically. Cleopatra authors the image of Antony as the eternal conqueror, taking the role of the living chronicler of their glorious past and, as we will see, she also attempts to author her own image to suit their nostalgic fantasy. Caesar needs not only to divest Cleopatra of her power to incite nostalgia for the chivalric past but also, more importantly, to author the image of the queen which would complement his side of the story. With her protector Antony dead, Cleopatra is left vulnerable to the invading Romans. Yet the long-standing conflict between Caesar and Cleopatra has just begun to intensify, a competition for representation to which Shakespeare devotes the entire final act of the play.

The competition for representing the queen

Throughout the play, Cleopatra is portrayed differently by other characters and accorded various epithets; while she is denigrated as 'gipsy' (1.1.10) and 'witch' (4.12.47), for example, she is also hailed as 'a most triumphant lady' (2.2.194) or, more ambiguously, as 'royal wench' (2.2.236) and 'lass unparalleled' (5.2.315). In particular, the rivals at odds offer contrasting images of the queen; while, in Egypt, Cleopatra styles herself the supreme mistress of her Roman hero Antony as well as the revered goddess of the Egyptian people, Caesar has his own version of Cleopatra to propagate in Rome – a belligerent 'whore' (3.6.68) who seduces the Roman hero and exploits his achievements, sowing discord among the Romans. While Plutarch writes that Caesar 'made the people to abolishe the power and Empire of Antonius, bicause he had before given it uppe unto a woman', Shakespeare significantly changes Plutarch's 'woman' into 'whore' in Caesar's speech: 'He hath given his empire / Up to a whore, who now are levying / The kings o'th' earth for war' (3.6.67–69).[43] She is a dangerous Circe who goads her enchanted Roman lover into war with his mother country. Maecenas echoes his captain's view, denigrating her as 'a trull / That noises it against us' (3.6.97–98). Agrippa, Caesar's right-hand officer, also recounts Cleopatra's relationship with Julius Caesar in explicitly sexual terms, reducing the image of the supreme mistress into that of a sexual enchantress: 'She made great Caesar lay his sword to bed. / He ploughed her, and she cropped' (2.2.237–38). Caesar and his followers thus downplay the chivalric fantasy of Cleopatra and Antony by portraying her not as the fairy queen but as the fairy 'quean' – a dangerous seductress who sets his fellow countrymen against each other. Caesar thus inverts the glorious image of the warlike queen as Cleopatra styles herself before the battle at Actium. In this regard, Caesar's struggle with Antony's Roman wife Fulvia earlier in the play offers a backdrop to his fight against Cleopatra. Fulvia is a warlike woman who waged war with Caesar to attract Antony's attention; she stirred 'too much disquiet' (2.2.75) in Rome and Caesar found it necessary to subdue her in order to maintain peace in Rome.[44] Caesar sees Cleopatra as another warlike woman who unsettles the stability of his world order; he justifies his war on Cleopatra by branding her as the monstrous fairy 'quean' who needs to be contained.

While, in Plutarch, Caesar is keen to capture Cleopatra alive not only because her presence in Rome would furnish his triumphal return to Rome but also because 'otherwise all the treasure [in Cleopatra's possession] would be lost', Shakespeare's Caesar, in a striking contrast, cares little about her possessions; as he puts it, 'Caesar's no merchant to make prize with you / Of things that merchants sold' (5.2.182–83).[45] Caesar provides one clear motive to keep her alive: 'for her life in Rome / Would be eternal in our triumph'. Caesar's eagerness to bring the defeated queen to Rome can be seen as part of his persistent campaign to author the image of Cleopatra; bringing Cleopatra to Rome is essential for Shakespeare's Caesar as it gives him total control over how the queen is seen in public. Earlier in the play, Caesar frustratedly recounts that, in Egypt, Cleopatra publicizes her image as the divine queen by appearing 'in the public eye' in 'th'habiliments of the goddess Isis' (3.6.11–17). By taking her away from her homeland, Caesar can divest her of her power to represent herself in such a manner; in Rome, he can present the miserable, captured queen in front of the citizens, debasing and rewriting the image of the magnificent queen Cleopatra has authored for herself. As Antony warns her beforehand, Caesar can have Cleopatra 'follow his chariot like the greatest spot / Of all thy sex; most monster-like be shown / For poor'st diminutives' (4.7.35–37), replacing the image of female ruler with that of monster.

Cleopatra sees through Caesar's intention. After Caesar's military victory, what disturbs Cleopatra most is how she is to be displayed by Caesar to 'let the world see / His nobleness well acted, which your [Cleopatra's] death / Will never let come forth' (5.2.43–45). Cleopatra believes that, if she is brought to Rome alive, Caesar will exhibit her as his 'scutcheons' and 'signs of conquest' (5.2.134) for his political interests, and she envisions that she is to be denigrated in Rome and personified by a squeaking boy actor in the 'posture of a whore' (5.2.220). Therefore, even before the death of Antony, she starts to think about suicide in order to make herself inaccessible to the conqueror:

CLEOPATRA
                    Not th'imperious show
        Of the full-fortuned Caesar ever shall
        Be brooched with me. If knife, drugs, serpents, have
        Edge, sting, or operation, I am safe.

                                                (4.15.24–27)

In Plutarch, Cleopatra makes it clear that she intends to end her life because, if she is brought to Rome, she will not be able to share the grave with Antony: 'I feare me they will make us chaunge our contries. For as thou being a Romane hast bene buried in Egypt: even so wretched creature I, an Egyptian, shall be buried in Italie'.[46] In Mary Sidney's *Antonius*, Cleopatra's chief motive for suicide also appears to have little to do with her fear of being humiliated in Rome and more with her desire to follow her lover and to be buried with him: 'Die *Cleopatra* then no longer stay / From *Antony*, who thee at *Styx* attends: / Go ioyne thy Ghost with his, and sob no more / Without his loue within these tombes enclos'd'.[47] By contrast, by emphasizing Cleopatra's persistent fear and strong defiance towards Caesar's attempt to use her as his 'Egyptian puppet' (5.2.207), Shakespeare's play gives us the impression that Cleopatra's decision to swiftly end her life is not prompted chiefly by her love for Antony but rather by her determination to counter Caesar's attempt.

Cleopatra carefully stages her suicide. Shutting herself and her women inside the monument – the Egyptian tomb she has constructed – Cleopatra instructs Iras to bring her robe and crown ('My best attires') and to 'show' her 'like a queen' (5.2.226–27). Cleopatra thus attempts to author how she would be seen after her own death. Charmian, the other servant, also plays a key role; she invites the audience to see the dead Cleopatra as the beloved royal mistress by replicating the conventional metaphor in Petrarchan love-poetry: 'Downy windows, close, / And golden Phoebus, never be beheld / Of eyes again so royal!' (5.2.315–17). The last thing Charmian does before her own death is to mend the crown on the head of her dead mistress ('Your crown's awry; / I'll mend it' [5.2.317–18]), adding a finishing touch to the body as if it is a work of art – as she puts it, the work is 'well done' and 'fitting for a princess / Descended of so many royal kings' (5.2.325–26). Cleopatra thus fulfils her 'immortal longings' (5.2.280); with the help of Iras and Charmian, she transforms her body into a royal effigy, an effigy of the stately queen surrounded by her loyal women. By turning herself into a fixed monument of magnificence, Cleopatra thus thwarts Caesar's plan to convey and display her 'in what place you [Caesar] please' (5.2.135) and to exploit her as a living, manipulable image.

This is where Caesar's final speech begins to acquire a symbolic significance. While being shocked by Cleopatra's suicide – 'the dreaded act which' he 'sought'st to hinder' (5.2.330–31) – and admitting that she has certainly outwitted him, Caesar quickly devises a countermeasure. In the closing speech of the play, he commands his officers to take up the bed on which Cleopatra's body lies and to remove the bodies of her women away from the monument. Caesar unfixes the crowned statue from its resting place, disturbing, as it were, the still tableau Cleopatra has authored. Caesar then proclaims that Cleopatra's funeral shall be conducted in a Roman military manner as if to rewrite Cleopatra's death in his own language.[48] Caesar's order to conduct Cleopatra's funeral in a Roman fashion can be seen as his calculated attempt to contain and nullify the power of the female ruler within the Roman patriarchal framework. Caesar's male soldiers clear the three women from the stage, completing the transference of power from women to men. Caesar shows himself, despite Cleopatra's best efforts, to be in control of authoring Cleopatra's image, regulating the way in which she is to be seen and remembered hereafter. Though once outmanoeuvred by her death, Caesar thus attempts to assert control over the posthumous image of the Egyptian queen.

Nevertheless, Shakespeare does not present Caesar's attempt as wholly successful; on the contrary, he allows us to question its effectiveness. What the final scene of the play highlights for the audience is not the controllability of the posthumous image of the famous queen but rather its uncontrollability. Caesar's response when he confronts Cleopatra's dead body – lines specific to Shakespeare's text – is a key to understanding the critical cross-current in the final scene:

CAESAR
                    she looks like sleep,
        As she would catch another Antony
        In her strong toil of grace.

                                        (5.2.345–47)

After Antony's death, Cleopatra strongly longs for sleep so that she can freely dream of encountering 'such another man' (5.2.77). Then, when applying an asp to her breast, she compares herself to a nurse who is brought to sleep by her suckling infants – 'Does thou not see my baby at my breast / That sucks the nurse asleep?' (5.2.308–9) – welcoming her approaching death not as the ultimate end of her life but rather as sleep, the counterfeit of death. In this regard, Caesar confirms that Cleopatra has fulfilled her wishes. Cleopatra appears to Caesar not as dead but as a sleeping queen who entices 'another Antony' with her undiminished charm. Earlier in the play, Cleopatra playfully remarks that as a pastime she would catch 'tawny-finned fishes' with her hook as if every one of them is 'an Antony', effectively anticipating Caesar's line ('As she would catch another Antony'):

CLEOPATRA
My music playing far off, I will betray
Tawny-finned fishes. My bended hook shall pierce
Their slimy jaws, and, as I draw them up,
I'll think them every one an Antony,
And say 'Ah, ha! You're caught!'

(2.5.11–15)

Just as when she played the seductress of a Roman, her sleeping statue, as Caesar observes, retains that power to attract and catch 'an Antony'. We might also recall that Enobarbus, in his nostalgic, idealized account of Cleopatra, recounts a time when she hopped through the public street and lost her breath, marvelling at the way in which, though she was 'breathless', she was able to 'pour breath forth' (2.2.242). Indeed, in distinct contrast to Caesar's sister Octavia, who 'shows a body rather than a life, / A statue than a breather' (3.3.20–21) and is thereby praised as the ideal of Roman womanhood (2.6.124–26), Cleopatra is 'a breather' and remains to be so even after her death; the dead Cleopatra is not an Octavia-like lifeless statue but an animate one. The death does not end her power to influence others; on the contrary, it eternizes Cleopatra as a queen who, in her unbreakable sleep, continues to mesmerize Roman soldiers. The image of Cleopatra as the fairy queen has survived Caesar's constant attempts to discredit it, becoming the potent symbol of the glorious chivalric past and the object of nostalgia, reminiscent of the way in which Elizabeth became the object of nostalgia and continued to live in the minds of Jacobeans.

Shakespeare's representation of Cleopatra as the sleeping queen has a strong resonance with the Jacobean discourse of Elizabeth. One of the elegies published in 1603, for example, commemorates Elizabeth as a sleeping queen whose honour and glory would live on, expressing the wish that she would rise up again:

Sleepe dearest Queene, your vertue neuer sleepeth:
Rest in your bed of earth, your honour waketh:

> Slumber securely, for your glorie keepeth
> Continuall guard; and liuing ioy partaketh:
>> Dearest of deare, a rising doth remaine;
>> For Sunnes that sleeping set, must rise againe.[49]

Several writers who witnessed Elizabeth's funeral procession through the streets of London expressed admiration for the lifelike effigy of Elizabeth and described it as a sleeping figure. In *Expicedium* (1603), Richard Niccols describes 'the liuely picture of her Maiesties whole body in her Parliament robes with a Crowne on her head, and a Scepter in her hand, lying on the corpes inshrin'd in leade' – a description which resonates with Shakespeare's crowned and sceptred corpse of Cleopatra – and writes: 'hadst thou seene her figure as she slept, / In memorie, thou would'st her semblance beare / Whose deere remembrance would so touch thy minde'.[50] In *Elizabetha Quasi Viuens* (1603), Henry Petowe, another witness, also admires the way in which her effigy was 'tryumphant drawne in robes so richly wrought' and adorned with a 'crowne on her head, in hand her Scepter'. Petowe writes that the effigy makes him believe that Elizabeth is not actually dead but merely sleeping:

>> her Princely head
> Lay on a pillowe of a crimson dye,
> Like a sweet beauty in a harmlesse slumber:
> She is not dead, no sure it cannot be.[51]

He even claims that 'a man of iudgement' 'would haue sworne and said, / To Parliament rides this sweet slumbring Maide'. The dead Cleopatra, who 'looks like sleep / As she would catch another Antony', evokes England's sleeping queen, whom Petowe called 'Faire Englands Queene, euen to the life thogh dead'.[52] Shakespeare thus allows the audience to see the iconographical analogy between his Cleopatra and Elizabeth.

In Jacobean theatres, Shakespeare was not alone in responding to the ways in which Elizabeth became the focus of nostalgia and was beginning to gain eternal life as a symbol in the first decade of James's reign; contemporary plays such as John Marston's *Sophonisba* (1605) and Thomas Middleton's *The Lady's Tragedy* (1611), also known as *The Second Maiden's Tragedy*, also featured the commemoration of the dead queen on stage. In *Sophonisba*, Marston dramatizes the tragic suicide of Sophonisba, the princess of Carthage. Departing from his main historical sources by Livy and Appian, Marston presents Sophonisba as a virtuous woman, who is recently married to the heroic warrior Massinissa. Carthage is attacked and conquered by the Roman general Scipio, who mercilessly claims Sophonisba as a war prize, leaving her husband no choice but to surrender her. Sophonisba, however, honours her own chastity and defies the Roman conqueror by taking her own life with poison and making herself inaccessible to him. Her death saves her honour from her vanquisher in much the same way as Cleopatra's suicide frees her from Caesar. Significantly, in the final scene – Marston's invention – the warrior Massinissa adorns the corpse of the eponymous heroine with a 'crown', a 'robe of triumph', a 'conquest's wreath' and a 'sceptre' (5.4.44–46), commemorating her as the 'loved creature of a deathless fame' (5.4.53).[53] The grieving warrior thus creates a royal effigy which will incite in its viewers 'women's right wonder, and just shame of men' (5.4.59), a phrase which, I suggest, evokes the way in which some of the elegies composed upon the death of Elizabeth commemorated her; she was praised, for example, as *'The pride of all her sex, all womens boast: / The worlds wonder, that they wondred most'*.[54] By evoking the contemporary discourse of Elizabeth, Marston thus dramatizes the symbolic process in which the dead woman acquires 'a deathless fame' and becomes an icon of female royalty.

Similarly, Middleton's *The Lady's Tragedy* – which will be further discussed in Chapter 4 – features the dead body of the faithful Lady, who has taken her own life in order to protect herself from the lustful Tyrant. At the end of the play, Govianus, her husband and the legitimate king, who has reclaimed the

throne from the dead Tyrant, gives a surprising order; 'in memory /
Of her admirèd mistress', he instructs his men to install her
corpse on the throne and to 'crown her our queen':

GOVIANUS
                                in memory
        Of her admirèd mistress, 'tis our will
        It receive honour dead, as it took part
        With us in all afflictions when it lived.
        Here place her in this throne, crown her our queen,
        The first and last that ever we make ours,
        Her constancy strikes so much firmness in us.
        [*The* LADY's *body is placed on the throne and crowned*]
                                        (5.2.197–203)[55]

The virtuous and pious Lady, who has won a 'virgin victory'
(3.1.177) over the lustful Tyrant, is thus turned into a royal
effigy; Govianus's eulogy ensures that the dead Lady, now the
queen, will continue to live in the minds of her subjects and
that the memory of her 'constancy' will become the guiding
principle of the kingdom.[56] As if to make this point clearer,
Middleton even introduces the spirit/ghost of the queen
after this eulogy: the stage direction reads, '*The Spirit* [*of the*
LADY] *enters again and stays to go out with the body, as it
were attending it*' (5.2.206 SD). The queen is dead, yet her
lingering presence is still felt by the survivors. These plays
variously attest to the Jacobeans' growing fascination with
commemoration of Elizabeth. Shakespeare's play strikes a
chord with these contemporary plays. Like Marston and
Middleton, Shakespeare turns the dead queen into a royal
effigy, an icon of magnificent female royalty, similarly to the
way in which Elizabeth was turned into such an icon by the
Jacobeans.
    Yet Shakespeare probes deeper into the phenomenon of
nostalgia than these fellow playwrights. First, *Antony and
Cleopatra* does not simply replicate the nostalgic discourse
of Elizabeth; it also harks back to the negative assessment

of Elizabeth by her contemporaries. During her reign, Elizabeth was cited for her lack of enthusiasm for military ventures; criticism was directed not only towards Elizabeth's reluctance to pursue militant policies but also towards the court culture she sustained, where militant courtiers were urged to engage in the futile game of courtly love – like Antony, who no longer engages in military wars but in amorous wars at Cleopatra's court.[57] Clearly, the empress of the seas, who was fully supportive of her subjects' military ambitions, as some Jacobeans attempted to portray her, was an idealized and politicized image of Elizabeth. In Shakespeare's play, Cleopatra performs the role of the glorious empress of the Roman warrior, yet, as is apparent to the audience, she is also the faint-hearted leader who refuses to engage in battles and, as Caesar and his men put it, the enchantress who has corrupted the heroic Roman. I would suggest, then, that while the play reproduces the nostalgic discourse of Elizabeth, it simultaneously addresses the gap between the historical queen and the queen represented in that discourse. By presenting the two conflicting assessments of Cleopatra, the play effectively illuminates the fictionality of, and the politics behind, the contemporary nostalgia for Elizabeth.

Furthermore, *Antony and Cleopatra* highlights not only the symbolic power of the dead queen but also the ongoing competition for appropriating that power among the Jacobeans by drawing our attention to Caesar's struggle for authoring the image of Cleopatra. Shakespeare's play does not present Caesar's attempt as wholly successful. Cleopatra transforms herself into a statue and protects herself from Caesar's attempt to rewrite her image; in Caesar's eyes, she appears to be asleep and seems to retain her power to charm 'another Antony'. In fact, in the final act of the play, Cleopatra is shown to have already attracted 'another Antony' under Caesar's nose – another Roman who adores her as his mistress and carries out her command. Caesar's trusted officer Dolabella confesses to Cleopatra, whom he calls the 'most noble empress' (5.2.70), that her fall gives him 'a grief that smites / My very heart at root' (5.2.103–5). Meaningfully, Dolabella presents himself as Cleopatra's servant ('I, your servant' [5.2.204]) and takes, though for a short period, the role of her faithful knight, undertaking her request to be secretly informed, 'as thereto sworn by your command, / Which my love makes religion to obey' (5.2.197–98) – a language evocative of that of chivalric romance. Prompted by his honourable love for Cleopatra, Dolabella reveals Caesar's plan to his mistress, implicitly encouraging Cleopatra to take immediate action. Dolabella thus sides with Cleopatra, frustrating Caesar's ambition and thereby protecting the honour of his mistress. Cleopatra's penetrating charm is indeed beyond Caesar's control; Dolabella's devotion to Cleopatra shows that the fairy queen continues to exert influence over Caesar's men. Unlike Caesar in Daniel's *The Tragedie of Cleopatra*, who rebukes Dolabella for his infatuation with the queen ('What in a passion *Dolabella*? what take heed: / Let others fresh examples be thy warning; / What mischiefes these, so idle humors breed'), Shakespeare's Caesar does not even notice Dolabella's feeling for Cleopatra.[58] Surprisingly, although the audience has just witnessed Dolabella's betrayal of Caesar, it is Dolabella, out of '*all his train*' (5.2.331 SD), whom the ignorant Caesar appoints to oversee Cleopatra's funeral: 'Come, Dolabella, see / High order in this great solemnity' (5.2.364–65). Caesar unwittingly ensures that Cleopatra's funeral will be authored by her ardent follower, who reveres her as his fairy queen.

In this regard, Caesar's final speech does not demonstrate his control over the dead queen; rather, it suggests that, though he himself may not be aware, Caesar has eventually failed to take control of the queen. In Plutarch, Caesar creates the image of Cleopatra to display in his triumphal return: 'in his triumphe he caried Cleopatraes image, with an Aspicke byting of her arme'.[59] Whether or not he captures her alive, Caesar is shown to have successfully appropriated her image as his political tool. By contrast, Shakespeare allows the audience to see Caesar's campaign to control her image as failure. In Jacobean England, Elizabeth continued to be commemorated as the warlike queen beloved by her courageous English soldiers; John Speed, for example, harked back to Elizabeth's appearance at Tilbury in *The Theatre of the Empire of Great Britaine* (1612), representing her as the '*Amazonian* Empresse' who filled her soldiers with 'manly spirit':

> thither her Maiesty in person vpon the ninth of August repaired, full of Princely resolution, and more then feminine courage, whose louely presence and imperiall speeches, as shee passed like some *Amazonian* Empresse through all her Army, were so acceptable and gratious, that Her souldiers, full-fraught with manly spirit, yet receiued an accesse of hardinesse from so alacrious a patterne in their *Mayden Queene*: and both they perceiued so well the loue of their Prince, and shee saw what it was to haue the loue of her subiects, that the harmony of both their affections was admirable, both of them professing resolution, and willing to sacrifice their liues in that most rightfull quarrel.[60]

By drawing our attention to Caesar's struggle to control the image of Cleopatra, the play provides an insightful examination of the ways in which the representation of Elizabeth continued to evoke nostalgia for her famed reign when Elizabethan militarism supposedly flourished, despite various attempts by James and his supporters to downplay militaristic aspects of her reign, attempts which will be further discussed in Chapter 3.

Indeed, while *Antony and Cleopatra* was performed on stage, the spectre of militant Elizabeth had already found her strong follower. Militant Protestants began to hail Prince Henry, James's elder son, as the restorer of Elizabethan militarism, seeing him as the long-awaited chivalric knight who was sent to finish unaccomplished missions that Elizabeth's 'knights' had started – the battle to rescue the imperilled Protestants on the continent and the expansion of overseas dominions. As the Venetian ambassador puts it, Prince Henry 'protected the colony of Virginia, and under his auspices the ships sailed for the north-west passage to the Indies. He had begun to put the navy in order and raised the number of sailors. He was hostile to Spain and had claims in France'.[61] In Ben Jonson's *Prince Henry's Barriers* (1610), Merlin makes a prophecy on Prince Henry:

> MERLIN
> And this young knight, that now puts forth so soon
> Into the world, shall in your names achieve
> More garlands for this state.[62]

Prince Henry styled himself the future conquering hero and attempted to follow the footsteps of his spiritual predecessors, such as Philip Sidney and Essex.[63] In Jonson's *Oberon* (1611), Prince Henry even masqued as the fairy prince, presenting himself, as Anne Barton puts it, as the 'true descendent of the Faerie Queene: anti-Spanish, anti-Catholic, martial, chivalric and unafraid'.[64] Indeed, Smuts observes that, under the reign of James, 'medieval warrior-kings and references to England's maritime power virtually disappeared from court masques and poems', adding, however, 'except for those written for James's warlike son Henry'.[65] Prince Henry was beginning to emerge as a knight of England's dead fairy queen, the spiritual patron of his militaristic ambitions.

The dead Elizabeth continued to remain a symbol of Elizabethan militarism, refuelling militaristic sentiments among those who were dissatisfied with James's conciliatory approach to religion and diplomatic relations. By dramatizing Caesar's attempt to control Cleopatra's symbolic power and his difficulty in doing so, *Antony and Cleopatra* engages the audience with the politics behind the growing nostalgia for Elizabeth, highlighting, in particular, the way in which her increasingly influential power intensified competition for authoring her image among Jacobeans during the first decade of James's reign.

Notes

1   Julia M. Walker, 'Reading the Tombs of Elizabeth I', *English Literary Renaissance* 26, no. 3 (1996): 510–30 (esp. 527).

2   Julia M. Walker, 'Bones of Contention: Posthumous Images of Elizabeth and Stuart Politics', in *Dissing Elizabeth: Negative Representations of Gloriana*, ed. Julia M. Walker (Durham, NC: Duke University Press, 1998), 252–76 (esp. 257). For the date of *Antony and Cleopatra*, see esp. Leeds Barroll, 'The Chronology of Shakespeare's Jacobean Plays and the Dating of *Antony and Cleopatra*', in *Essays on Shakespeare*, ed. Gordon Ross Smith (University Park: Pennsylvania State University Press, 1965), 115–62 and Wells and Taylor, *A Textual Companion*, 129–30.

3   Julia M. Walker, *Medusa's Mirrors: Spenser, Shakespeare, Milton, and the Metamorphosis of the Female Self* (Newark, NJ: University of Delaware Press, 1998), 150.

4   See Paulina Kewes, '"A Fit Memorial for the Times to Come …": Admonition and Topical Application in Mary Sidney's *Antonius* and Samuel Daniel's *Cleopatra*', *Review of English Studies* 63 (2012): 243–64. For studies of the ways in which the representation of Cleopatra by Sidney and Daniel specifically evokes Elizabeth, see also Pascale Aebischer, 'The Properties of Whiteness: Renaissance Cleopatras from Jodelle to Shakespeare', *Shakespeare Survey* 65 (2012): 221–38 (esp. 229–36).

5   For the possible sources of *Antony and Cleopatra*, see Geoffrey Bullough, ed., *Narrative and Dramatic Sources of Shakespeare*, vol. 5 (London: Routledge; New York: Columbia University Press, 1966), 254–449. For the closet dramas of Sidney and Daniel as Shakespeare's possible sources, see esp. Bullough, ed., *Sources*, 5:229–36.

6   *A Dedication to Sir Philip Sidney*, in *The Prose Works of Fulke Greville, Lord Brooke*, ed. John Gouws (Oxford: Clarendon Press, 1985), 62.

7   For Greville's representation of Elizabeth and its Jacobean implication, see also Lisa Richardson, 'Elizabeth in Arcadia: Fulke Greville and John Hayward's Construction of Elizabeth, 1610–12', in *The Myth of Elizabeth*, 99–119 (esp. 99–101).

8 See also Samuel Daniel's 1607 addition to his *Cleopatra*, which
   provides another fair example of the way in which the story
   of Cleopatra assumed political significance in the Jacobean
   period; Paul Yachnin points out that Daniel's addition serves as
   'transparent political allegory in which ancient Rome stands for
   the Spanish-Catholic domination of Europe' and, in this context,
   'Cleopatra irresistibly evokes the memory of the militantly
   anti-Catholic Queen of England' ('"Courtiers of Beauteous
   Freedom": *Antony and Cleopatra* in Its Time', *Renaissance and
   Reformation* 15, no. 1 [1991]: 8).

9 On this point, see also Helen Morris, 'Queen Elizabeth I
   "Shadowed" in Cleopatra', *Huntington Library Quarterly* 32
   (1969): 271–78 (esp. 276–77).

10 See esp. Morris, 'Queen Elizabeth I "Shadowed" in Cleopatra',
   271–78 and Keith Rinehart, 'Shakespeare's Cleopatra and
   England's Elizabeth', *Shakespeare Quarterly* 23, no. 1 (1972):
   81–86.

11 As Michael L. Hays puts it, the primary function of the
   mistress in chivalric romance 'is to prompt chivalric adventure
   by motivating the knight to perform great deeds through her
   beauty, moral superiority, and the possibility of winning her
   love' (*Shakespearean Tragedy as Chivalric Romance: Rethinking
   'Macbeth', 'Hamlet', 'Othello', and 'King Lear'* [Woodbridge:
   Brewer, 2003], 87). For chivalric romance in early modern
   England and its popularity across the social spectrum, see esp.
   Hays, *Shakespearean Tragedy as Chivalric Romance*, 2–5,
   66–93. As Hays notes, chivalric romances 'were available and
   familiar to, and popular with, much of the late Elizabethan and
   early Jacobean populace' (3).

12 *The Princely Pleasures at Kenelworth Castle*, in *The Complete
   Works of George Gascoigne*, ed. John W. Cunliffe, vol. 2 (New
   York: Greenwood Press, 1969), 99.

13 *The Poems of Sir Walter Ralegh: A Historical Edition*, ed.
   Michael Rudick (Tempe: Arizona Center for Medieval and
   Renaissance Studies, 1999), 106, 19.

14 For the framework of chivalric romance as applied to Elizabeth's
   relationship to her courtiers, see also Arthur B. Ferguson, *The
   Chivalric Tradition in Renaissance England* (Washington, DC:
   Folger Shakespeare Library, 1986), 66–82 and Frances A. Yates,

Astraea: The Imperial Theme in the Sixteenth Century (London: Routledge, 1975), 88–111.

15 Henry Raymonde, *The Maiden Queene* (London, 1607), C2r.

16 R. Malcolm Smuts, *Court Culture and the Origins of a Royalist Tradition in Early Stuart England* (Philadelphia: University of Pennsylvania Press, 1987), 20.

17 See esp. Jennifer R. Goodman, *Chivalry and Exploration, 1298–1630* (Woodbridge: Boydell Press, 1998), 168–91 and Smuts, *Court Culture*, 20.

18 For the representation of Elizabeth's subjects as sea-knights, see Joan Pong Linton, *The Romance of the New World: Gender and the Literary Formations of English Colonialism* (Cambridge: Cambridge University Press, 1998), 39–61.

19 Robert Johnson, *Nova Britannia* (London, 1609), B1v.

20 Thomas Heywood, *Troia Britanica: Or, Great Britaines Troy* (London, 1609), Q3r.

21 Edmund Spenser, *Colin Clouts Come Home Againe* (London, 1595), B1v. For the representation of Elizabeth as Cynthia, see esp. Elkin Calhoun Wilson, *England's Eliza* (Cambridge, MA: Harvard University Press, 1939), 273–320.

22 Raphael Holinshed, *Holinshed's Chronicles of England, Scotland, and Ireland*, vol. 4 (London: J. Johnson, 1808), 647.

23 William Browne, *Britannia's Pastorals. The Second Booke* (London, 1616), E2r. Samuel Daniel, *The Vision of the 12. Goddesses* (London, 1604), A3v.

24 As Michael Neill notes, 'even in 1606 the word ["gests"] had a slightly archaic, chivalric ring to it' (Neill, ed., *The Tragedy of Anthony and Cleopatra* [Oxford: Oxford University Press, 1994], 274n).

25 Francis Bacon, *The Felicity of Queen Elizabeth* (London, 1651), 39. Bacon's original Latin version written in 1608 circulated extensively in manuscript. For the representation of Elizabeth as the fairy queen, see esp. Helen Cooper, *The English Romance in Time: Transforming Motifs from Geoffrey of Monmouth to the Death of Shakespeare* (Oxford: Oxford University Press, 2004), 173–217 and Matthew Woodcock, *Fairy in 'The Faerie Queene': Renaissance Elf-Fashioning and Elizabethan Myth-Making* (Aldershot: Ashgate, 2004), 88–115.

26 *Sorrowes Ioy*, in Nichols, *Progresses of Elizabeth*, 4:765.

27 George Chapman, *Bussy D'Ambois* (London, 1607), B1v.

28 Chapman, *Bussy D'Ambois*, B1v.

29 Chapman, *Bussy D'Ambois*, B2r.

30 For Chapman's engagement with the phenomenon of nostalgia for Elizabeth, see also Anne Barton, 'Harking Back to Elizabeth: Ben Jonson and Caroline Nostalgia', *English Literary History* 48, no. 4 (1981): 712–14.

31 Michael Neill notes that Act 3 Scene 1 is 'often cut in modern productions for its seeming insignificance' (Neill, ed., *The Tragedy of Anthony and Cleopatra*, 219n). Marvin Rosenberg also observes that 'the scene is usually cut, reducing this part of Shakespeare's complex glance at war and warriors' (*The Masks of 'Anthony and Cleopatra'*, ed. Mary Rosenberg [Newark, NJ: University of Delaware Press, 2006], 227).

32 Paul A. Cantor, *Shakespeare's Rome: Republic and Empire* (Ithaca, NY: Cornell University Press, 1976), 133.

33 Simon Goulart, *The Lives of Epaminondas ... and of Octavius Caesar Avgvstvs*, in Plutarch, *The Lives of the Noble Grecians and Romaines* (London, 1603), 59.

34 For the classic study of this association, see H. Neville Davies, 'Jacobean *Antony and Cleopatra*', *Shakespeare Studies* 17 (1985): 123–58 and Yachnin, '"Courtiers of Beauteous Freedom"', 1–20.

35 See, for example, Yachnin, '"Courtiers of Beauteous Freedom"', 12.

36 Keith M. Brown, 'The Vanishing Emperor: British Kingship and Its Decline', in *Scots and Britons: Scottish Political Thought and the Union of 1603*, ed. Roger A. Mason (Cambridge: Cambridge University Press, 1994), 79. For the representation of James as the British Augustus, see esp. Howard Erskine-Hill, *The Augustan Idea in English Literature* (London: Edward Arnold, 1983), 164–69.

37 James VI and I, *Political Writings*, 133–35.

38 *Calendar of State Papers, Venice*, 10:504.

39 Mervyn James, *Society, Politics and Culture: Studies in Early Modern England* (Cambridge: Cambridge University Press, 1986), 308–415.

40 For this comparison, see esp. Brinkley, *Arthurian Legend*, 20–22.

41 Smuts, *Court Culture*, 24–25.

42 Michael Drayton, 'Rowlands Song in Praise of the Fairest Beta', in *Englands Helicon*, ed. John Bodenham (London, 1600), E1r.

43 Plutarch, *The Lives of the Noble Grecians and Romans*, in Bullough, ed., *Sources*, 5:295.

44 For the warlike image of Fulvia, see also Theodora A. Jankowski, *Women in Power in the Early Modern Drama* (Urbana: University of Illinois Press, 1992), 156.

45 Plutarch, *Lives*, in Bullough, ed., *Sources*, 5:311.

46 Plutarch, *Lives*, in Bullough, ed., *Sources*, 5:315.

47 Mary Sidney, *The Tragedie of Antonie. Doone into English by the Countesse of Pembroke* (London, 1595), G4v–G5r.

48 On this point, see also Chris Laoutaris, *Shakespearean Maternities: Crises of Conception in Early Modern England* (Edinburgh: Edinburgh University Press, 2008), 237.

49 *Sorrowes Ioy*, in Nichols, *Progresses of Elizabeth*, 4:753.

50 Richard Niccols, *Expicedium* (London, 1603), C2v–C3r.

51 Petowe, *Elizabetha Quasi Viuens*, B3r.

52 Petowe, *Elizabetha Quasi Viuens*, B3r.

53 *Sophonisba*, in *The Selected Plays of John Marston*, ed. Macdonald P. Jackson and Michael Neill (Cambridge: Cambridge University Press, 1986).

54 Fenton, *King Iames His Welcome to London*, B2v.

55 I quote *The Lady's Tragedy* from the manuscript text edited by Julia Briggs (*Thomas Middleton: The Collected Works*, ed. Gary Taylor and John Lavagnino [Oxford: Oxford University Press, 2007]).

56 For a more political reading of the crowned corpse of the Lady, see also Chapter 4 and Simon Shepherd, *Amazons and Warrior Women: Varieties of Feminism in Seventeenth-Century Drama* (Brighton: Harvester Press, 1981), 128.

57 For literary examinations of this issue, see, for example, Susan Frye, *Elizabeth I: The Competition for Representation* (Oxford: Oxford University Press, 1993), 78–86; Richard McCabe,

Spenser's Monstrous Regiment: Elizabethan Ireland and the Poetics of Difference (Oxford: Oxford University Press, 2002), 7–27, 79–100; and David Norbrook, *Poetry and Politics in the English Renaissance*, rev. ed. (Oxford: Oxford University Press, 2002), 97–139 (esp. 103–5). For the negative representation of Elizabeth during and after her reign, see also Julia M. Walker, ed., *Dissing Elizabeth*.

58 Samuel Daniel, *The Tragedie of Cleopatra*, in *The Poeticall Essayes of Sam. Danyel* (London, 1599), F1r.

59 Plutarch, *Lives*, in Bullough, ed., *Sources*, 5:316.

60 John Speed, *The Theatre of the Empire of Great Britaine* (London, 1612), 862.

61 *Calendar of State Papers Relating to English Affairs in the Archives of Venice*, ed. Horatio F. Brown, vol. 12 (London: Her Majesty's Stationery Office, 1905), 450.

62 *The Speeches at Prince Henry's Barriers*, in *The Cambridge Edition of the Works of Ben Jonson*, ed. David Bevington, Martin Butler and Ian Donaldson, 7 vols. (Cambridge: Cambridge University Press, 2012), 3:539.

63 For the representation of Prince Henry, see esp. Parry, *The Golden Age Restor'd*, 64–94 and J. W. Williamson, *The Myth of the Conqueror: Prince Henry Stuart, a Study of Seventeenth Century Personation* (New York: AMS Press, 1978).

64 Anne Barton, *Ben Jonson, Dramatist* (Cambridge: Cambridge University Press, 1984), 310.

65 Smuts, *Court Culture*, 24.

3

Coriolanus: Disarming the Memory of Elizabethan England

Volumnia's triumphal procession

In *Antony and Cleopatra*, Shakespeare offers a dramatic examination of the ways in which the chivalric discourse of Queen Elizabeth and her court became the cornerstone of nostalgia for Elizabethan militarism. Indeed, outside the theatre, the idealized memory of Elizabeth continued to refuel militaristic sentiments among those who were dissatisfied with James I's conciliatory policy. James and his supporters could neither suppress nor ignore the growing tide of militaristic sentiments; thus they needed to implement an effective way to tackle the glorification of Elizabethan militarism, a process extensively examined in Shakespeare's subsequent Roman play, *Coriolanus*. In *Coriolanus*, Shakespeare makes full use of the anthropomorphic understanding of a state as a female body (Chapter 1) as well as the representation of a warlike patroness and her heroic soldier (Chapter 2), probing further into the malleability and multivalency of Elizabethan images and motifs deployed during the first decade of James's reign.

In contrast to his preceding Roman tragedy, which ends with the deaths of the female protagonist and her female servants, Shakespeare features the victory of Roman women in the final act of *Coriolanus*. In Act 5, Caius Martius Coriolanus allies himself with the enemy of Rome, the Volscians, and leads their army to destroy his mother country. After the entreaties of his former general Cominius and his old friend Menenius are flatly dismissed by the vengeful Coriolanus, the Roman women headed by his mother Volumnia are sent to his camp as a last resort. Although Coriolanus initially refuses to listen, Volumnia urges him to forsake his arms and kneels before him, successfully changing his mind; Coriolanus agrees to sign a peace treaty, a self-immolating decision which, as he himself is well aware, pits him against the Volscians. The Romans rejoice at the news of Volumnia's victory over Coriolanus, and her triumphal entry into Rome is staged in Act 5 Scene 5:

> *Enter two Senators, with Ladies, passing ouer the Stage, with other Lords.*
>
> SENATOR
> Behold our Patronesse, the life of Rome:
> Call all your Tribes together, praise the Gods,
> And make triumphant fires, strew Flowers before them:
> Vnshoot the noise that Banish'd *Martius*;
> Repeale him, with the welcome of his Mother:
> Cry welcome, Ladies, welcome.
> ALL   Welcome Ladies, welcome.
> *A Flourish with Drummes and Trumpets.*[1]

In the next and final scene of the play, Coriolanus returns to Corioles, a Volscian city, where he is branded as a traitor and brutally stabbed to death; his fatal entry to Corioles markedly contrasts with Volumnia's victorious return to Rome in the preceding scene. Yet many studies have failed to take note of this contrast, effectively ignoring Volumnia's triumphal march across the stage in Scene 5 and treating it as in effect a redundant, transitional scene without much significance of its own.[2]

The stage direction, '*A Flourish with Drummes and Trumpets*', indicates that Act 5 Scene 5 is designed to be staged as a celebratory and ceremonial scene. However, the idea that a mother can thus triumphantly march across the stage after knowingly or unknowingly putting the life of her son at risk is an odd one, to say the least. Volumnia has often been seen, particularly in psychoanalytical readings of the play, as a monstrous mother who devours her own son.[3] Others have attempted to defend Volumnia by focusing on the fact that Volumnia remains silent throughout Act 5 Scene 5. Grace Latham, for example, interprets Volumnia's silence as her effort to conceal her internal struggle, seeing Volumnia as a patient mother who suffers from the loss of her son: 'she has made the greatest of all sacrifices for her country; and just as she would not show her anxiety when her Marcius was at the wars, so now she hides her pain and goes home to weep'.[4] Christina Luckyj also argues that Volumnia's silence suggests that she is not a triumphant virago but rather a devastated mother with complex emotions, challenging studies which regard her as an unnatural, cruel mother.[5] Several key productions in the second half of the twentieth century also attempted to 'humanize' Volumnia by presenting her as a devastated, weeping mother and reinterpreting her procession as an 'untriumphal' procession, thereby giving Act 5 Scene 5 a new role to reveal the inner struggle and suffering of a mother.[6]

Modern productions – often by adding gestures and backdrops that are not specified in Shakespeare's text – produced different versions of Volumnia. It is important to note, however, that, as R. B. Parker puts it, Volumnia's triumphant return to Rome 'must contrast ironically with Martius' subsequent entry into Antium however it is played'.[7] The fundamental framework of this scene – the public celebration of the defender of Rome – remains unaltered, regardless of how Volumnia expresses her inner struggle, if she has any, during the procession. I would suggest, then, that it is necessary to reflect on the significance of Volumnia's procession prior to the tragic death of the protagonist, presuming that the scene was performed as a moment of celebration, as the stage direction in the Folio text suggests. What was the significance of staging Volumnia's celebratory procession on the Jacobean stage?

One of the most lively topics at the time of first performances of *Coriolanus* in 1608–9 was James's foreign policy.[8] James had successfully maintained peace with Spain since he concluded a peace treaty with the Spanish in 1604. His foreign policy, however, was not popular in England, and some writers reflected their anti-peace sentiments in their writings. James and supporters of his peace policy were not oblivious to these anti-peace publications; they too published political pamphlets defending James's policy and refuting the arguments of the war party.[9] Just as the Roman senators in *Coriolanus* are engaged in a hot debate about foreign policy in the Capitol ('one but of my ordinance stood up / To speak of peace or war' [3.2.12–13]), the debate over war and peace was heating up in Jacobean England. It is key to my discussion, as it was in the last chapter, that, in this debate, Jacobean writers turned to Elizabethan symbolism and ideology in order to articulate and convey their political views.

The confrontation between the war party and the peace party was nothing new in England; the last years of Elizabeth's reign saw a growing antagonism between the two parties. The Earl of Essex, for example, openly argued for war with Spain and became a symbol of aggressive militarism, particularly after his successful campaign against Cadiz in 1596. Although direct antagonism between the peace party led by Robert Cecil and the war party led by Essex subsided when the latter was executed for treason in 1601, his death did not entirely crush the spirit of the war party. After the accession of James, the late earl was mythologized as a heroic conqueror who embodied the militant Protestant ideal. Robert Pricket's *Honors Fame in Triumph Riding* (1604), for example, nostalgically praises Essex as a heroic warrior – '*Englands* sunne' and '*Spaines* thunder' – whose 'glorie seemde a matchlesse Excellence', asserting that 'the hope of England on his Sword relyde'.[10] Militant Protestant sentiments were projected not only onto the memory of an Elizabethan courtier, such as Philip Sidney and the Earls of Leicester and Essex, but also onto James's elder son Prince Henry, who was regarded as the spiritual heir of Elizabethan militarism. The independent court of Prince Henry was known to have supported militant Protestants who failed to curry favour with the peace-loving king. Prince Henry, although he was still young at the time, was already hailed as a future conqueror and the hope of militant Protestantism; the Venetian ambassador reports that 'many predictions centred round his person, and he seemed marked out for great events. His whole talk was of arms and war. His authority was great, and he was obeyed and lauded by the military party'.[11] A number of plays, masques and political pamphlets associated Prince Henry with the oceanic and chivalric imagery of Elizabethan militarism, casting him in the role of Elizabeth's spiritual heir and knight. Despite James's official conciliatory stance, writers were able to project their militant Protestant sentiments on the representations of these warlike figures.

It was not only representation of heroic men but, as I discussed in Chapter 2, also representation of Elizabeth that played crucial roles in the militant Protestant discourse of the Jacobean period. Although Elizabeth herself was known to have been reluctant to adopt an aggressive foreign policy during her reign, those who argued for war with Spain and military intervention in the Netherlands compared her to a goddess of war, emphatically praising James's predecessor as the supporter of militant Englishmen. In *Nova Britannia* (1609), Robert Johnson reimagines Elizabeth as the belligerent queen who actively pursued the Protestant cause; as he recounts, Elizabeth's 'hand was euer lending, to distressed neighbour Princes, and her sword vnsheathed continually, repulsing forraine enemies'.[12] Given that Elizabeth appeared to be unwilling to provide military aid to the Protestants in the Netherlands and in Ireland throughout her reign, Johnson's account of Elizabeth's reign was, to say the least, one-sided. Yet providing an accurate historical account was not the aim of these writers; rather, by presenting the popular image of the triumphant queen, regardless of its historical accuracy, they aimed to encourage James to emulate his predecessor and to adopt a more aggressive foreign policy. The representation of Elizabeth as a belligerent queen who patronized and was protected by her heroic subjects and that of her warlike heroes became a combined icon of militant Protestantism and symbol of the glorious warlike age in the Jacobean period. It is this popular representation of the warlike patron/soldier pairing, I wish to argue, that is key to understanding the Jacobean significance of *Coriolanus*.

The warlike patron and her heroic soldier

Throughout the play, Coriolanus is compared to mythical heroes, to Hercules and to the war god Mars – the most revered war god in ancient Rome – from whom he takes his second name Martius.[13] Coriolanus amply demonstrates his martial excellence in his conquest of Corioles, a victory from which he earns his surname; when he triumphantly returns to Rome, he is hailed as a demigod and the nobles bend their knees 'as to Jove's statue' (2.1.260). When he joins the Volscians, Rome's militant rival tribe, after his banishment from Rome, the Volscian senators 'stand bald before him' (4.5.197) and deify him 'as if he were son and heir to Mars' (4.5.194–95). Their soldiers idolize Coriolanus, substituting his name for that of their god in their prayers ('Your soldiers use him as the grace fore meat, / Their talk at table and their thanks at end' [4.7.3–4]), and Cominius also reports that Coriolanus 'is their god. He leads them like a thing / Made by some other deity than nature / That shapes man better' (4.6.91–93). As

Menenius puts it, Coriolanus 'wants nothing of a god but eternity and a heaven to throne in' (5.4.23–24).

Shakespeare's representation of Coriolanus as a war god has an important Jacobean significance. As will be discussed later in this chapter, the deification of Coriolanus, for example, echoes the glorification of Essex, who was similarly praised for his warlike spirit and hailed as 'braue Mars of men' in Jacobean discourse.[14] Shakespeare's representation of the heroic conqueror is not only comparable to the way in which Essex was commemorated at this time but also to the representation of Prince Henry, as he was also frequently compared to a war god.[15] For the celebration of Prince Henry's investiture in 1610, for example, Ben Jonson composed *Prince Henry's Barriers*, in which the Lady of the Lake praises Prince Henry as Mars ('Does he not sit like Mars, or one that had / The better of him, in his armour clad?'), aligning Prince Henry with Elizabethan militant heroes.[16] Thus, in the local contexts of 1608–9, Coriolanus can be linked to the glorification of heroic militarism in Jacobean England.

The Jacobean significance of Shakespeare's representation of Volumnia, on the other hand, has not attracted much critical attention, despite the fact that Shakespeare invested great interest in developing her character. Both in Plutarch's *Lives* and Livy's *The Romane Historie* (translated by Philemon Holland and published in 1600) – Shakespeare's historical sources – Volumnia features only towards the ends of their accounts: that is, when she is sent to persuade Coriolanus not to attack Rome.[17] By contrast, Shakespeare gives his Volumnia a prominent role from the start of the play, representing her as a belligerent, domineering mother who sends her son to the battlefield without hesitation and rejoices when he comes home wounded. Shakespeare's Volumnia proudly announces that it is her encouragement which has made Coriolanus a successful soldier and that she is the source of his valour: 'Thy valiantness was mine, thou suck'st it from me' (3.2.130). As she also puts it later in the play, 'Thou art my warrior. / I holp to frame thee' (5.3.62–63). When Coriolanus triumphantly returns from Corioles, he kneels before his mother and thanks her for her support – a behaviour not in Shakespeare's sources – to which Volumnia replies, 'my good soldier, up' (2.1.166) as if she had just knighted him as her faithful subject. Shakespeare's Volumnia is thus distinctly portrayed as a warlike patron of the heroic warrior.

One of the few studies which attempted to situate this representation of the warlike mother in the Jacobean context is that of Robin Headlam Wells, who suggests that Volumnia evoked James's wife Queen Anne in the minds of the Jacobean audience. He points out similarities between Volumnia and Queen Anne by drawing on the biographical account of the latter by the eighteenth-century historian Thomas Birch; in his account, Birch portrayed Queen Anne as a possessive mother who encouraged her son to pursue his interest in military affairs.[18] I would suggest, however, that Queen Anne is relevant to the discussion of *Coriolanus* not because of the supposed biographical similarities with Volumnia but because she attempted to appropriate the memory of Elizabeth and continuously styled herself the warlike patron of heroic soldiers – the role which is iconographically similar to that of Volumnia. From the time of her arrival in London, Queen Anne styled herself a warlike queen. Court masques functioned as sites of her image-making. In Samuel Daniel's *The Vision of the Twelve Goddesses* (1604), for example, the twelve goddesses, including Astraea, Pallas, Diana and Vesta, signify, as Martin Butler puts it, 'the repertoire of roles that Elizabeth herself had used and which would have unavoidably evoked her memory'.[19] Among these Elizabethan personas, Queen Anne specifically chose to play Pallas Athena, a goddess of war; during the performance, Queen Anne 'was attired in a blew mantle, with a siluer imbrodry of all weapons and engines of war, with a helmet-dressing on her head, and presents a Launce and Target'.[20] Notably, in this performance, Queen Anne and her ladies wore costumes which had belonged to Elizabeth – a symbolic gesture that was in line with Anne's attempt to present herself as a successor to Elizabeth's persona as England's mighty queen.[21] Then, in Daniel's *Tethys' Festival* (1610), a court masque sponsored by Anne for the investiture of Henry as Prince of Wales and performed in her court, Queen Anne personated Tethys, Goddess-Queen of the Ocean. Symbolically, Tethys bestows the sword which belongs to Astraea on Meliades, the British warrior prince (personated by Prince Henry). Astraea is the goddess of justice to whom Elizabeth was often compared; Queen Anne thus passes Astraea's/Elizabeth's sword to Prince Henry and validates his role as a warrior prince – a symbolic and political gesture which is comparable to that of Spenser's Astraea in Book V of *The Faerie Queene*, who bestows her sword on Artegall, the knight of justice, for his fight against infidels – by which Spenser in fact means Ireland and Spain.[22] Queen Anne thus styled herself the successor to Elizabeth's role as a warlike queen who encourages her knight to pursue a militant course.

Queen Anne's self-stylization as warlike patron of her militant son is suggestive, as it illuminates the way in which her court masques appropriated the memory of Elizabeth and, indeed, some of the courtly audience of *Coriolanus* might have associated Shakespeare's Volumnia directly with the incumbent queen. In this chapter, however, I wish to suggest that it was not Queen Anne's courtly self-stylization but the memory of Elizabeth which had a greater relevance to Shakespeare's characterization of Volumnia. Although Queen Anne fashioned herself as Pallas and Tethys, not all audiences of *Coriolanus* in public theatres would have associated her with Volumnia since Queen Anne's masques were performed only at court and some of the printed texts were not available at the time of first performances of Shakespeare's play. The popularized image of Elizabeth as the patron of militant soldiers, a motif which Shakespeare examined in the figures of Cleopatra and her knight Antony in his preceding Roman play, could have been more recognizable to Jacobean theatregoers who attended *Coriolanus*.

As I have noted, Coriolanus does not exclusively evoke Prince Henry but rather the general notion of Elizabethan heroic warriors whom militant Protestants encouraged Prince Henry to emulate. What bound these idealized heroes together was their patron goddess Elizabeth. Indeed, in the Jacobean nostalgic discourse, both the late Earl of Essex and his Jacobean surrogate Prince Henry were praised as Elizabeth's heroic knights who would not only protect besieged Protestant England but also extend their arms to the distressed European Protestants on the continent. Volumnia and Coriolanus, like Cleopatra and Antony, evoke the Elizabethan chivalric framework which was at the basis of nostalgia for Elizabeth and her reign; Shakespeare's representation of Volumnia wilfully foregrounds the image of the warlike queen, an image which for the audience harked back to Elizabethan militarism. Furthermore, Volumnia's warlike mother status is not the only feature that evokes the representation of Elizabeth. As will be discussed further, when Rome is besieged by the Volscian army, Volumnia presents herself as the besieged nation-mother subject to male violence, reminiscent of the way in which the representation of the besieged Elizabeth signified the besieged status of England – the representation of Queen Anne, on the other hand, was rarely deployed to symbolize England's body politic in this way. Although earlier studies of *Coriolanus* have not noticed the significant link between Volumnia and the memory of Elizabeth, I would argue that this symbolic link is highly important in understanding the significance of Shakespeare's representation of Volumnia and that of her procession in Act 5 Scene 5.

That Volumnia and Coriolanus evoke the memory of Elizabethan England on multiple levels can be illustrated by the fact that they provoke not only the specific memories of Elizabeth and her militant followers – the prominent focal points of nostalgia – but also a generalized memory of ordinary Elizabethan warlike mother/son pairings as reimagined by Jacobean writers. Thomas Dekker's *The Whore of Babylon*, for example, offers a nostalgic portrayal of a mother and son at the time of the Armada attack:

PARTHENOPHIL
Old grandams that on crutches beare vp age,
Full nimbly buckled Armours on their sonnes,
And when twas on, she clapt him on his backe,
And spake thus, runne my boye, fight till th'art dead,
Thy bloud can neuer be more brauely shed.

(5.2.195–99)

In this play, Dekker not only represents Elizabeth as a warlike queen in the figure of Titania, but also offers an image of an Elizabethan mother among commoners who, like Volumnia (1.3.20–25), willingly arms her son at a time of war without showing any reluctance to sacrifice his life for the sake of his mother country. Yet, in contrast to *The Whore of Babylon* and other instances of nostalgic discourse of Elizabeth, Shakespeare's play does not take full part in reinforcing militant nostalgia for Elizabeth's reign. While evoking the reimagined militant past of Elizabethan England, Shakespeare significantly transforms the representation of the warlike patron Volumnia towards the end of the play, a dramatic transformation through which Shakespeare probes into the politics of reconstructing the memory of Elizabeth in Jacobean England.

Disarming the memory of Elizabethan England

The death of Coriolanus and the triumphal return of Volumnia are iconographically presented as the fall of one divinity and the rise of another. When Coriolanus first joins the Volscian side, Aufidius affectionately calls him Mars (4.5.120); upon his return to Corioles with the Volscian troops after abandoning the war, however, Coriolanus discovers that his second-in-command no longer reveres him as such:

AUFIDIUS
                    at his nurse's tears
He whined and roared away your victory
That pages blushed at him and men of heart
Looked wondering each at others.
CORIOLANUS   Hear'st thou, Mars?
AUFIDIUS   Name not the god, thou boy of tears.
                                          (5.6.99–103)

Aufidius pronounces that Coriolanus no longer deserves to
voice the name of Mars, deriding the erstwhile hero, who
has failed to live up to the ideal of the war god, as a 'boy of
tears' who 'whined and roared away' the victory 'at his nurse's
tears'. By choosing peace, Coriolanus deprives himself of the
divine status of Mars, revealing himself as an ordinary mortal
susceptible to human feelings.

     In the final scene, Aufidius and his conspirators stab
Coriolanus in front of the citizens and Aufidius tramples on
his body; as Shakespeare's elaborate stage direction in the Folio
puts it, '*Draw both the Conspirators, and kils Martius, who
falles, Auffidius stands on him*'.[23] The Volscians thus bring down
the man who was even compared to a winged dragon to earth
('This Martius is grown from man to dragon. He has wings; he's
more than a creeping thing' [5.4.12–14]), staging the dramatic
fall of the inhuman power. It is important to note that, even
though Coriolanus decided not to fight against Rome, he enters
the final scene, still styling himself a soldier: 'I am returned your
soldier, / No more infected with my country's love / Than when
I parted hence' (5.6.71–73). Accordingly, the stage direction,
'*Enter Coriolanus marching with Drumme, and Colours. The
Commoners being with him*', dictates that Coriolanus appears
on stage with drums and colours, followed by the commoners
as if he is still the heroic war god the Volscians revere.[24] The
play thus stresses that it is the god of war who is destroyed by
Aufidius and his supporters in the final scene.

     Volumnia's assumption that Coriolanus's decision to
conclude peace should be welcomed by the Volscians proves

wrong; neither do the Romans 'give the all-hail to' Coriolanus or bless him 'for making up this peace' (5.3.139–40). The Romans never show respect or gratitude to Coriolanus's decision to spare Rome; they celebrate Coriolanus's retreat from Rome as the merriest moment in the history of Rome ('The Volscians are dislodged and Martius gone. / A merrier day did never yet greet Rome' [5.4.41–42]), yet it is Volumnia, not her son, who is blessed and hailed as peacemaker. While Virgilia and Valeria, the two ladies who accompany Volumnia, also receive considerable commendations, it is Volumnia who is counted on as the most promising negotiator and is eventually venerated as the main agency of their success. In Plutarch, it is the group of the ladies who receive commendations and no specific praise is given to Volumnia: '[the Romans] were all throughly persuaded, and dyd certenly beleeve, that the ladyes only were cause of the saving of the cittie ... Whereupon the Senate ordeined, that the magistrates to gratifie and honour these ladyes, should graunte them all that they would require'.[25] Furthermore, Shakespeare omits Plutarch's account of the key contribution of Valeria, who receives omens from the gods and masterminds the ladies' delegate to Coriolanus, crediting thereby Coriolanus's capitulation mainly to his mother.[26] Accordingly, Menenius remarks that 'this Volumnia / Is worth of consuls, senators, patricians, / A city full' (5.4.52–54) and Aufidius also stresses that it is Volumnia ('his nurse') who subdued Coriolanus.

In this light, it is significant that Volumnia is called by her own name for the first time when she returns to the city in Shakespeare's play ('This Volumnia ... '). Up to this moment, Volumnia is known to the audience as Coriolanus's mother but, after expelling her son from the city gate, she begins to assert her own identity separate from that of Coriolanus. In Act 5 Scene 5, then, she is given a new name and identity: 'our patroness, the life of Rome' (5.5.1). The word 'patroness' comes from the Latin word, *patrōnissa*, which means the goddess of defence.[27] In this Roman context, it specifically refers to Juno, a protector of Rome – we may recall that the link between

Volumnia and this Roman goddess is hinted at when she voices the name of Juno twice in the play ('For the love of Juno, let's go' [2.1.98]; 'lament as I do, / In anger Juno-like' [4.2.52–53]). While Coriolanus is dramatically stripped of his divine status as the war god, Volumnia is deified by the Romans. In fact, as Peggy Muñoz Simonds points out, this symbolic replacement of Mars by Juno had a historical precedent in the famous ancient Roman annual ritual in which Juno expels her son Mars from the city of Rome and marks the arrival of peace.[28] By evoking this ritualistic replacement of Mars, the play shifts its focus from war to peace, and from conqueror to peacemaker.

This symbolic shift had a close thematic and iconographical link with the Jacobean contexts. In Plutarch, after the failure of several embassies to Coriolanus, the Romans prepare for an armed confrontation: 'it was determined in counsell … that they should watche and warde upon the walles, to repulse their enemies if they came to assault them'.[29] In Plutarch's supplication scene, Volumnia warns Coriolanus that he might lose the battle against the Romans and that, if he does, the Volscians, 'thy good friendes', might turn against him.[30] In contrast to its main source, Shakespeare's play does not refer to the possibility that Rome could win the battle against Coriolanus's Volscian force. In Shakespeare's Roman world, as Cominius stresses, 'desperation / Is all the policy, strength and defence / That Rome can make against them' (4.6.129–31). Indeed, Volumnia wins peace through negotiations and diplomacy in a situation in which, as Coriolanus puts it, 'all the swords / In Italy and her confederate arms / Could not have made this peace' (5.3.207–9). The play thus presents negotiation as the only solution to save the country from destruction, stressing the importance of Volumnia's role as reconciler and peacemaker – a symbolic role which resonates with James's much vaunted role as such.

James was often praised for resolving difficult political issues by peaceful means. In *A Panegyrike Congratulatorie to the Kings Maiestie* (1603), Samuel Daniel praises James as the monarch who finally resolved the centuries-old conflict between England and Scotland, calling his achievement 'what heretofore could neuer yet be wrought, / By all the swords of powre, by blood, by fire, / By ruine, and destruction' – a passage reminiscent of Coriolanus's praise of Volumnia ('all the swords ... ').[31] In *The Magnificent Entertainment Giuen to King Iames* (1604), Thomas Dekker's account of the entertainment for James's coronation entry into London, the female Genius of the city disarms the two armed knights, Saint George (England) and Saint Andrew (Scotland), announcing that they no longer need to bear arms by the accession of James ('why you beare (alone) th'ostent of Warre, / When all hands else reare *Oliue*-boughs and *Palme*: / And *Halcyonean* dayes assure all's calme'), a symbolic speech which is also meant to celebrate the peaceful union of England and Scotland under James.[32] Then, as I noted earlier, James was also known for his role in ending England's longstanding hostile relationship with Spain by negotiation not by force. In this context, Volumnia's lines spoken to her warlike son, 'each in either side / Give the all-hail to thee and cry "Be blest / For making up this peace!"' (5.3.138–40), resonate with the motto James adapted for his rule, *Beati Pacifici* ('Blessed are the peace makers').[33] By evoking the set of literary texts which praises James's political stance, the praise of Volumnia as a new peace-minded defender of the state thus associates the play with the theme of Jacobean peace.

Furthermore, Shakespeare's dramatization of the fall of Coriolanus/Mars also had famous symbolic precedents. Towards the end of the entertainment for James's coronation entry I mentioned earlier, an entry which was modelled on the style of Roman triumphal returns, James was presented with a Roman arch. In this Roman arch, actors performed an allegorical scene in which Mars is grovelling beneath the feet of Eirene (Peace) with his arms and armour scattered around him.[34] In his contribution to this entertainment, Ben Jonson writes:

> The first and principal person in the temple was IRENE, or Peace ... a wreath of olive on her head, on her shoulder a

silver dove; in her left hand she held forth an olive branch
with a handful of ripe ears, in the other a crown of laurel,
as notes of victory and plenty ... Beneath her feet lay
ENYALIUS, or Mars, grovelling, his armour scattered upon
him in several pieces, and sundry sorts of weapons broken
about him.[35]

The same image of Mars being defeated and laid down on
the ground – an image reminiscent of Coriolanus's being
trodden on by the Volscians at the end of the play – was later
reproduced on the title cover of James's *Workes* (1616).[36] It
was not only Eirene but James himself who was represented as
the vanquisher of Mars; he was hailed as a king who had finally
subdued and expelled Mars from London. In the entertainment
for James's coronation entry, the Genius of the City announced
James's victory over Mars: '[James's] strong and potent virtues
have defaced / Stern Mars his statues, and upon them placed /
His and the world's best blessings'.[37] William Herbert's *A
Prophesie of Cadwallader* (1604) similarly praises James for
bringing comfort to England by 'binding in chaines the sternest
god of warre'.[38] James's entry into London was thus presented
as a symbolic event that marks the death of Mars and the
arrival of long-sought peace. Against the backdrop of this
cultural symbolism, Volumnia's triumphal entry into Rome,
which celebrates her transformation from belligerent mother
to goddess of peace, can be seen as enacting a shift from
Elizabethan militarism to Jacobean peace, a shift which was
also the central theme of James's own Roman-style procession.

Volumnia's procession, however, is crucial to my discussion
not only because it highlights the theme of Jacobean peace
but also because it closely associates the play with the politics
of commemorating Elizabeth during this period. After the
discovery of the Gunpowder Plot in 1605, Elizabeth's victory
over the Armada in 1588 – a similar instance of national
victory over the Catholic menace – and her Roman-style
triumphal procession into London attracted much nostalgic
attention. Indeed, significant thematic parallels can be drawn

between this national celebration of victory, which was well documented at the time, and Volumnia's Roman-style procession. As John Stow writes, 19 November 1588 was 'kept holyday throughout the realme, with sermons, singing of psalms, bonefires, &c. for ioy, and a thanksgiuing unto God, for the ouerthrow of the Spanyards our enemies on the sea'.[39] Then, on 24 November, Elizabeth entered the city in triumph, riding in a chariot; as Richard Hakluyt puts it, Elizabeth, 'imitating the ancient Romans, rode into *London* in triumph, in regard of her owne and her subiects glorious deliuerance'.[40]

It has been generally assumed that Elizabeth after the victory over the Armada was represented as a victorious, warlike queen. It is true that some writers and painters represented her as such; James Aske's *Elizabetha Triumphans* (1588) describes Elizabeth at Tilbury as 'an *Amazonian* Queene' who, 'heaving oft to Skies her war-like hands, / Did make her selfe *Bellona*-like renown'd'.[41] However, the victory over the Armada was not always linked to militant sentiments in the late Elizabethan and the early Jacobean periods. In fact, Elizabeth was careful enough to prevent the war party from capitalizing on this national victory, making sure that England's victory was seen not as the result of a successful military campaign, which she was reluctant to fund, but rather as definite proof that England was protected by God against the formidable enemy. In her prayer of thanksgiving in 1588, she thanked God 'for that the weakest sex hath been so fortified by Thy strongest help that neither my people find lack by my weakness nor foreigners triumph at my ruin'.[42] *A Psalme and Collect of Thankesgiuing* (1588), published by Christopher Barker, Elizabeth's official printer, and used across the churches, similarly stresses that England could not have defended herself against the mighty Armada without the protection of God: 'surely their coming was so sudden (their multitude, power, and cruelty so great) that, had we not believed verily to see the goodness of God and put our trust in His defense and protection, they might have utterly destroyed us'.[43] Therefore, according to Hakluyt, 'all people thorowout *England* prostrated themselues with humble prayers and supplications vnto God ... especially the outlandish Churches ... enioyned to their people continuall fastings and supplications ... knowing right well, that prayer was the onely refuge against all enemies, calamities, and necessities'.[44]

In the national celebration of victory, Elizabeth presented herself as a pious queen, kneeling and thanking God for his protection. In her triumphant entry into London in 1588, Elizabeth, dismounting from her chariot, 'on hir knees made hir hartie praiers to God', commanding her subjects to follow her example.[45] As Hakluyt puts it, 'with her owne princely voice she most Christianly exhorted the people to doe the same'.[46] Even after this national celebration, Elizabeth continued to urge her people to offer humble prayers to God: 'Also a while after the Spanish Fleet was departed, there was in *England,* by the commandement of her Maiestie, and in the vnited Prouinces, by the direction of the States, a solemne festiuall day publikely appointed, wherein all persons were enioyned to resort vnto the Church, and there to render thanks and praises vnto God'.[47] In fact, Aske's pamphlet praises Elizabeth not only as a *'Bellona*-like' queen but also as a pious, kneeling queen: 'Our gracious Queene (for this Gods mercie shew'd / To her, her land ...) / Doth yeeld him thankes deuoutly on her knees, / And wills her Subiects throughout all her land / To fast and pray for this his prouidence'.[48] In *Coriolanus,* after Volumnia's victory, the Romans similarly express their 'thankfulness' (5.4.59) to the gods. Meaningfully, a senator urges them to 'praise the gods, / And make triumphant fires' (5.5.2–3) during Volumnia's triumphal procession. There is no reference to fires in Plutarch's account of the celebration. Indeed, as Lee Bliss puts it, lighting bonfires was 'a common Elizabethan expression of thankful celebration, as at the defeat of the Spanish Armada'.[49] Thus, Shakespeare's reference to triumphant fires, reminiscent of bonfires lit in celebration of Elizabeth's victory over the Armada, also serves to connect the scene with the memory of her reign.

In the supplication scene, Volumnia reprovingly asks Coriolanus, 'Alas, how can we for our country pray, / Whereto we are bound', criticizing her son for denying 'our prayers to the gods' (5.3.105–8); she then kneels on stage, urging others to follow suit. It soon turns out that their knees prove more potent than the sword. At this point, the audience might recall Menenius's admonitory line spoken to the rioting plebeians early in the play, 'Your knees to them, not arms, must help' (1.1.69), which, we come to realize, prophetically summarizes the central motif of Act 5 and confirms the symbolic importance of kneeling in this play. I would argue that the representation of Volumnia, whose knees, not arms, defend her city from invasion, has a striking thematic and symbolic parallel with the memory of England's kneeling state mother.

In this context, Volumnia's identification of Rome with her own body assumes a profound significance; in the supplication scene, Volumnia gives an emphatic warning to her son:

VOLUMNIA

              If I cannot persuade thee
Rather to show a noble grace to both parts
Than seek the end of one, thou shalt no sooner
March to assault thy country than to tread –
Trust to't, thou shalt not – on thy mother's womb
That brought thee to this world.

                                (5.3.120–25)

Volumnia warns him that what he is about to destroy is not just the body politic of Rome but the body of his own mother.[50] Volumnia also compares the attack on Rome to an act of 'tearing / His country's bowels out' (5.3.102–3). Here, the mother Rome is represented as a woman who attempts to defend her body from male violence/invasion. Before his planned attack on Rome, Coriolanus expresses his desire to 'stand / As if a man were author of himself / And knew no other kin' (5.3.35–37). Only by destroying the womb of Rome/ his own mother from which he was born – living proof that he is authored by his mother – is he able, in his own mind at least, to become the 'author of himself' who 'knew no other kin'. It is highly symbolic that he is called 'viper' at critical moments in the play ('Where is this viper, / That would depopulate the city' [3.1.265–66]; 'This viperous traitor' [3.1.285]), since in early modern England young vipers were believed to eat their way out of their mother's womb.[51] The representation of Coriolanus as a threat to his mother's womb thus serves to represent Volumnia/Rome as a mother striving to defend her body from male violence.

As I discussed in Chapter 1, Elizabeth was often identified with mother England. Peter Stallybrass points out that Elizabeth's virginity was pictured as 'the emblem of the perfect and impermeable container' and the state under Elizabeth was seen as 'a *hortus conclusus*, an enclosed garden walled off from enemies'.[52] In other words, Elizabeth's body symbolized the impenetrability of England. Indeed, she was commemorated as 'the wall and bulwark' of England in some of the elegies composed upon her death.[53] The representation of Volumnia as a woman defending her womb evokes the apotheosized image of the queen – an Elizabethan propagandistic myth in which England was represented as Elizabeth's insurmountable and impregnable body. Volumnia, who, of course, is not a virgin in the literal sense of the word, is presented as the representative of the Roman ladies who are determined to defend their wombs from the Volscian army. Throughout the play, war is represented as male violence on the wombs of the female citizens ('wars in some sort may be said to be a ravisher' [4.5.229–30]), a common rhetoric during Shakespeare's time; the Armada's attempted invasion, for example, was seen as the Spanish attempt to 'deflower our virgins'.[54] By striving to stop war – 'a ravisher' of women – Volumnia, flanked by Virgilia, who also manifests her determination to defend her womb from Coriolanus's destruction (5.3.125), symbolically presents herself as the defender of the impenetrable womb(s) of Rome. In this respect, the presence of Valeria in the supplication scene is also meaningful. Although she has no lines in the scene, her presence on the stage is crucial as she is significantly compared to 'the moon of Rome, chaste as the icicle' (5.3.65) – the chaste moon Diana, one of the symbolic personas of the virgin Elizabeth. The representation of Volumnia, accompanying the symbolism of Diana, thus enables the audience to associate Volumnia's attempt to defend the womb of the state from invasion with Elizabeth's.

In this context, Volumnia's name, which is, as I pointed out earlier, first pronounced just before her triumphal procession, acquires a deeper significance. In historical accounts by Livy and Florus, Coriolanus's mother has a different name, Veturia.[55] In Livy's account, Volumnia is in fact the name of his wife. On this point, Shakespeare chooses to follow Plutarch by naming Coriolanus's mother Volumnia. Interestingly, the word Volumnia, as Simonds points out, originally comes from the word meaning 'enclosed space'.[56] Although the mother's name derives from Plutarch, Shakespeare's representation of her as besieged mother/Rome activates the latent significance of the name; given that Elizabeth's body politic, England, was often compared to an enclosed space, particularly an enclosed garden, the name 'Volumnia' Shakespeare appropriately chooses for the mother who attempts to guard her body/ state against violence, I would suggest, can also be linked to the memory of Elizabeth and her England. Shakespeare's representation of Volumnia in Act 5 can be thus associated with the image of Elizabeth as a woman who, by kneeling and praying, successfully defended the womb of England from the invading army.

As we have seen, Aske's 1588 pamphlet, *Elizabetha Triumphans*, presents two images of Elizabeth at the time of the Armada attack: the besieged queen whose only shield against the attacker was her piety and the '*Bellona*-like' queen who worked as the main agent for the victory over the Armada. During her reign, these two images reflected the complex, often contradictory, views of English subjects about their queen, and the Jacobeans continued to develop these images of Elizabeth. While the war party praised her as England's warlike monarch, the peace party attempted to counter burgeoning militant nostalgia by focusing on a more moderate image of Elizabeth, who credited England's victory not to her military might but to God. Lodowick Lloyd's *The Tragicocomedie of Serpents* (1607), for example, retrospectively credits Elizabeth's victory over the Armada solely to her piety, not to her army, emphasizing that it was God who gave Elizabeth the victory: 'the windes, weathers, stormes, tempests, rockes, and stones of the earth sung, and gaue the victorie to Queen *Elizabeth* against the Spaniards'.[57] In *In Felicem Memoriam Elizabethae* (1608), Francis Bacon re-assesses Elizabeth's reign and praises her as a peace-minded monarch who successfully led her country by curbing the 'warlike and stout' faction in her court:

> That is not also to be forgotten what kinde of People she governed ... for all this inclination of her people longing for war, & of their rest impatient, she was never hindred from loving and keeping of peace, which will of hers was seconded with success, I reckon among her chiefest praises.[58]

Although Bacon was formerly known as a supporter of Essex and his militant Protestantism, he switched sides upon the accession of James, and attempted to represent Elizabeth as a peace-loving monarch – a representation which Curtis Perry calls 'the King James's version of Elizabeth' – rewriting her memory in order to counter the growing nostalgia for the warlike Elizabeth.[59] Similarly, Richard Crakanthorpe's sermon preached in 1609 stressed that England's 'long tranquility and happie peace, with all the blessings and blessed fruites of peace' was first bestowed by God 'at the ioyful entrance of our late Soueraigne QVEENE ELIZABETH, whose Sacred spirite doth now rest and raigne with the Lord', and that England 'enioyed long and happy peace, vnder her long and happy raigne'.[60] D. R. Woolf points out that by the 1620s it was impossible for James to prevent the warlike image of Elizabeth from appearing in a range of texts; he argues that 'at this stage, the best way to counteract the growing image of Elizabeth the protestant crusader was simply to present a convincing alternative', and he cites the representation of the peace-minded Elizabeth in William Camden's *Annales*, a work commissioned by James (the first part of which was published in 1615 and the second in 1625).[61] As the examples from Bacon's writing and Crakanthorpe's sermon suggest, however, supporters of James's peace policy had already started to present an alternative image of Elizabeth in the first decade of James's reign.

James found it increasingly difficult to counter the popular discourse of militarism. Its spiritual leader Prince Henry was not to be counselled by his father on matters of his militant political stance. James's attempts to directly refute the argument of the war party – for example, his order for Robert Cotton to write a counter-argument against an anonymous pamphlet entitled 'Propositions of War and Peace Delivered to His Highness Prince Henry by Some of His Military Servants' (1608), which harshly criticizes the pacific policy of James's regime and openly argues for war with France and Spain – failed to check the growing popularity of the militant discourse.[62] Indeed, the peace party needed to change their tactics. The representation of the warlike Elizabeth was appropriated to promote the militant Protestant cause and to lead Prince Henry into the path of aggressive Protestantism. James and his supporters then resorted to counter-tactics; they attempted to adjust the representation of Elizabeth as a prudent, peace-minded monarch, appropriating her iconic power in order to advance their own cause. In this Jacobean context for representing Elizabeth, rewriting Volumnia, the breeder and spiritual supporter of her heroic warrior, as the state mother who instructs her soldier to curb his warlike spirit is highly symbolic. Coriolanus has followed the path of the heroic warrior that Volumnia has laid out for him but, in Act 5 Scene 3, the same Volumnia assumes the role of peacemaker, instructing her soldier to change the course of his militant action. In this regard, Shakespeare's representation of Volumnia can be read in the contexts of Jacobeans' competition for authoring the memory of Elizabeth; in particular, her carefully choreographed transformation from the belligerent patron of the heroic warrior to the reconciler/peacemaker can be associated with the ongoing attempts to rewrite the representation of Elizabeth – the spiritual patron of aggressive militarism – as the patroness of peace.

Despite its complexity, *Coriolanus* has sometimes been read as an anti-James play. Many attempts have been made to examine the topicality of *Coriolanus*; certain local contexts for the play – uprisings in the West Midlands and conflict between James and the Commons – have received a good deal of critical attention over a sustained period.[63] Yet some of these topical readings treated the play as a critical commentary on James by citing possible biographical similarities between Coriolanus and James – for example, their disdain towards the common people.[64] As I have shown, the focus on the representation of Volumnia in Act 5 can correct this critical bias by suggesting a possibility of revisiting the play from the Jacobean pro-peace perspective. It is, however, equally inappropriate to interpret the play as Shakespeare's full support for James's peace policy.[65] Shakespeare's representations of Volumnia and Coriolanus do not provide straight answers to the complex political issues of war and peace that Jacobean England was facing at the time.

Questioning peace and commemorating the warrior

Shakespeare carefully draws an alternative perspective from which the audience can sharply question the validity and credibility of the representation of Volumnia as peacemaker; to this extent, we need to pay particular attention to Shakespeare's representation of Coriolanus, which is far more complicated than Plutarch's in the extent to which the peace Volumnia establishes at the end of the play begins to appear insubstantial and illusory.

Plutarch writes that, after the conclusion of the peace treaty and Coriolanus's death, the Volscians attacked Rome and that

Rome won the battle and subjugated the Volscian state as a Roman dependency: 'the Romannes overcame them in battell, in which Tullus [Aufidius] was slaine in the field ... so that they were compelled to accept most shamefull conditions of peace, in yelding them selves subject unto the conquerers'.[66] Plutarch thus makes it clear that Coriolanus was, after all, not indispensable to the defence of Rome. In contrast, throughout Shakespeare's play, Coriolanus is represented as indispensable to the defence of Rome and as an integral part of the body politic of Rome. In Act 1, while the Volscians seek 'to take in many towns, ere, almost, Rome / Should know we were a-foot' (1.2.24–25) and then to penetrate Rome itself, Coriolanus keeps the state alert ('Martius, 'tis true that you have lately told us, / The Volsces are in arms' [1.1.222–23]), preparing his army to defend Rome from possible invasions. With Coriolanus in charge, Rome is strongly defended against Volscian plots, and the Romans are not only able to defend themselves but also able to carry out a pre-emptive attack on Corioles. However, once Coriolanus is banished from Rome in Act 3, Rome suddenly reveals its vulnerability to external threat. Brutus, one of the two tribunes, remarks that 'Rome / Sits safe and still without him [Coriolanus]' (4.6.36–37). Ironically, though, his lines are followed by the news that the Volscians are invading the Roman territories. While the two tribunes who mastermind the banishment of Coriolanus accuse him of attempting to take away liberty from themselves and the plebeians, the Volscians' invasion reveals that it is Coriolanus who has been the guardian of the independence and freedom of Rome, fighting against foreign armies which would have confined the Roman 'franchises ... / Into an auger's bore' (4.6.87–88). Indeed, as a Volscian watchman deridingly remarks, 'you have pushed out your gates the very defender of them and in a violent popular ignorance given your enemy your shield' (5.2.40–42). Sicinius, the other tribune, asserts that Coriolanus is 'a disease that must be cut away' (3.1.296) but, as Menenius retorts, 'he's a limb that has but a disease: / Mortal to cut it off' (3.1.297–98). However flawed and menacing Coriolanus appears in the eyes of the Roman plebeians and tribunes, he is represented as the irreplaceable part of the body politic of Rome. When mother Rome loses her mighty limb, that is, the power to protect herself from invaders (as it happens when the citizens banish Coriolanus from the city), then, 'desperation / Is all the policy, strength and defence / That Rome can make against them'.

Furthermore, while stressing the importance of the military defender, Shakespeare also highlights the belligerency and unreliability of the Volscians, representing them as a formidable threat to Rome. In Act 1, the Volscians are badly defeated in the battle in and outside Corioles, but they swiftly make 'new head' (3.1.1) and attempt the second invasion of the Roman territory. When the Volscian invasion is reported after the banishment of Coriolanus in Act 4 Scene 6, Menenius reminds the incredulous tribunes that the Volscians broke the treaties and invaded Rome three times in his lifetime alone:

> BRUTUS   [*to the Aedile*]
>   Go see this rumourer whipped. It cannot be
>   The Volsces dare break with us.
> MENENIUS   Cannot be?
>   We have record that very well it can,
>   And three examples of the like hath been
>   Within my age.
>
>   (4.6.47–51)

Menenius's lines, which are not in Plutarch, lead us to doubt the validity and effect of the peace treaty that Volumnia helps to conclude with the Volscians at the end of the play. How can the Romans be sure that the Volscians will not break the treaty and attack Rome, a country which is no longer guarded by the mighty military defender? Indeed, according to Plutarch's account, that is what historically happened to Rome after Coriolanus's death; the Volscians attacked Rome again but they were badly defeated and eventually subjugated by the Romans. Shakespeare's play, however, does not include Plutarch's account of Rome's final military victory over the

Volscians. Instead, by highlighting the indispensability of Coriolanus and putting an extra stress on the unreliability of the Volscians, the play leaves the fate of post-Coriolanus Rome totally uncertain; the peace Volumnia has brought home, then, appears fragile and insubstantial.

In this regard, we should note that, at the end of the play, the Romans express their gratitude towards Volumnia in the same way as they thanked the two tribunes who banished Coriolanus, praying for them on their knees and hailing them as peacemakers ('Ourselves, our wives and children, on our knees / Are bound to pray for you both' [4.6.22–23]). Furthermore, Volumnia's procession is staged with the sounds of 'the trumpets, sackbuts, psalteries and fifes, / Tabors and cymbals and the shouting Romans' (5.4.49–50). As editors of the play have noted, this list of instruments significantly corresponds with that in Daniel 3:5, where the people indulge themselves in idolatry with 'the cornet, trumpet, harpe, sackebut, psalteries, dulcimer, and all instruments of musicke', worshipping a golden idol set up by Nebuchadnezzar.[67] This uncanny association might suggest that the Roman citizens are mistakenly worshipping Volumnia as their peace goddess just as they blindly worshipped the two tribunes as their guardians earlier in the play. The play thus alerts us to weigh the disconcerting possibility that, just as the arrival of peace after the banishment of Coriolanus in Act 3 turned out to be an illusion, peace in the final scene is also an illusion, and thus so too is the representation of Volumnia as peacemaker.

This sceptical view of peace and of the peacemaker resonates with the anxiety shared among opponents of James's foreign policy. James attempted to defend his kingdom from possible Catholic attacks, not by military might, but by concluding a peace treaty with Spain; his opponents, however, repeatedly expressed their concern that the Catholic powers on the continent were not to be trusted. Several Protestant pamphlets circulating at the time of first performances of *Coriolanus* emphasized how Spain and Rome needed to be seen as a threat, expressing their scepticism towards the validity of James's peace treaty. Joachim Beringer's *The Romane Conclaue* (1609), for example, argues that there are ample precedents to demonstrate the unreliability of the Pope, who has recently urged Spain to carry out a second Armada invasion ('The world I hope is againe and againe satisfied with the proofe hereof. It yet freshly remembreth, what ouertures were made, euen but yesterday, and by whome, vnto the Spanish king for a second Inuasion'), echoing Menenius's warning about the belligerent and unreliable Volscians.[68] The citizens' uneasiness regarding England's reconciliation with Spain was articulated even in city comedies; for example, in Ben Jonson's *The Alchemist* (1610), a comedy set in contemporary London, Dame Pliant openly expresses her anti-Spanish sentiment:

PLIANT
    Truly, I shall never brook a Spaniard.
SUBTLE   No?
PLIANT   Never sin' eighty-eight could I abide 'em,
    And that was some three year afore I was born, in truth.
                                            (4.4.28–30)[69]

The 'eighty-eight', of course, refers to the Armada attack. This comic banter illuminates the way in which the memory of Spain's attempted invasion was still ingrained in the minds of the Jacobeans, including those who had not been born in 1588, showing that the citizens did not feel truly reconciled with the Spaniards even after the peace treaty. Situated in this cultural atmosphere, the ambiguous presentation of peace in the final scene of *Coriolanus* can be aligned with the sceptical view of some Jacobeans on James's peace policy and the peace he claimed to have established with Spain.

Finally, the play does not end with Volumnia's triumphal return but with the death of the heroic warrior and his funeral procession. After the brutal killing of Coriolanus, Aufidius's envy of him and the citizens' strong hatred quickly disappear, and Coriolanus is hailed as a paragon of a noble warrior and instantly made into an object of mourning:

> 1 LORD
> Bear from hence his body
> And mourn you for him. Let him be regarded
> As the most noble corpse that ever herald
> Did follow to his urn.
>
> (5.6.143–46)

The Volscian lord urges the citizens to mourn Coriolanus and to treat his body ('the most noble corpse') with the highest respect, despite the fact that Coriolanus has been accused by the Volscians of committing treason against their state. Aufidius then joins in, declaring that he will host a solemn funeral for his rival and commemorate the war god by erecting a tomb: 'he shall have a noble memory' (5.6.155). Coriolanus's prediction of his own fate earlier in the play – 'I shall be loved when I am lacked' (4.1.15) – thus proves true.

It has been suggested that Aufidius's elaborate instructions for the funeral, such as 'trail your steel pikes' (5.6.152), are not in Shakespeare's sources and that they evoke not Roman but Elizabethan military funerals, specifically the state funeral of Philip Sidney in 1587.[70] Indeed, according to a contemporary account, military officers in their military habits trailed their pikes, truncheons and halberds on the ground at Sidney's funeral, in a manner similar to that in which the mourners of Coriolanus are ordered to trail their pikes.[71] This apparent resemblance between the two is not surprising given that, as I have argued, Coriolanus can be closely associated with the memory of Elizabethan heroic militarism. Aufidius's lines reinforce Coriolanus's symbolic significance, suggesting to the audience that it is an Elizabethan heroic warrior who is buried and commemorated at the end of the play.

As I have already noted, James's peace policy was not welcomed by all. In *Coriolanus*, the Volscian commoners disdain peace, admiring Coriolanus's heroism:

2 SERVINGMAN
> This peace is nothing, but to rust iron, increase tailors
> and breed ballad-makers.

1 SERVINGMAN
> Let me have war, say I. It exceeds peace as far as day
> does night. It's sprightly walking, audible and full of
> vent. Peace is a very apoplexy, lethargy, mulled, deaf,
> sleepy, insensible, a getter of more bastard children than
> war's a destroyer of men.

$$(4.5.222-31)$$

Although this exchange is between the Volscians, whom
Shakespeare represents as belligerent, this anti-peace sentiment
was shared by some of the English people under James's rule.
Some writers, for example, warned of the danger of peacetime
slumber in similar terms; in *A Souldiers Wish* (1603), Pricket
writes that peace has made the English people 'such great
strangers vnto warre: / That want of skill wil worke thy
[James's] kingdoms wrong'.[72] Others even praised war; in
Four Paradoxes, or Politique Discourse (1604), Dudley Digges
compares foreign war to 'souereigne medicines' for the state
since war 'will soon withdraw mens mindes from intestine
garboiles to resist the generall mischief' and, surprisingly,
praises the 'wise proceeding of the *Senate* of *Rome* in
Coriolanus time that by this means [foreign war] appeased all
diuisions'.[73]

Then, as I noted at the beginning of this chapter, there was
a growing support for the revival of Elizabethan militarism, as
manifested in the glorification of militant heroes such as Essex
and Prince Henry. In particular, the late Essex was attracting
increasing popularity as a symbol of lost Elizabethan
militarism in the first decade of James's reign. At one point,
Essex's reputation seemed irrecoverable; after his failed
treason against Elizabeth and his execution, no one dared to
publicly praise this fallen hero during her reign. However, he
began to be favourably represented after James's accession;
Elizabeth's death seemed to have opened up opportunities

for English writers to reflect on Essex.[74] The year of James's accession saw the publication of *An Apologie of the Earle of Essex* (written and circulated in manuscript in 1598), in which Essex attempts to defend his aggressive militant stance and argues for war with Spain, regarding war as a necessary physic. The popularity of the late earl in the early years of James's reign was such that Bacon found it necessary to defend himself, by composing *Sir Francis Bacon His Apologie, in Certaine Imputations Concerning the Late Earle of Essex* (1604), from the allegation that he betrayed Essex. James's government occasionally found it necessary to react to the growing popularity of Essex, seeing the glorification of Essex's militant activism and the sympathetic account of Essex's downfall alarming, and showing considerable concern about the call for military confrontation with Spain that accompanied nostalgia for Essex; for example, Pricket, who praised Essex in *Honors Fame in Triumph Riding* (1604), was imprisoned by the order of the Privy Council, which also interrogated the publisher and recalled the copies of the verse. Yet militant Protestant sentiments continued to be projected not only onto the memory of Elizabeth but also on the memory of Essex. William Herbert's *Englands Sorrowe or, A Farewell to Essex* (1606) nostalgically praises Essex as England's immaculate militant hero whose name or greatness shall never die: 'Was never age, nor ever time did see, / So valiant and so brave a Gentleman, / So mightie, iust, so good and great as hee; / The forraigne spoiles and conquests which he wan, / Were like to those of *Scipio African*'.[75] Likewise, in *Troia Britanica* (1609), Thomas Heywood hailed Essex as a 'warlike' and 'renowned' hero 'at whose warlike feete / *Spaines* countlesse spoyles and Trophyes haue been told', while carefully omitting the inconvenient account of Essex's rebellion.[76]

The fact that *Coriolanus* does not end with the triumph of the peacemaker but with the commemoration of the heroic warrior is meaningful in this context of the Jacobeans' commemorative practice of glorifying the lost Elizabethan hero. I would suggest that, in the final scene of the play, Shakespeare offers a careful observation of the persistent nostalgia for Elizabethan militarism. *Coriolanus* cannot be simply read as Shakespeare's denunciation of militarism as some critics argue.[77] Not only Volumnia, the peace goddess, but also Coriolanus, the war god, is venerated in the last act of the play; these are problematic venerations which can be read from both the pro-peace and militant perspectives. Unlike Plutarch, Shakespeare does not dismiss Coriolanus as a flawed, replaceable general, leaving the political role of Coriolanus open to interpretation. The play does not offer simple answers to the difficult questions of war and peace, but rather questions and problematizes simplistic solutions and ideologies that both militant Protestants and supporters of James's peace policy advocated.

Revisiting Volumnia's silence

As I have argued in this chapter, there is a consistent parallel relationship between Shakespeare's representation of Volumnia and the place of Elizabeth in Jacobean discourse. Volumnia can be situated in the context of James's attempt to rewrite the militarized memory of Elizabeth and her England. The play, however, does not fully endorse the representation of Volumnia as peacemaker, as Shakespeare allows us to take a critical view of the arrival of peace at the end of the play. It is left to the audience to decide whether they see the Roman peace as success or illusion, or whether they see the veneration of Volumnia as peacemaker as legitimate or unfounded. Shakespeare's dramatization of Volumnia thus functions as an intersection of unresolved conflicting ideologies, alerting the audience to the complexity of the issues of foreign policy, highly contentious issues in Jacobean England.

I began this chapter by registering my uneasiness with the triumphal procession of the mother whose son is to be murdered in the next scene. My urge to probe into the awkwardness of her triumphal procession has led me to examine the context that lay behind this scene: that is, the ongoing competition for reconstructing the memory of Elizabeth. However, there is another important aspect of the procession which generates even deeper uneasiness: Volumnia's total silence. After she successfully disarms Coriolanus in Act 5 Scene 3, she never speaks a word; she remains totally silent throughout her procession in Act 5 Scene 5. Like the silence Isabella maintains towards the Duke at the end of *Measure for Measure* (1604) or that which Hermione maintains towards King Leontes at the end of *The Winter's Tale* (1610–11), Volumnia's silence inevitably creates a degree of uncertainty in this seemingly celebratory procession.[78] On the Jacobean stage, Volumnia might have marched across the stage exultant at her achievement or she might have appeared devastated by the prospect of losing her son forever. However, as I pointed out at the beginning of this chapter, whatever emotions or gestures she shows in this scene, the fundamental nature and political significance of her procession does not change – the moment of the national victory. I have focused on the representation of Volumnia as peacemaker, yet, importantly, it is not her self-stylization; it is the senators of Rome who introduce her onto the stage and prompt others to venerate her as their peace goddess. Volumnia is venerated as a symbol of peace, irrespective of her own feelings and thoughts; unlike James, who fashioned himself as peacemaker, she has no say in how she is represented or what she represents. In Act 5 Scene 5, Volumnia is an object; she is there to be represented and interpreted by others.

In this regard, Volumnia's situation curiously illustrates the way in which Elizabeth was represented in the Jacobean period. Jacobean writers created various, often conflicting, images of Elizabeth, projecting their own views of the Elizabethan past and the Jacobean present onto the queen. These Elizabeths were inevitably coloured by their political views, not necessarily by Elizabeth's own political standpoint. Political significance was imposed on her by those who represented her. Elizabeth left a specific request that her tomb would not be carved with any political messages; according to Bacon, Elizabeth desired not to have her tomb furnished with 'long Titles, or shadows of glory' and expressed that 'a line or two would be enough for her memory'.[79] Elizabeth seemed to have been aware of the prospect that, once she was deceased, her iconography was to be freely appropriated by others. Elizabeth was right; the iconic power of Elizabeth's image, whether that image was originally authored by herself or by others, was appropriated by Jacobeans in order to advance their own causes. *Antony and Cleopatra* suggests that the dead queen still speaks; the statue of the queen continues to speak to survivors, inciting nostalgia for the lost chivalric past and propelling some to action. Yet Volumnia's silence brings to light the apparent fact that the dead Elizabeth does not have her own voice – a fact which was often masked by the undiminishing iconic power of her posthumous image. The Jacobeans commemorated Elizabeth and gave her the voice that spoke back to themselves. The silent Volumnia in Act 5 Scene 5 evokes this dead, voiceless queen – or, to use Cleopatra's phrase, a 'puppet' (5.2.207) – who no longer had control over how her iconic power was to be used or how her image was to be posthumously interpreted.

It is not surprising that Volumnia's silence has led to various versions of Act 5 Scene 5 in stage productions; just as the Jacobeans did to the late Elizabeth, directors and actors are able to stage silent Volumnia according to their own interpretations of the play. There cannot be a definitive or correct way of staging and interpreting Volumnia in Act 5 Scene 5, just as there was no definitive way of representing Elizabeth within Jacobean discourse. *Coriolanus* thus invites us to reflect not only on complex political issues of war and peace but also on the representation of Elizabeth itself. Act 5 Scene 5, a scene which consists of fewer than ten lines, not only reveals the play's complex relationship to the Jacobean political context but also provides an in-depth, dramatic analysis of the representation of Elizabeth in the Jacobean period.

Notes

1   In order to restore the original stage directions, I quote the scene from the Folio text of *Coriolanus* (*Mr. William Shakespeares Comedies, Histories, and Tragedies Published According to the True Originall Copies* [London, 1623], Cc3r). Unless otherwise stated, the play is quoted from the Arden Third Series edition.

2   Alice V. Griffin's study of triumphal processions in Shakespeare's drama, for example, only focuses on Coriolanus's triumphal return from the conquest of Corioli in Act 2 Scene 1 (*Pageantry on the Shakespearean Stage* [New Haven, CT: College and University Press, 1951], 186–88).

3   See esp. Adelman, *Suffocating Mothers*, 146–64; Kahn, *Man's Estate*, 155–72; and Madelon Sprengnether, 'Annihilating Intimacy in *Coriolanus*', in *Women in the Middle Ages and the Renaissance: Literary and Historical Perspectives*, ed. Mary Beth Rose (Syracuse, NY: Syracuse University Press, 1986), 89–111.

4   Grace Latham, 'On Volumnia', *Transactions of New Shakspere Society, 1887–92* (London: Kegan Paul, 1887), 90.

5   Christina Luckyj, 'Volumnia's Silence', *Studies in English Literature, 1500–1900* 31, no. 2 (1991): 327–42.

6   For the performance history of Act 5 Scene 5, see Richard David, *Shakespeare in the Theatre* (Cambridge: Cambridge University Press, 1978), 146; Peter Holland, ed., *Coriolanus* (London: Arden Shakespeare, 2013), 437–38n; and John Ripley, *'Coriolanus' on Stage in England and America, 1609–1994* (Madison, WI: Fairleigh Dickinson University Press, 1998), 327.

7   R. B. Parker, ed., *The Tragedy of Coriolanus* (Oxford: Clarendon Press, 1994), 31. Parker supposes that the final scene is set in Antium instead of Corioles.

8   For the date of *Coriolanus*, see esp. Lee Bliss, introduction to *Coriolanus*, ed. Lee Bliss (Cambridge: Cambridge University Press, 2000), 7; Ripley, *'Coriolanus' on Stage*, 34–36; and Wells and Taylor, *A Textual Companion*, 131.

9   For James's struggle with anti-peace publications in 1608–9, see esp. Wells, *Shakespeare on Masculinity*, 152–54.

10 Robert Pricket, *Honors Fame in Triumph Riding. Or, the Life and Death of the Late Honorable Earle of Essex* (London, 1604), E1r, C4r.

11 *Calendar of State Papers, Venice*, 12:450.

12 Johnson, *Nova Britannia*, D1r.

13 The Latin meaning of Martius is 'pertaining to Mars'. See, for example, Philip Brockbank, ed., *Coriolanus* (London: Arden Shakespeare, 1976), 93n. For the close association between Coriolanus and Mars, see esp. Peggy Muñoz Simonds, '*Coriolanus* and the Myth of Juno and Mars', *Mosaic* 18, no. 2 (1985): 33–50 (esp. 41–46).

14 Raymonde, *The Maiden Queene*, C2r. For studies that associate Coriolanus with Essex, see, for example, Willet T. Conklin, 'Shakespeare, *Coriolanus*, and Essex', *Studies in English* 11 (1932): 42–47.

15 For studies that associate Coriolanus with Prince Henry, see also Wells, *Shakespeare on Masculinity*, 149–58.

16 Jonson, *The Speeches at Prince Henry's Barriers*, in *The Cambridge Edition*, 3:138–39.

17 For the possible sources of *Coriolanus*, see esp. Bullough, ed., *Sources*, 5:496–563. For Shakespeare's departure from his historical accounts of Volumnia, see also M. W. MacCallum, *Shakespeare's Roman Plays and Their Background* (London: Macmillan, 1910), 497 and William Rosen, *Shakespeare and the Craft of Tragedy* (Cambridge, MA: Harvard University Press, 1960), 188–90.

18 See Wells, *Shakespeare on Masculinity*, 157.

19 Butler, *The Stuart Court Masque*, 101. For the representation of Queen Anne, see esp. Peter Holbrook, 'Jacobean Masques and the Jacobean Peace', in *The Politics of the Stuart Court Masque*, ed. David Bevington and Peter Holbrook (Cambridge: Cambridge University Press, 1998), 67–87; Lewalski, *Writing Women in Jacobean England*, 18–19; and Kathryn Schwarz, 'Amazon Reflections in the Jacobean Queen's Masque', *Studies in English Literature, 1500–1900* 35, no. 2 (1995): 293–319 (esp. 300).

20 Daniel, *The Vision of the 12. Goddesses*, A4v.

21 For analysis of Anne's use of Elizabeth's clothes and her self-stylization as the second Elizabeth, see esp. McManus, *Women on the Renaissance Stage*, 106–11.

22 See Edmund Spenser, *The Faerie Queene*, ed. A. C. Hamilton, rev. 2nd ed. (Harlow: Pearson Longman, 2007), canto 1 stanzas 9–10.

23 *Mr. William Shakespeares Comedies, Histories, and Tragedies*, Cc3v.

24 *Mr. William Shakespeares Comedies, Histories, and Tragedies*, Cc3v.

25 Plutarch, *Lives*, in Bullough, ed., *Sources*, 5:537.

26 See Plutarch, *Lives*, in Bullough, ed., *Sources*, 5:537–38.

27 *The Oxford English Dictionary*, 2nd ed. (Oxford: Clarendon Press; Oxford: Oxford University Press, 1989).

28 See Simonds, '*Coriolanus* and the Myth of Juno and Mars', 47–48.

29 Plutarch, *Lives*, in Bullough, ed., *Sources*, 5:536.

30 Plutarch, *Lives*, in Bullough, ed., *Sources*, 5:540.

31 Daniel, *A Panegyrike Congratulatorie*, A1r.

32 Dekker, *The Magnificent Entertainment*, in *The Dramatic Works*, 2:255.

33 Matt. 5:9.

34 For the theme of peace in the coronation entry in 1604, see also Goldberg, *James I and the Politics of Literature*, 43–54 and Parry, *The Golden Age Restor'd*, 1–39.

35 *Ben Jonson His Part of King James His Royal and Magnificent Entertainment*, in *The Cambridge Edition*, 2:447–48. For Dekker's account of this theme, see Dekker, *The Magnificent Entertainment*, in *The Dramatic Works*, 2:253–303. The coronation pageant for James in 1604 is attributed to Dekker, Jonson, John Webster, Thomas Middleton and Stephen Harrison. While Dekker provides an account of the entire pageant, Jonson includes only his own contributions to the pageant in *Ben Jonson His Part of King James His Royal and Magnificent Entertainment* (1604).

36 See also Steven Marx, 'Shakespeare's Pacifism', *Renaissance Quarterly* 45, no. 1 (1992): 57.

37 *Ben Jonson His Part*, in *The Cambridge Edition*, 2:453.

38 Herbert, *A Prophesie of Cadwallader*, H1v.

39 John Stow, *The Annales of England* (London, 1592), 1281.

40 Richard Hakluyt, *The Principal Nauigations, Voyages, Traffiques and Discoueries of the English Nation* (London, 1599–1600), Ccc3r.

41 James Aske, *Elizabetha Triumphans*, in Nichols, *Progresses of Elizabeth*, 3:453, 459.

42 I quote Elizabeth's prayer of thanksgiving from Thomas Sorocold, *Supplications of Saints. A Booke of Prayers* (London, 1612), N8r.

43 Church of England, *A Psalme and Collect of Thankesgiuing* (London, 1588), A2v.

44 Hakluyt, *The Principal Nauigations*, Ccc2r.

45 Stow, *The Annales of England*, 1282.

46 Hakluyt, *The Principal Nauigations*, Ccc3r.

47 Hakluyt, *The Principal Nauigations*, Ccc3r. For the national celebration of the victory over the Armada, see also Cressy, *Bonfires and Bells*, 117–23.

48 Aske, *Elizabetha Triumphans*, in Nichols, *Progresses of Elizabeth*, 3:468.

49 Bliss, ed., *Coriolanus*, 265n.

50 For the identification of Volumnia with Rome, see also Reuben A. Brower, *Hero and Saint: Shakespeare and the Graeco-Roman Heroic Tradition* (Oxford: Clarendon Press, 1971), 369 and Cantor, *Shakespeare's Rome*, 105.

51 For the cultural significance of the viper in early modern England, see C. T. Onions, 'Animals', in *Shakespeare's England: An Account of the Life and Manners of His Age*, ed. Sidney Lee and C. T. Onions, vol. 1 (Oxford: Clarendon Press, 1916), 492.

52 Peter Stallybrass, 'Patriarchal Territories: The Body Enclosed', in *Rewriting the Renaissance: The Discourses of Sexual Difference in Early Modern Europe*, ed. Margaret W. Ferguson, Maureen Quilligan and Nancy J. Vickers (Chicago: University of Chicago Press, 1986), 129.

53 *Threno-Thriambeuticon*, in Nichols, *Progresses of Elizabeth*, 4:319. See also 4:351.

54 Thomas Deloney, *A Ioyful New Ballad* (London, 1588), 1.

55 *The Romane Historie of T. Livy*, in Bullough, ed., *Sources*, 5:504. *The Roman Histories of Lucius Florus*, in Bullough, ed., *Sources*, 5:550.

56 For the meaning of the name Volumnia, see Simonds, '*Coriolanus* and the Myth of Juno and Mars', 39.

57 Lodowick Lloyd, *The Tragicocomedie of Serpents* (London, 1607), C2r.

58 Bacon, *The Felicity of Queen Elizabeth*, 9. For Bacon's attempt to represent Elizabeth as the peace-minded queen, see also Perry, *The Making of Jacobean Culture*, 159–62.

59 Perry, *The Making of Jacobean Culture*, 164. For Bacon's inconsistent attitude to foreign policy, see esp. Ian Box, 'Politics and Philosophy: Bacon on the Values of War and Peace', *The Seventeenth Century* 7 (1992): 113–27.

60 Richard Crakanthorpe, *A Sermon at the Solemnizing of the Happie Inauguration of Our Most Gracious and Religious Soueraigne King Iames* (London, 1609), B4r.

61 D. R. Woolf, *The Idea of History in Early Stuart England: Erudition, Ideology and 'The Light of Truth' from the Accession of James I to the Civil War* (Toronto: University of Toronto Press, 1990), 123–24.

62 See also Wells, *Shakespeare on Masculinity*, 152–54.

63 For the link between the play and the Midlands uprising, see, for example, E. C. Pettet, '*Coriolanus* and the Midlands Insurrection of 1607', *Shakespeare Survey* 3 (1950): 34–42. For the link with the parliamentary debate, see, for example, W. Gordon Zeeveld, '*Coriolanus* and Jacobean Politics', *Modern Language Review* 57, no. 3 (1962): 321–34.

64 See, for example, Shannon Miller, 'Topicality and Subversion in William Shakespeare's *Coriolanus*', *Studies in English Literature, 1500–1900* 32, no. 2 (1992): 287–310.

65 For such readings, see Marx, 'Shakespeare's Pacifism', 49–95 (esp. 79–87) and Wells, *Shakespeare on Masculinity*, 144–76.

66 Plutarch, *Lives*, in Bullough, ed., *Sources*, 5:544.

67 See esp. W. A. Wright, ed., *Coriolanus* (Oxford: Clarendon Press, 1884), 251n.

68 Joachim Beringer, *The Romane Conclaue* (London, 1609), Bb4v.

69 Ben Jonson, *The Alchemist*, in *The Cambridge Edition*, vol. 3.

70 See, for example, W. J. Craig and R. H. Case, eds., *The Tragedy of Coriolanus* (London: Arden Shakespeare, 1922), 224n.

71 See the account of Sidney's funeral in Nichols, *Progresses of Elizabeth*, 3:283–340 (esp. 337–39).

72 Pricket, *A Souldiers Wish*, C1r.

73 Thomas Digges and Dudley Digges, *Foure Paradoxes, or Politique Discourses* (London, 1604), O1r, N4v.

74 On this point, see Maureen King, 'The Essex Myth in Jacobean England', in *The Accession of James I: Historical and Cultural Consequences*, ed. Glenn Burgess, Rowland Wymer and Jason Lawrence (Basingstoke: Palgrave Macmillan, 2006), 177–86 (esp. 179).

75 William Herbert, *Englands Sorrowe or, A Farewell to Essex* (London, 1606), B2v.

76 Heywood, *Troia Britanica*, Q3r.

77 See Marx, 'Shakespeare's Pacifism', 79–87 and Wells, *Shakespeare on Masculinity*, 144–76.

78 For indeterminate silences in Shakespeare's drama, see esp. Philip C. McGuire, *Speechless Dialect: Shakespeare's Open Silences* (Berkeley: University of California Press, 1985), xv–xxiii and Christina Luckyj, '*A Moving Rhetoricke*': *Gender and Silence in Early Modern England* (Manchester: Manchester University Press, 2002), 117–18n14.

79 Bacon, *The Felicity of Queen Elizabeth*, 24.

4

Cymbeline: The Politics of Remembering the Besieged Heroine

'My lord, I fear, has forgot Britain'

Cymbeline, a play set in ancient Britain, presents a prophecy; Jupiter, a Roman god, descends from above and visits downcast Posthumus, leaving him a book containing a riddling prophecy about the fate of the kingdom of Britain:

POSTHUMUS
> (*Reads.*) *Whenas a lion's whelp shall to himself unknown, without seeking find, and be embraced by a piece of tender air; and when from a stately cedar shall be lopped branches which, being dead many years, shall after revive, be jointed to the old stock, and freshly grow; then shall Posthumus end his miseries, Britain be fortunate and flourish in peace and plenty.*

> (5.4.108–15)

At the end of the play, a Roman soothsayer examines Jupiter's prophecy and announces that the prophecy has been fulfilled as the lost two princes of Britain – '*lopped branches*' – are discovered and restored to the royal household of King

Cymbeline – '*a stately cedar*'. Now that King Cymbeline has found his male heirs, the soothsayer proclaims, Britain will '*flourish in peace and plenty*'. As in *Macbeth*, the restoration of order is staged in the form of the prophecy and through the language of vegetation, which formed an essential part of Jacobean union-related discourse. While the prophecies in *Macbeth* illuminate the Jacobean political vision of creating Britain from Elizabethan England, the prophecy in *Cymbeline* complements that vision by representing Britain as a nation of peace, the ideal vision of James I.

Indeed, it has been a critical commonplace to read *Cymbeline* by way of its links to Jacobean political themes since G. Wilson Knight's influential 1947 study first highlighted the historical aspects of the play.[1] Jupiter's prophecy, repeated references to Milford Haven (the landing place of Henry Tudor, who heralded the union of York and Lancaster and to whom James compared himself) and the celebration of Britain's reunion with Rome and the arrival of peace at the end of the play have attracted much interest and have been the focus of analysis over the decades.[2] The focus on these aspects of the play has helped to illustrate its political topicality and enriched our understanding of Shakespeare's career as a Jacobean dramatist. Yet an important question remains. Did Jacobean audiences interpret the play politically as modern critics would like to believe that they did? Although I argue that they did, I also believe that we should not dismiss this question without carefully examining it. That this question is not as misplaced as it might sound is suggested by one contemporary source, an account – patchy, but immensely meaningful – of an original performance: an undated entry in Simon Forman's memoranda, 'The Book of Plays and Notes Thereof'. In his recollection of the performance he attended possibly at the Globe in 1611, Forman wrote down things that interested him in a random order.[3] Significantly, his memorandum on *Cymbeline* lacks any reference to the potentially spectacular scene of the descending Jupiter, who provides the prophecy about the fate of Britain, the deciphering of Jupiter's prophecy or the conclusion of peace between Britain and Rome. These highly topical British/Jacobean elements seem to have escaped his interest altogether.[4] In fact, Forman appears not to have been interested at all in the British theme of the play; he refers to Cymbeline as 'King of England', not 'King of Britain', and he never uses the word Britain in his account, opting to use 'England', despite Shakespeare's repeated references to Britain.[5] This may strike modern scholars as odd not only because the word England is not used anywhere in the play but also because the word Britain, which James publicized, featured prominently in a broad range of discourse and was one of the most topical words of the time. In the play, upon hearing the rumour that the exiled Posthumus has taken mistresses in Rome, Innogen (Cymbeline's daughter), though she will quickly realize that the rumour is false, cries out, 'My lord, I fear, / Has forgot Britain' (1.6.111–12). Ironically, Innogen's lines about a man forgetting Britain can be applied to Forman's apparent disregard for the British/Jacobean theme: how, we might wonder, could Forman forget to mention Britain and thus interpret the play politically?

Instead, Forman's account of the play centres on Innogen. Forman begins with the invasion of 'England' by Lucius's Roman army and Cymbeline's victory over the invaders, taking note that two of the three outlaws who helped Cymbeline are the lost heirs of the king. Then the rest of his memorandum focuses on Innogen, recording Iachimo's intrusion into her bedchamber in uncharacteristic detail. Forman then ends his account with the episode of Innogen's disguising herself as a man and her encounter with Lucius in Act 4 Scene 3 ('and how by eating a sleeping dram they thought she had been dead, and laid her in the woods and the body of Cloten by her, in her love's apparel that he left behind him, and how she was found by Lucius, etc.').[6] Forman's seeming negligence in ending his account with Act 4 Scene 3 does not have to be because the final scenes were cut from original public performances or because Forman had left in the middle of the performance (as the 'etc.' as well as the reference to Cymbeline's victory over Rome in the first lines of his account in any case makes clear) but rather because he invested so much of his attention and time in following and reconstructing Innogen's story. Act 4 Scene 3 is, in fact, the final scene in which, as we will see, Innogen features as a popular type of suffering heroine, and for a number of reasons it should not be surprising that Forman ends his account at that point. The abrupt ending of his memorandum shows the extent to which at least one Jacobean audience member saw Innogen and the story of her hardship as central to the play and, given the popularity and significance of the representations of besieged, suffering princesses during this period, Forman's primary focus on the besieged Innogen before Act 4 Scene 3 may not have been an unusual response to the play at the time of its first performances.

Although Forman could not have been alone among his fellow Jacobean audience members in taking an interest in the heroine rather than the British theme, Innogen, a key figure in the assessment I will offer here of the play's intricate links to its Jacobean contexts, has not featured as fully as might be expected in Shakespearean scholarship, and her political and cultural significance within *Cymbeline* still requires critical examination. By naming his heroine Innogen – the name of the wife of Brutus, the legendary founder of Britain – Shakespeare associates her with the mother of the British people and consistently represents her as the symbol of the British polity. In order to illuminate the complex significance of Shakespeare's Innogen, I will situate the play in a specific Jacobean context that has not adequately featured in earlier studies, that is, the context of the politics of negotiating the memory of Elizabeth I and her reign.[7]

Innogen is not the only character who merits contextual re-examination. An equally important female character in the play is the Queen (Cymbeline's wife) – a warlike queen – with whom I will begin my reading of the play. The domineering Queen, the de-facto leader of Britain, not only suffers a terrible death but also has her posthumous reputation completely tarnished by the survivors, who demonize her and attempt to write her out of the history of Britain. The excision of the Queen reminds us of the underlying theme of *Macbeth*: the male fantasy of excising female agency in order to fashion an ordered, male-controlled polity. On this point, Jodi Mikalachki's instrumental reading of the play supports my view; Mikalachki has convincingly argued that the excision of the Queen is necessitated by the politics of male-centred historiography and that the play excludes the Queen in order to forge an origin for an exclusively masculine Britain.[8] What Mikalachki has not fully examined in her insightful study, however, is the way in which this vision of the exclusively masculine Britain was specifically Jacobean. It is not only the Queen but also Innogen herself who needs to be fully analysed in the context of the political fantasy of regendering and pacifying the British polity. Through the examination of the Queen, I will first outline the play's overarching framework of this political fantasy, a specifically Jacobean framework within which I will later situate and examine Shakespeare's Innogen.

Regendering and pacifying Britain

When Lucius, the Roman general, comes from Augustus Caesar with a demand that Britain should resume paying tribute to the empire, the Queen is the first to voice opposition to Rome; in defiance of Caesar, she counsels the king not to fear Lucius's threat of invasion, delivering an ostentatiously nationalistic speech:

QUEEN
                Remember sir, my liege,
The kings your ancestors, together with
The natural bravery of your isle, which stands
As Neptune's park, ribbed and paled in
With oaks unscalable and roaring waters,

> With sands that will not bear your enemies' boats,
> But suck them up to th'topmast.
>
> (3.1.16–22)

The Queen urges Cymbeline to take up defensive arms and goes on to describe how Julius Caesar, before he finally conquered Britain, was 'twice beaten', to his shame, and how his ships 'on our terrible seas, / Like eggshells moved upon their surges, cracked / As easily 'gainst our rocks' (3.1.27–29). The Queen then recounts how King Cassibelan celebrated the victory by making 'Lud's town with rejoicing fires bright' (3.1.32). The reference to fire is not in Shakespeare's main historical source, Raphael Holinshed's *Chronicles*, in which Holinshed simply writes that 'Cassibellane made a great feast at London, and there did sacrifice to the gods'.[9] Thus the celebration of Cassibelan's victory as recalled by the Queen could have been specifically evocative of the national celebration in which Elizabeth and her people celebrated the victory over the invading Armada with bonfires in 1588.[10]

In this regard, it is also meaningful that the Queen's nationalistic speech has a specific thematic correspondence with the chivalric discourse of Elizabeth. The Queen urges Cymbeline to defy Rome by addressing him as 'my liege' – a traditional address to a knight in chivalric romance. The Queen's speech incites chivalric sentiments by presenting Cymbeline as her valiant knight and herself as Cymbeline's supreme mistress, a relationship reminiscent of that of Antony and Cleopatra. Similarly to the way in which Cleopatra encourages Antony to lead the army against the invading forces, the Queen incites her knight to take courageous action against the Romans. In portraying the Queen's relationship to Cymbeline, the play replicates the framework of female-centred chivalric romance, which, as I discussed in Chapter 2, informed the nostalgic representation of Elizabeth as the commanding mistress of her militant courtiers. Her speech thus reinforces the image of Cymbeline's Britain as a version of the wartime Elizabethan England as reconstructed and propagated by some Jacobeans, an England where its warlike leader marshalled her lords to fight against Spain and Rome.

Significantly, though, *Cymbeline* recalls the militarized memory of Elizabethan England in this way only to undermine it towards the end of the play. As the Queen has advocated, Cymbeline enters into war with Rome and, against all the odds, defeats the invading Roman army, a victory through which Britain successfully rebrands itself as a full-fledged kingdom, seemingly putting itself on equal terms with the sometime superior Roman Empire. The Queen's wish has certainly been fulfilled and her call for armed confrontation proves to have been timely and successful. In the final scene of resolution, however, Cymbeline accuses the Queen – now deceased – for her belligerent speech I quoted earlier and castigates her as the cause of all confusion. Cymbeline's proclamation of peace is a case in point; even though his soldiers have just defeated the Roman army, Cymbeline voluntarily submits to Rome, stating his intention to prioritize peace and harmony:

CYMBELINE
    My peace we will begin. And Caius Lucius,
    Although the victor, we submit to Caesar,
    And to the Roman empire, promising
    To pay our wonted tribute, from the which
    We were dissuaded by our wicked queen,
    Whom heavens in justice both on her and hers
    Have laid most heavy hand.

                                    (5.5.458–64)

Cymbeline blames the breakout of war between Britain and Rome solely on the Queen, whose agonizing death has just been announced, claiming that he was dissuaded by the 'most delicate fiend' (5.5.47) from paying 'our wonted tribute'. What Cymbeline does in this speech is to rewrite the past in his favour. Although it is Cymbeline who made the final decision to defy Rome because the Britons 'will not endure his [Augustus Caesar's] yoke, and for ourself / To show less sovereignty than they must needs / Appear unkinglike' (3.5.5–7), he now claims that he was actually willing to pay the tribute rather than fight and that he was wilfully misled by the warlike enchantress into the war. In Cymbeline's revisionist commemoration of the dead Queen, Britain would never have been at odds with Rome if it were not for the warlike, seditious woman. The Queen's nationalistic speech, which has momentarily evoked the glorious memory of the warlike England at the time of the Armada invasion, is redefined as a destructive spell cast over peaceful Britain. Cymbeline thus justifies the restoration of peace with Rome by rewriting the Queen as a destructive, belligerent enchantress and by obliterating her from the history of peaceful Britain, proclaiming that 'she was naught' (5.5.270).[11]

In the words of one of his observant subjects, the king was 'governed' by the Queen (2.1.57). Foreign policy, for example, was known as a king's prerogative among the Jacobean audience, yet it is the Queen who, before the war, virtually dictated Britain's course of action against Rome.[12] Britain was not the king's realm but the Queen's. In the final scene, therefore, Cymbeline attempts to rebrand his kingdom as a male-controlled polity and himself as its masculine leader. In order to do so, Cymbeline not only tarnishes the memory of the Queen but also dismantles the framework of female-centred chivalric romance. Upon severing his emotional tie with the Queen, his sometime supreme mistress, Cymbeline restores another tie, this time, not with a powerful woman but with a powerful man: that is, Augustus Caesar. Earlier in the play, Cymbeline tells us that he was knighted by Caesar: 'Caesar knighted me; my youth I spent / Much under him; of him I gathered honour' (3.1.69–70). In the final scene, then, Cymbeline changes his allegiance from his commanding mistress to his surrogate father Caesar. As Janet Adelman puts it, 'Cymbeline demonstrates his autonomy – his independence from the will of his queen – by his submission to Caesar, his merger with a male will larger than his own'.[13] Cymbeline's/Britain's reunion with Caesar/Rome indicates that Cymbeline finally frees himself and Britain from domineering womanhood. In this regard, it is also significant that Cymbeline refashions himself not only as Caesar's knight but also as the father of British knights. After their military victory over the Romans, Cymbeline, anachronistically to the ancient British setting, knights the three warlike British soldiers, demonstrating thereby the monarchical authority he has regained: 'Bow your knees. / Arise, my knights o'th' battle' (5.5.19–20). In this restored kingdom, it is Cymbeline, not the Queen, who controls British knights. Cymbeline's resumption of power thus creates an exclusively masculine framework for the relationship of monarch and subject, an alternative model to the framework of Elizabethan chivalric romance in which men are swayed by a supreme mistress (as they were at the beginning of *Cymbeline*).

By staging the restoration of peace and the male authority through the excision of the warlike Queen and the dismantling of the female-centred chivalric framework, the play, like *Antony and Cleopatra*, evokes James's ideological conflict with the practice of commemorating Elizabeth as the warlike supreme mistress of England's heroic knights. The vision of the regendered and pacified Britain is in many ways James's own vision of the male-controlled, peaceful Britain, a vision which he attempted to protect from the powerful nostalgia for the warlike Elizabeth among his people. As I discussed in the Introduction, Jacobean theatres successively featured warlike queen figures in the aftermath of the failed Gunpowder Plot; these characters, such as Heywood's Elizabeth in *If You Know Not Me, You Know Nobody, Part II* and Dekker's Titania in *The Whore of Babylon*, evoked the militarized memory of England's responses to Catholic aggression: in particular, the response to the Armada attack. *Cymbeline* initially replicates the same approach to its own warlike queen figure; by giving the Queen the emphatically nationalistic speech in which she incites men to courageously defend her state from her enemy, the play similarly evokes the memory of the warlike Elizabeth/ England. However, that memory is not glorified in *Cymbeline*; rather, the play downplays that memory by branding the Queen as female monstrosity. The warlike Queen is not there to be commemorated but rather to be erased from the collective memory of the kingdom.

Shakespeare was not the only Jacobean playwright during this period to present a warlike queen figure as the memory to be erased rather than as the memory to be glorified. John Fletcher similarly dramatized the process of discrediting and side-lining the memory of a warlike queen. At the beginning of *Bonduca* (1611–14), a play set in ancient Britain, Bonduca, the warrior queen of the Iceni, delivers a nationalistic speech, urging British soldiers to bravely confront the invading Romans:

BONDUCA
> Twice we have beat 'em, *Nennius*, scatter'd 'em,
> And through their big-bon'd *Germans*, on whose Pikes
> The honour of their actions sit in triumph,
> Made Themes for songs to shame 'em, and a woman,
> A woman beat 'em, *Nennius*; a weak woman,
> A woman beat these *Romanes*.

$$(1.1.12–17)^{14}$$

The warrior queen boasts of her past victory over the Romans, yet Caratach, the general of Britain, quickly corrects the queen, reminding her that the victory was not her doing but the work of the gods: "'Tis a truth, / That *Rome* has fled before us twice, and routed; / A truth we ought to crown the gods for, Lady, / And not our tongues' (1.1.24–27). Like Shakespeare's Cymbeline, Caratach is pro-Rome. Having been defeated, he eventually submits himself to Rome at the end of the play and becomes Rome's authorized ruler of Britain. In stark contrast, when the Roman army overwhelms its British counterpart, Bonduca takes her own life in order not to be captured alive; she then disappears from the play and is referred to only when Caratach denounces her as the cause of Britain's downfall: 'O thou woman, / Thou agent for adversities' (5.1.3–4). The warlike queen is not an object of nostalgia but merely a symbol of an aggressive and unsettling female agency.

The derogatory representation of Bonduca on the Jacobean stage is significant not least because Elizabeth was often associated with this historical warlike queen. In his account of Elizabeth at the time of the Armada attack in *Elizabetha Triumphans* (1588), for example, James Aske evokes Voada (Bonduca) to praise Elizabeth's warlike valour:

Now *Voada* once *Englands* happie Queene,
Through *Romans* flight by her constrain'd to flie:
Who making way amidst the slaughtered corps,
Pursued her foes with honor of the day
With *Vodice* her daughter (her too like,
Who vrging wounds with constant courage died)
Are now reuiu'd, their vertues liue (I say)
Through this our Queene, now *Englands* happie Queene.[15]

Both in *Bonduca* and *Cymbeline*, a warlike queen figure evokes the memory of the warlike Elizabeth, and the process of the restoration of masculine order and peace is staged through the excision of this queen, whose key function in these Jacobean plays is to be demonized and then erased from the history of Britain.[16]

The process of debasing the memory of a warlike queen, as enacted in these two plays, recalls the persistent attempts by James and his supporters to protect James's vision of peaceful Britain from the militarized memory of Elizabethan England by downplaying and rewriting Elizabeth's iconographical role. Nevertheless, the ways in which Shakespeare's play interacted with Jacobeans' negotiation of the memory of Elizabeth are far more complex than I have illustrated so far. In order to probe further into this interaction, I will now turn to the other key female character in *Cymbeline*. The warlike queen figure is not the only unsettling female agency in this play; Princess Innogen is represented as an equally unsettling presence and also needs to be resituated in the process of the regendering and pacifying of Britain.

Taming and containing
female agency

From the beginning of the play, Innogen does not conform
to the stereotype of the 'good daughter'; the play opens with
two gentlemen discussing a political upheaval that Innogen
has stirred in the kingdom. Although Cymbeline has arranged
to marry his daughter to Cloten (the Queen's son), Innogen
openly defies her father by wedding Posthumus, a man of her
own choice, without her father's consent; indeed, even critics
who extol her as the embodiment of virtue admit that her
disobedience to her father is problematic; for example, Carroll
Camden notes that 'the only fault which could possibly be
charged against Imogen is that she failed to obey her father'.[17]
Her decision to marry Posthumus is particularly unsettling, given
that Innogen is the sole heir of Britain and that Cymbeline's
dynastic continuity and the future of Britain entirely depends
on her. Posthumus is a 'poor' gentleman (1.1.7), whom the king
calls the 'basest thing' (1.1.126) and 'a beggar' (1.1.142); by
marrying Posthumus, Innogen, as Cymbeline accuses her, turns
his throne into 'a seat for baseness' (1.1.143). Furthermore,
during the Jacobean period, not only foreign policy but also the
arrangement of marriages for the king's children was regarded
as an inviolable royal prerogative. As Edward Coke put it
in Parliament, 'the indisputable prerogatives of the king are,
to make peace, war, and marriages for his children'.[18] In this
regard, Innogen's action could have been seen as undermining
Cymbeline's royal authority in the same way as the Queen
undermines it by dictating Britain's foreign policy. Innogen,
however, never sounds apologetic; when she is confronted
by her father, she eloquently defends herself, provocatively
asserting that, by choosing Posthumus, she has 'rather added /
A lustre to' Cymbeline's throne (1.1.143–44). Innogen was
not the only heroine to defy her arranged marriage during
this period. In Francis Beaumont and John Fletcher's *Philaster*
(1609), Arethusa, the only heir of the King of Sicily, refuses

to marry a Spanish prince of her father's choice, frustrating her father's plan to forge an alliance with Spain, while, in *Mucedorus* (1590), a popular anonymous Elizabethan play which was performed by the King's Men in 1610, Amadine, the only heir of the King of Aragon, similarly refuses to marry Segasto, whom her father has chosen in order to alleviate his own financial difficulty. Nevertheless, these princesses unwittingly choose men of royal birth, thereby actually, if not knowingly, avoiding tainting the purity of royal blood, and, in the end, they acquire the kings' blessings to continue their royal lineages. In striking contrast, Innogen has chosen and married a 'rootless' gentleman, making her choice all the more unsettling in the patriarchal dynastic context.

In fact, Innogen's problematic action has another crucial, though less noticeable, implication within the play; her choice of the inferior Posthumus creates male anxiety on the part of Posthumus. A good starting point is to note the way in which Posthumus's attitude to Innogen is defined and limited by her higher status and his sense of inferiority. As Ann Thompson puts it, 'Imogen's problem is quite simply that she is "worth more" than her husband, a point which is constantly emphasized throughout the play'.[19] Posthumus's rootlessness, which contrasts with Innogen's royal blood, is gossiped about not only among gentlemen in Cymbeline's court ('I cannot delve him to the root' [1.1.28]) but also in Rome, where Iachimo describes Innogen's marriage as 'taking a beggar without less quality' (1.4.22–23). Cloten echoes Cymbeline when he reminds Innogen of her duty as a royal heir, taunting Posthumus as 'a base slave': 'you are curbed from that enlargement by / The consequence o'th' crown, and must not foil / The precious note of it with a base slave' (2.3.120–22). More importantly, however, just like Othello, Posthumus himself inhabits the views of those around him, seeing the marriage as 'infinite loss' on Innogen's part, believing that even his love token cannot surpass Innogen's: 'As I my poor self did exchange for you / To your so infinite loss, so in our trifles / I still win of you' (1.1.120–22). Posthumus directly addresses her only as 'my queen, my mistress' (1.1.93) throughout the first scene as if he cannot see her as other than his superior. Posthumus's last words before he departs Britain are, as Pisanio reports, 'his queen, his queen' (1.3.5). Innogen's royal birth makes it implausible for Posthumus to identify himself as her husband or lord, or as more than merely her devotee and admirer.

In this regard, the wager scene, in which Iachimo and Posthumus bet on Innogen's fidelity, is a case in point. In this scene, Posthumus eloquently defends 'the honour of my mistress' (1.4.98) in front of other men; in praising his 'unparagoned mistress' (1.4.83), Posthumus styles himself 'her adorer', not 'her friend', that is, her husband or lover: 'I would abate her nothing, though I profess myself her adorer, not her friend' (1.4.70–71). For Posthumus, the matter of his mistress's honour is not of 'slight and trivial a nature' (1.4.43) so that, being challenged, he willingly proposes the dispute 'be put to the arbitrement of swords' (1.4.50–51). As Iachimo puts it later in the play, Posthumus is indeed Innogen's 'true knight, / No lesser of her honour confident' (5.5.186–87), a knight who is ready to stake his life to defend the honour of his mistress. Understandably, Posthumus himself later calls Innogen Britain's 'mistress' (5.1.20); as a devoted knight, Posthumus attempts to defend Britain's mistress from the slanderous tongues of foreigners. The wager plot thus frames Posthumus's relationship to Innogen as that of a knight to his immaculate mistress. This chivalric framework not only conveniently masks Posthumus's inferiority to Innogen in rank – the source of his male anxiety – but also aligns the relationship of the couple with that of the Queen and Cymbeline.

It is not surprising, then, that the male-centred narrative in the play, in the process of restoring patriarchal order and regendering the polity, moves to act not only against the Queen but also against Innogen, who similarly undermines male authority not only by defying her father but also, though unwittingly, by assuming the role of the presiding 'queen' of her British 'knight'. Nevertheless, in contrast to the warlike Queen, who is unambiguously portrayed as a stock evil character and can be easily vilified as a female deviant and erased from the play, it is apparently more difficult for the play to relegate and marginalize Innogen without appearing contrived and unconvincing. That is because she is, unlike the Queen, sympathetically portrayed as virtuous, and members of the public audience like Forman must have found themselves siding and sympathizing with her. The play therefore has to find a subtler way to 'tame' Innogen and contain her instead of totally excising her. The solution the play proposes is, unsurprisingly, rather theatrical. The play gradually transforms Innogen from an assertive, authoritative heroine into a submissive one, presenting this transformation as a self-motivated – not enforced – change, and this transformation is visibly signalled by the change of costumes and roles. When she secretly leaves the court to join Posthumus at Milford Haven, Innogen takes off her royal clothing once and for all, changing into 'a riding suit no costlier than would fit / A franklin's housewife' (3.2.76–77). Then, when she learns that Posthumus is wrongly accusing her of adultery and demanding that Pisanio murder her, she decides to follow the latter's plan that she should disguise herself as a man and fake her death; Pisanio advises her to change not only her clothes and her gender but also, significantly, her entire princely outlook: 'You must forget to be a woman: change / Command into obedience' (3.4.154–55). The disguised Innogen then takes up the role of 'housewife' (4.2.45) to the three men in the Welsh cave and afterwards becomes a faithful page of the Roman general Lucius, who later extols her as 'a page so kind, so duteous, diligent, / So tender over his occasions, true, / So feat, so nurse-like' (5.5.86–88).

The final scene completes Innogen's change of roles. Guiderius and Arviragus are revealed to be the lost sons of Cymbeline, a discovery which significantly diminishes her role within Cymbeline's household, as she is no longer 'the heir of's kingdom' (1.1.4), which she has been known as in the court up to then. Now that she has lost the prospect of being the female ruler of Britain, her role is that of a subservient woman; as the Roman soothsayer who decodes Jupiter's prophecy puts it, she is no more than Cymbeline's 'virtuous daughter' (5.5.445) and Posthumus's 'most constant wife' (5.5.448). Innogen then kneels before her father, asking for his blessing ('[*Kneels.*] Your blessing, sir' [5.5.265]), demonstrating her obedience to her father-king. Significantly, all this while, Innogen remains in the guise of a page; she is audibly Innogen – 'the tune of Innogen' (5.5.238) – but visually she remains the faithful page Fidele, presenting herself as a symbol of faithful servitude. Her last word in this play, which is directed to Lucius, is symbolic in this regard: 'My good master, / I will yet do you service' (5.5.402–3). The play thus deftly stages the change of Innogen from commanding princess to subservient daughter/ wife/page.

Innogen is no longer a future queen but merely a lady at court, over whom Posthumus can finally feel comfortable to claim lordship. Jupiter's prophecy – 'He shall be lord of Lady Innogen' (5.4.77) – is thus fulfilled. The play signals their changed relationship in a striking manner; when the yet undisclosed Fidele approaches the grieving Posthumus, he knocks down the 'scornful page' in front of other characters:

POSTHUMUS
                              O Innogen!
    My queen, my life, my wife. O Innogen,
    Innogen, Innogen.
INNOGEN   Peace, my lord. Hear, hear –
POSTHUMUS
    Shall's have a play of this? Thou scornful page,
    There lie thy part. [*He strikes her and she falls.*]
PISANIO   O gentleman, help!
    Mine and your mistress! O my Lord Posthumus,
    You ne'er killed Innogen till now. Help, help!
                                                (5.5.225–31)

Posthumus's sudden violence against Innogen may baffle modern audiences and readers. Yet, however repelling Posthumus's violence may seem to us, this scene can be seen as brutally necessary to the dramatic logic if the play is to announce Posthumus's authority over his sometime superior 'queen'; by knocking down Innogen at this moment, Posthumus symbolically kills his superior mistress and, though neither Posthumus nor Innogen may be aware of its significance, unwittingly and physically demonstrates to the audience that Innogen's role has now irrevocably changed from 'command into obedience'.

Both the Queen and Princess Innogen are deprived of power over their 'knights', power which the men in turn claim in the final scene. Through the excision of the Queen and the taming of Innogen, the play completes the restoration of male authority and creates a regendered Britain. However, a closer examination of Innogen will show that there is a further Jacobean implication in the taming of Innogen; importantly, an unsettling mistress/daughter is not the only role Innogen is initially given in this play.

Rewriting the Jacobean heroine

The suffering of vulnerable princesses was one of the most popular themes among the theatre audience and readers in the Jacobean period.[20] In particular, John Foxe's representation of Princess Elizabeth as a persecuted, besieged, but never yielding princess had been hugely popular and influential since Elizabeth's reign.[21] Imperilled heroines, modelled on the Foxean representation of Princess Elizabeth, strongly appealed to the public, as the success of Thomas Heywood's *If You Know Not Me, You Know Nobody, Part I* attests. Even at the time of first performances of *Cymbeline*, heroines of this type continued to attract audiences and readers; for example, Heywood achieved another commercial success with his new play, *The Rape of Lucrece* (first performed in 1607, printed in 1608 and reprinted in 1609, 1614, 1630 and 1638) – a play which features the suffering of Lucrece, the prototype of an imperilled, vulnerable heroine. Importantly, Shakespeare's pronounced focus on Innogen's besieged and helpless status situates her within this popular trend of representing imperilled heroines.

Innogen suffers greatly in Cymbeline's court, where she is alienated because of her firm refusal to annul her marriage with Posthumus. First, she is besieged by the nagging suitor Cloten, who urges her to forgo the 'base wretch' (2.3.113) and remarry none but himself. At one point, Cloten and his musicians literally besiege her bedchamber and play music outside the door, trying to open up her mind. His aggressive suit, which Innogen describes as a 'love-suit ... / As fearful as a siege' (3.4.133–34), has the backing of her royal father, who demands that she remarry Cloten and, when she refuses, even invokes a curse on his disobedient daughter: 'let her languish / A drop of blood a day and, being aged, / Die of this folly' (1.1.157–59). Innogen stands alone; no one dares to publicly side with her in the matter of her marriage. More troublingly, Innogen is besieged not only by her fellow Britons but also by a foreigner – the Roman seducer Iachimo, who is determined to destroy her reputation and wreck her marriage with Posthumus. Again, Innogen has to defend herself on her own. The only man who understands her predicament and offers support is Pisanio, the servant Posthumus has left with her. Nevertheless, Innogen finds herself totally alone and vulnerable when Iachimo seduces her and attempts to kiss her. Having discovered Iachimo's intention to despoil her chastity, Innogen feels threatened and calls for Pisanio's help as many as three times ('What ho, Pisanio!' [1.6.138; 1.6.147; 1.6.154]), yet Pisanio never appears before them. Innogen is temporarily freed from Iachimo's increasingly aggressive seduction only because Iachimo strategically backs down. Pisanio's failure to answer his mistress thus brings Innogen's vulnerability into sharp relief.

Innogen's ordeal does not end there, and a nightmarish scenario awaits her. Iachimo successfully sneaks into Innogen's bedchamber at night by hiding himself in a trunk and has the sleeping Innogen, totally unattended and defenceless, at his disposal. Tellingly, he compares himself to Tarquin, who is about to rape Lucrece ('Our Tarquin thus / Did softly press the rushes ere he wakened / The chastity he wounded' [2.2.12–14]), a comparison which automatically invites the audience to see Innogen as a version of Lucrece. Like Lucrece, Innogen vulnerably lies in her bed, and the intruder Iachimo takes advantage of her defencelessness; he kisses her, takes her ring and carries out what can be described as the voyeuristic rape of her body, discovering a mole on her breast, a piece of private information which would attest that he has enjoyed her. Although Iachimo has not physically raped Innogen, the scene between Innogen and Iachimo, which has many of the hallmarks of a classical seduction and rape narrative, thus gives the impression that he has at least metaphorically ravished her.[22] In this regard, Cloten's attempts to 'penetrate' (2.3.14) and '[assail] her with music' (2.3.39) in the next scene, followed by his vivid illustration of his fantasy of raping her (3.5.137–46; 4.1.15–20), also serve to represent Innogen as a Lucrece figure in this play. Iachimo's voyeuristic rape takes its toll on Innogen. Falsely believing that Innogen has given in to Iachimo, even her loved one Posthumus turns against her, ordering Pisanio to murder her. While Lucrece has supporters to revenge Tarquin's wrongdoing, Innogen is further isolated by Iachimo's 'rape'. Besieging Innogen on all sides, the play thus stresses her helplessness and vulnerability and the perseverance she shows in enduring these misfortunes – notable characteristics which were embodied by popular heroines at the time.

The image of besieged virtue had political and religious connotations in the Jacobean context. Most notably, the imperilled Elizabeth, as in Heywood's dramatization of Princess Elizabeth, directly symbolized English Protestantism besieged by menacing Catholics. Yet it is not only direct representations of Elizabeth which had such connotations. Imperilled heroines, such as Samuel Rowley's dramatization of Catherine Parr, who is hounded by Henry VIII's Catholic advisers, in *When You*

See Me, You Know Me (1605) and Thomas Dekker and John Webster's dramatization of Lady Jane Grey in *Sir Thomas Wyatt* (a late Elizabethan play first performed in 1602 and published in 1607), also followed the model of Princess Elizabeth, symbolizing besieged English Protestantism.[23] These heroines whom writers and playwrights portray with great sympathy can be associated with contemporary political and religious discourse. During Elizabeth's reign, the representation of the distressed Elizabeth served as a call for Englishmen to rush to defend their vulnerable queen and their mother country from the Catholic powers. For example, in the aftermath of the failed Armada invasion, William Averell reminds his countrymen of the besieged status of Elizabeth and incites them to 'manfully defend' her from the Catholic menace and to requite her love:

> Remember howe many daungers her sacred person hath sustayned and often endured, for defending both you & yours from Popery ... doe you agayne naturally requite her, and manfully defend her, with liues, landes, and goods, that shee may thinke her selfe happie of so good subiectes, and you not vnworthie of so gracious a Quéene.[24]

The representation of the besieged Elizabeth in need of protection recurred in post-Armada discourse and seemed to appeal to the anti-Catholic sentiments of the English people.[25] Crucially, this representation continued to have symbolic power over Jacobeans.[26] Although James attempted to implement his conciliatory policy towards Catholic Europe, the failed Gunpowder Plot by English Catholics in 1605 renewed the memory of Elizabethan England at the time of the Armada attack and confirmed many Jacobeans' fear that, despite James's show of reconciliation and harmony, Protestant England was still under siege by the Catholic powers and needed to be defended.[27] The imperilled Elizabeth did not belong to the Elizabethan past but rather spoke directly to Jacobeans about the danger which English Protestantism continued to face. The popularity of the besieged Elizabeth and similarly besieged heroines, a popularity which showed no sign of waning nearly a decade into James's reign, both reflected and informed Jacobeans' deep-seated anxiety towards the Catholic powers.

Cymbeline closely evokes this specific Jacobean significance of imperilled heroines. Most notably, Iachimo's attack on Innogen is given a religious significance comparable to the representation of the imperilled Elizabeth. When Iachimo first attempts to seduce her, Innogen repels him, describing him as 'a saucy stranger' who came from 'a Romish stew' 'to expound / His beastly mind to us' (1.6.150–52), in other words, a corrupter of her countrymen. As several editors have noted, the phrase 'Romish stew' was often used in anti-Catholic discourse for describing the Roman Catholic Church as the source of moral corruption.[28] Iachimo's attempt to seduce and corrupt Innogen closely follows the framework of the anti-Catholic polemic. It is, therefore, not surprising that Donna B. Hamilton sees Innogen as an allegory of the imperilled Protestant Church; as she puts it, the plot concerning Innogen 'replicates the narrative patterns that had been legitimated by Jewel, Foxe, and Spenser – but were now newly in vogue – to tell the story of the struggles of the true church against the false church'.[29] In this regard, Dekker's *The Whore of Babylon*, one of the notable theatrical examples in which the Catholic Church is represented as the corrupter and invader of Protestant England, offers another important backdrop for the embattlement of Innogen. The empress of Babylon (the allegory of Catholic Rome) orders three Catholic kings to seduce and corrupt Titania (Elizabeth), the true defender of the faith, and, when the seduction has failed, sends out the fleets to invade and penetrate into Titania's fairy land (England) (1.1.97–114; 1.2.81–208).[30] Here, Titania's body is identified with the body politic of her fairy land, just as Elizabeth's body was with the body politic of England, and the planned invasion of Titania's fairy land is envisaged as the rape of her body. Similarly, in *Cymbeline*, Innogen's body is closely linked to the body politic of Britain. Iachimo's failure to seduce the princess is followed not only by his invasion of her bedchamber – his metaphorical rape of Innogen – but also by the Roman soldiers' invasion of Britain, which is, as critics have pointed out, imagined as the invasion of a female body.[31] Just as the image of the imperilled Elizabeth symbolized England under siege by the mighty European Catholic powers, Innogen also symbolizes the body politic under siege by a powerful foreign power, in this case, the Roman Empire (which is anachronistically and meaningfully associated with the contemporary, corrupted/corrupting Italy) and, as with other Jacobean imperilled heroines, can be linked to the memory of Elizabeth's imperilled Protestant England.[32]

Furthermore, Shakespeare's portrayal of Innogen should also be examined in the specific context of the first decade of James's reign when the memory of the imperilled Elizabeth assumed added political significance. After the failed Gunpowder Plot and the implementation of the Oath of Allegiance in 1606, polemical conflicts between Protestants and Catholic exiles intensified and religious pamphlets were successively published from both sides.[33] While the Pope, bishops and exiled English preachers such as Robert Persons – a prolific Jesuit writer and the chief proponent of the Counter-Reformation publishing campaign – strongly condemned the Oath of Allegiance, a group of Protestant polemists defended the oath, condemning, in turn, recusant Catholics and portraying Roman Catholicism as an omnipresent menace to English Protestantism.[34] These polemical conflicts offer an important backdrop for my discussion not only because controversies of this kind involved ordinary citizens, including dramatists and their audiences, as well as clergy and government officials but also because the memory of Elizabeth significantly featured in this polemical war, becoming the prime target of Persons's notorious anti-Protestant campaign.[35] In his publications, Persons continually harks back to Elizabeth's reign and vehemently attacks Elizabeth and her policy in an attempt to tarnish the history and legitimacy of English Protestantism and to warn James and his people not to follow her example. In *An Answere to the Fifth Part of Reportes* (1606), for example, Persons harshly criticizes Elizabeth's persecution of Catholics, stating that her policy against Catholics had no legal or spiritual legitimacy since '*Q. Elizabeth* being a woman could not haue any supreame spirituall power or Iurisdiction in Ecclesiasticall matters'.[36] In *The Judgment of a Catholicke English-Man* (1608), Persons quickly rebuts James's comment in *Triplici Nodo* (1608) that 'the late Queene of famous memory, neuer punished any Papist for Religion' and intensifies his attack on Elizabeth, reviling her as heretic, tyrannical and illegitimate.[37] Exactly as she had been during her lifetime, Elizabeth was again besieged by Roman Catholicism, this time, specifically in print, and, for English Protestants, the late queen became the symbol of the Protestant principle that needed to be defended.

Meaningfully, Persons's attack on the dead queen was seen by some Protestants as a sacrilegious act of desecrating the dead. In *An Answer to a Catholike English-Man* (1609), for example, William Barlow rushes to defend Elizabeth, whom '*Parsons, famous* for nothing but Capitall *Infamies,* hath defiled', as 'a *Carefull Gouernour* ... an *example* of vertue for her owne to follow, and a *Load-starre* for other *Nations* to admire', harshly criticizing Persons as 'a *Carrionly Curre,* entring her Tombe, and exenterrating her very bowels to stanch his rage'.[38] Barlow writes, 'cannot SHE bee suffered to rest? and is *there no end of barbarous malice?* but a currish, Blood-hound must rouse her, and teare her, from top to toe, within and without, from *Birth* to *Death?*' arguing that the late queen who has been recently 'gloriously entombed by her MOST ROYALL SVCCESSOR' should now be left in peace.[39] Thomas Middleton's *The Lady's Tragedy* (1611), the play I briefly discussed in Chapter 2, featured contemporaries' fear that the dead queen was being symbolically and ideologically desecrated by Catholic detractors. The Lady, the unnamed heroine, is presented as a besieged virgin; although she is betrothed to the legitimate king Govianus, the Tyrant, usurper of Govianus's throne, seduces her and attempts to coerce her into marrying him. The Lady steadfastly refuses and, when the Tyrant decides to take her by force, the heroine literally besieged by the Tyrant's soldiers outside the house frees herself by taking her own life. However, even after she is dead and entombed by Govianus, she continues to be beset by the lustful Tyrant, who steals her body from her tomb and attempts to ravish her posthumously. The play adds a distinctly religious dimension to the Tyrant's action against the Lady by portraying her as a pious Protestant martyr; before her suicide, the Lady styles herself a martyr, kneeling down to pray (3.1.107–10) and, after her death, she reappears as a ghost in the habiliment of a religious martyr ('*all in white, stuck with jewels and a great crucifix on her breast*' [4.4.42 SD]).[40] On the other hand, the Tyrant is presented as a corrupted/corrupting Catholic. As Julia Briggs rightly points out, 'the Tyrant's illegitimacy, lustfulness, and acts of desecration and idolatry link him with the Catholic Church as it appeared to committed Protestants like Middleton, while the sombrely dressed Lady represents the reformed Church, persecuted but unafraid'.[41] In this regard, the Tyrant's desecration of the Lady's body could have evoked Catholics' symbolic desecration of Elizabeth as it appeared to some Jacobean Protestants; when Govianus cries out, 'O, thou sacrilegious villain, / Thou thief of rest, robber of monuments! / Cannot the body after funeral / Sleep in the grave for thee?' (5.2.127–30), he effectively echoes Protestants' anger towards Persons's notoriously vindictive polemics, as shown in Barlow's impassioned call that the entombed queen should not be attacked.

Significantly, when Iachimo intrudes into Innogen's bedchamber in order to carry out the voyeuristic rape and to smear her reputation, Iachimo meaningfully associates the sleeping Innogen with a monument in a chapel:

IACHIMO
    O sleep, thou ape of death, lie dull upon her,
    And be her sense but as a monument
    Thus in a chapel lying.

                                        (2.2.31–33)

Iachimo imagines Innogen's bedchamber as a chapel and her body as a monument in it, that is, as Martin Butler glosses, 'a recumbent marble effigy, on a tomb'.[42] Shakespeare reinforces this image of Innogen as an effigy later in the play when Guiderius and Arviragus grieve over the 'dead' body of Innogen, whom they still believe to be Fidele. Arviragus recounts in detail the posture of 'dead' Innogen he has found lying on the floor, describing her body as a recumbent effigy sleeping/lying on its bed/grave (4.2.209–16). These descriptions of the sleeping Innogen, I would suggest, could have had a specific Jacobean significance. Elizabeth's new tomb with her recumbent effigy was installed in Westminster Abbey in 1606 and the image of her tomb was known to many Jacobeans. According to the seventeenth-century historian Thomas Fuller, drawings of Elizabeth's tomb with her effigy were placed 'in most London and many country churches, every parish being proud of the shadow of her tomb'.[43] Many Jacobeans, each of whom, as Fuller observes, 'erected a mournful monument for her in his heart', were thus possibly well acquainted with the image of her marble effigy, which constituted the official monument.[44] It is possible therefore that the representation of Innogen as an effigy recalled Elizabeth's effigy in some members of the audience and that Iachimo's attempt to desecrate the sleeping Innogen in the sacred chapel and defame her evoked the desecration/defamation of the late Elizabeth allegedly carried out by Catholic dissidents at the time of first performances of the play.

The imperilled Elizabeth did not belong to the Elizabethan past; nor was this image the mere object of nostalgia. James's reign did not end religious conflict and Elizabeth, as a symbol of English Protestantism, continued to be besieged as she had been during her lifetime. The besieged Elizabeth and similarly besieged princess figures in print and on stage served as a pointed reminder to Jacobeans that, despite James's show of unity and reconciliation, their Protestant state was still embattled by the omnipresent Catholic menace and that England and Europe continued to be divided religiously as well as politically. I would suggest that Innogen was a highly symbolic presence at the time of first performances of the play because of her close links with this politically charged representation of an imperilled English Protestantism. Like the imperilled Elizabeth, Shakespeare's portrayal of Innogen not only evokes the memory of the besieged Elizabethan England but also directly addresses the religious and political fissures which James attempted to play down to maintain his vision of British and European peace. Significantly, the play not only transforms Princess Innogen into a submissive daughter/wife/ page, thereby pronouncing the transfer of power from women to men, but also rewrites the besieged Innogen – symbol of the besieged state – in a way that illustrates James's strategy to adjust the memory of Elizabeth and her England.

As a starting point for this discussion, let us return to Innogen's 'death' in Act 4 Scene 3. After her arduous journey into Wales, Innogen finally finds shelter in the Welsh cave where, feeling unwell, she unknowingly swallows a drug which temporarily incapacitates her bodily functions. Believing that she is dead, Guiderius, Arviragus and Belarius conduct a funeral and, from that moment on, the play shifts its central focus from the sufferings of Innogen to the Britons' defensive war against the Romans. Innogen no longer commands the central attention of the audience as she is relegated into the backdrop of the play; Innogen as the imperilled heroine has symbolically died and she revives only to become a servant of the Roman general (as I noted at the beginning of the chapter, Forman abruptly ends his account at this point: 'And how she was found by Lucius, etc.'). When the play brings her back to the centre of the play in the final scene, the revived Innogen assumes a new symbolic role. As the previously imperilled Britain reconciles itself with and voluntarily submits itself to Rome, Innogen – the voluntary servant of the Roman general – comes to symbolize the restored polity of Britain. Her pledge of continued allegiance to Lucius ('My good master, / I will yet do you service') accurately describes Britain's renewed allegiance to its master, Rome. Innogen thus becomes a symbol of Britain's reconciliation and peace with Rome.

The play invites the audience to see the new Innogen as a symbol of harmony and unity. In the final scene, the seemingly unrelated or previously separated characters all find themselves linked to Fidele, and the revelation of Fidele's true identity as Innogen instantly brings these characters closer to one another. Innogen reunites father and sons and reconciles Rome and Britain. Cymbeline draws our attention to this new role of Innogen:

CYMBELINE
                    See,
Posthumus anchors upon Innogen,
And she, like harmless lightning, throws her eye
On him, her brothers, me, her master, hitting
Each object with a joy. The counterchange
Is severally in all.

                                        (5.5.391–96)

Cymbeline describes Innogen as shining on all the characters 'like harmless lightning', bringing joy to every character, including the general of the invading army ('her master'). Those who have been at odds – Britain and Rome, Cymbeline and Posthumus, and Cymbeline and Belarius – are now reconciled under the gaze of Innogen. While Innogen loses her hereditary right to succession, the play thus gives her an equally important role in Cymbeline's restored Britain, turning her into a symbol of both British solidarity and harmony between Britain and Rome.

Cymbeline significantly rewrites Innogen, whom it initially characterizes as a symbol of besieged Protestant England, as a symbol of reconciliation and harmony – a symbol which effectively represents Cymbeline's vision of peaceful Britain reconciled with Rome. As I discussed in Chapter 3, *Coriolanus* draws our attention to the way in which some Jacobeans attempted to rewrite the militarized memory of Elizabeth; just as the Roman senators give Volumnia a role of reconciler, thereby transforming the warlike mother into the usher of peace, James and the supporters of his peace policy attempted to adjust the Jacobeans' perception of Elizabeth as warlike by focusing on Elizabeth's achievements as the peace-minded monarch, thereby publicizing a counter-image of Elizabeth as the peacemaker like James. It is this Jacobean politics of negotiating the memory of Elizabeth, I would suggest, that Shakespeare further examines in *Cymbeline*. In *Cymbeline*, it is not only the representation of the warlike queen that is the object of adjustment but that of the imperilled, helpless princess. Shakespeare brings into sharp relief, as he similarly does in *Coriolanus*, the ways in which those who supported James's policy attempted to simplify the memory of Elizabeth and her reign and to represent her as a symbol of peace so that they could overshadow other popular versions of Elizabeth, such as the warlike and the besieged, which inconveniently pointed at the religious and political fissures both in England and Europe.

Yet this is not to suggest that the play merely replicates their attempts to appropriate the memory of Elizabeth. On the contrary, the play problematizes them. Cymbeline dismisses the warlike Queen and finally takes back the monarchical power from his sometime domineering mistress, staging a containment of militarism and female agency as embodied by the Queen at the same time as he appropriates the image of his daughter as the symbol of his restored Britain. The play, however, allows us to question not only Cymbeline's restored authority but also his vision of peaceful Britain, a sceptical viewpoint which inevitably weakens Innogen's new symbolic role. In particular, *Cymbeline*, as will be shown, questions the vision of peace by presenting militarism as an essential principle that is necessary to assert and maintain national integrity and also by presenting that vision in the form of a potentially unreliable prophetic vision. Although excising the warlike Queen and rewriting Innogen as a symbol of peace and reconciliation seem to reinforce James's much publicized vision of peaceful Britain, there are powerful cross-currents within the play which problematize it.

Against the Jacobean vision
of Britain

In the preceding chapters on *Antony and Cleopatra* and *Coriolanus*, I argued that, in these plays, although warlike queen/mother figures disappear in the end, nostalgia for Elizabethan militarism was not entirely suppressed but rather was left simmering in the background of the plays' seemingly conclusive restoration of peace. I would suggest that *Cymbeline* also presents an alternative perspective which conflicts with the final resolution of peace and harmony.

First, although the play demonizes the warlike Queen as the source of strife and discord, it significantly falls short of denouncing the Queen's militarism itself. On the contrary, in its staging of the battle between the Britons and the Romans, the play fuels militant sentiments the Queen has incited by representing Guiderius, Arviragus and Belarius as the heroic guardians of vulnerable Britain. In the final scene, Cymbeline praises these warlike men as the 'preservers of my throne' (5.5.2) and acknowledges that they are 'the liver, heart, and brain of Britain' (5.5.14), without which Britain cannot sustain herself ('by whom, I grant, she lives' [5.5.15]); they are the ones who have defended his kingdom from invasion and thus retained its integrity. While highlighting the importance of Britain's defence capability and the indispensability of these soldiers in this way, the play repeatedly directs our attention to Cymbeline's incompetence as commander during the war. When the news arrives that the Roman legion has landed at Milford Haven, Cymbeline is distraught at the prospect of leading the counter-force without the counsel of the Queen and her son Cloten ('Now for the counsel of my son and Queen, / I am amazed with matter' [4.3.27–28]) and he is mildly chided by one of his lords, who implores him to remain calm and 'to put those powers in motion / That long to move' (4.3.31–32). In the battle scene, to add to his humiliation, Cymbeline is briefly captured by the Romans before he is rescued by the warlike Britons (5.2.11–13). Thus the play not only glorifies the prowess and courage of these warlike men but also undermines Cymbeline's fatherly authority by exposing his utter dependence on them.

In this regard, Cymbeline's proclamation of peace at the climax of the play can be seen as his attempt to restore both his monarchical and fatherly authority. As I noted earlier, 'to make peace', as Edward Coke puts it, was seen as one of 'the indisputable prerogatives of the king' among the Jacobean audience. However, Cymbeline's sudden announcement that he will make peace with Rome is highly problematic in many respects. Before war breaks out, for example, Cymbeline stresses the eagerness of his people to shake off the Roman yoke, stating that, if he does not answer their expectations, he would 'show less sovereignty than they' and must 'appear unkinglike'. Yet what he does in the final scene is to voluntarily stoop to the Romans whom the warlike Britons have just defeated and to agree to resume paying tribute to Augustus Caesar. By proclaiming peace in this way, Cymbeline, to use his own words, inevitably makes himself 'appear unkinglike' to his subjects. In other words, Cymbeline's declaration of peace appears nothing but the show of his 'unkinglike' inconsistency rather than the demonstration of his monarchical or fatherly authority. It would not be surprising, then, if the audience were not only to see Britain's voluntary subjugation to Rome as humiliating but also to see Cymbeline's two warrior princes as more competent and kingly leaders than their father.

The play also seems to question Cymbeline's vision of Britain by highlighting the precariousness of the peace Cymbeline proudly initiates. The return of the warrior princes to Britain's royal household inevitably makes the peace between Britain and the Roman Empire look markedly fragile. Indeed, according to Holinshed, it was not Cymbeline but Guiderius who started all-out war with the Roman Empire; Guiderius, 'being a man of stout courage, gave occasion of breach of peace betwixt the Britains and Romans, denieing to paie them tribute, and procuring the people to new insurrections, which by one meane or other made open rebellion'.[45] The audience who knew this historical background might have seen Guiderius's return to the royal court of Britain as foreboding the breakdown of Cymbeline's peace. After all, the Britons are repeatedly described as warlike and defiant; in fact, it is Cymbeline himself who states that the Britons are 'a warlike people' (3.1.52). The play thus asks how these warlike people can or should remain subjugated to and yoked to Rome, allowing the audience to question the effectiveness or even desirability of Cymbeline's peace.

The scepticism towards peace that *Cymbeline* raises evokes the Jacobeans' similar scepticism towards England's peace with Spain. As I discussed in Chapter 3, the peace treaty with Spain was not welcomed by all; militant Protestants expressed dissatisfaction with James's conciliatory policy – for example, his controversial decision to downsize England's maritime activities in order to maintain peace with Spain. Just as Cymbeline's Queen hails the warlike feats of the Britons in the past in her nationalistic speech, they stressed the warlike nature of the English people and evoked England's militant past in order to advance their cause. As Robert Pricket puts it in a pamphlet addressed to James, 'your Englands nation hath in times past, been accounted famous in the exercise of Armes, and your people, for their magnanimious valour in warlike cheualry haue, not onely beene admired, but feared of all the kingdoms in Christendome'.[46] In this regard, the play's ambiguous attitudes to Cymbeline's peace point to the contemporary scepticism towards James's policy. When Cymbeline suddenly announces that he will resume paying tribute to Rome and secure peace between the two states, proclaiming that 'my peace we will begin', it is literally Cymbeline's peace – note his use of the personal possessive – not necessarily that of future Britons, and certainly not of his heirs, in the same way that James's peace was seen by militant Protestants who looked to his warlike heir Prince Henry to defend Protestantism both in England and Europe.

As in his earlier tragedies, Shakespeare thus incorporates an alternative viewpoint which allows the audience to question the authorized political vision of peace and unity; importantly, he does so not only by representing militarism in a positive light and stressing the precariousness of peace but also by articulating the ideal view of peaceful Britain through spectacle and prophecy, key mediums which Shakespeare deployed to problematize James's political vision in *Macbeth*. As I noted at the beginning of this chapter, Cymbeline's peaceful Britain is first articulated by Jupiter, who descends from above and foretells that Britain will '*be fortunate and flourish in peace and plenty*'. Critics have registered unease with Jupiter's scene. Heather James, for example, points out that 'the play's strongest assertion of authority, from none other than the father of the gods, is also its clumsiest theatrical display'.[47] Indeed, the scene of Jupiter, involving his descending and ascending on the eagle and his throwing a thunderbolt, is the most conspicuous theatrical spectacle in the play. It is likely that this contrived spectacle incited not only awe but also a sense of disbelief in some members of the audience. It would not be surprising if those audience members reacted to Jupiter's prophetic vision of peaceful Britain with a certain degree of scepticism.

The deeper problem, however, lies with the fact that Cymbeline's peace is ushered in and legitimized by the contrived decoding of prophecy and prophetic vision. In the final scene, the Roman soothsayer unveils his interpretation of Jupiter's prophecy to Cymbeline. The soothsayer decodes the first part of the prophecy concerning Posthumus's reunion with Innogen by stating that 'the piece of tender air' indicates Innogen since its Latin form, '*mollis aer*' or '*mulier*', signifies woman (5.5.445–48), an interpretation which is, to say the least, contrived. The strain in the soothsayer's interpretation has been noted in earlier studies. Brian Gibbons, for example, points at the 'hint of absurdity in solving of the final riddle', noting that the soothsayer's interpretation 'is in the worst tradition of allegorical exegesis, depending on extracting an excruciating pun from the words "mollis aer"'.[48] Leah S. Marcus also reads his decipherment as the 'niggling, labored mode of interpretation', which 'can easily be understood as mockery of the play's own process of "wondering" decipherment of riddles and emblems of state'.[49]

The rather dubious soothsayer then explains to Cymbeline that the second part of the prophecy ensures that the discovery of his heirs 'promises Britain peace and plenty' (5.5.457). Upon hearing the words of the soothsayer, Cymbeline proclaims the peace with Rome. As if to further reassure Cymbeline that his decision is appropriate, the soothsayer unveils to Cymbeline the prophetic vision he claims to have received from the Roman gods before the war ('I saw Jove's bird, the Roman eagle, winged / From the spongy south to this part of the west, / There vanished in the sunbeams' [4.2.347–49]) and interprets it as portending the reunion of Cymbeline and Caesar, thereby validating Cymbeline's decision to secure peace with Rome. The soothsayer, who is appropriately named 'Philharmonus' (5.5.432), that is, lover of harmony, is the real author of the final scene of reconciliation; he is the one who orchestrates the peace between Britain and Rome and validates it as the divine will, proclaiming that 'the fingers of the powers above do tune / The harmony of this peace' [5.5.465–66]). Yet, again, one cannot help noticing the contrivance of the interpretation of the Roman soothsayer. We might recall that the soothsayer, before the battle, initially interprets the same vision for the Roman general as portending 'success to th' Roman host' (4.2.351), that is, apparently, the victory of the Roman army; yet, upon the defeat of the Roman soldiers, he adjusts his interpretation by claiming that the vision actually foretells the reconciliation between Cymbeline and Caesar, which, only in an oblique sense, can be seen as 'success to th' Roman host' as Britain will resume paying tribute to Caesar. In this regard, the Roman soothsayer appears not as an authoritative conveyer of divine will but rather as a political manipulator who seems to be determined to extract the interpretation which would prompt and support Cymbeline's action to secure peace with Rome.

As I discussed in Chapter 1, while James's supporters extensively re-edited and reinterpreted ancient prophecies, claiming that James's succession and his British union project were pre-ordained by these prophecies and therefore legitimate, some of his English subjects shared the scepticism towards political prophecy. Indeed, Shakespeare was not the only playwright to address this contemporary scepticism on the Jacobean stage. Ben Jonson's *Catiline His Conspiracy* (1611), a King's Men play contemporaneous with *Cymbeline*, features the way in which prophecy can be used as a political tool. Catiline attempts to win support from his fellow patrician Lentulus for his ambitious plan to overthrow the Roman Republic; in order to keep Lentulus on his side, Catiline finds a prophecy in 'the Sibyl's books' and commissions the augurs to concoct an interpretation which would please Lentulus:

CATILINE
                                I have to do
With many men and many natures. Some
That must be blown and soothed, as Lentulus,
Whom I have heaved with magnifying his blood
And a vain dream, out of the Sibyl's books,
That a third man of that great family
Whereof he is descended, the Cornelli,
Should be a king in Rome – which I have hired
The flattering augurs to interpret him,
Cinna and Sulla dead.

                                        (1.1.131–40)[50]

While Plutarch's *Lives*, one of the sources for the play, only mentions that Catiline's prophecy was a forgery, Jonson goes further and highlights the way in which Catiline attempts to win political support by bribing the 'flattering augurs' to produce an interpretation of the prophecy. Catiline's political manoeuvre pays off; the forged interpretation of the prophecy successfully unites Lentulus and Catiline's other supporters. The play thus exposes the dubiousness of political prophecy, the kind of dubiousness which some Jacobeans perceived in the use of political prophecy by James and his supporters.

Macbeth evokes James's vision of succession and union through the witches' prophecies and allows the audience to question its legitimacy as well as its idealism. *Cymbeline* too, I would suggest, problematizes James's vision of peace by articulating it through the prophecy of the pagan god. As in *Macbeth* and *Catiline*, the dubiousness of prophecy as a medium for justifying a political initiative is specifically stressed by the way in which the prophecy is shown to be interpreted in a conspicuously contrived manner. Not all Jacobeans supported or sympathized with James's much vaunted role as Britain's peacemaker, a role which he and his supporters attempted to legitimize and publicize not only by adjusting the memory of Elizabeth but also by utilizing political prophecy. By drawing the attention of the audience to the soothsayer's strained mode of interpretation, the play allows them to question James's attempts to reinterpret ancient prophecies to validate his role as peacemaker. In this regard, the play can be read as incorporating contemporaries' sceptical views both of Jacobean peace and of the ways in which it was promoted.

It might not be a coincidence, then, that Jupiter's spectacle, the soothsayer's interpretation of prophecy and prophetic vision and Cymbeline's proclamation of peace did not elicit any response from Forman. His account suggests that some audience members, despite the play's emphasis on these scenes, were not interested in the theme of British peace. Instead, Forman's attention is drawn to the two invasions, Rome's invasion of 'England' and Iachimo's invasion of Innogen's bedchamber, showing particularly strong fascination with the latter. In the final section, therefore, I will return to Innogen and consider what it could have meant for the Jacobean audience to remember Innogen and her hardship instead of the play's emphasis on the theme of British peace.

The politics of remembering the besieged heroine

The political symbolism of Innogen is indeed multifaceted in this play. Through Innogen, the play characterizes the two images of the state, both of which were familiar to the Jacobean audience: the besieged England and the peaceful Britain. Innogen, as a princess besieged by a Roman male, symbolizes the body politic of the kingdom besieged by the Roman Empire, while, in the final scene, Innogen symbolizes the polity reconciled with the outside world. In this regard, the representation of Innogen can be associated with the ways in which Elizabeth and her England were recalled to represent various, often conflicting, views of the Jacobean state. As I argued in this chapter, the play does not present the final phase of Britain – the peaceful Britain with Innogen as a symbol of peace and harmony – as the uncontested vision of the state; while it seemingly celebrates Cymbeline's peace, the play simultaneously allows the audience to question it. Shakespeare's play functions as the contested field where the different representations of the state and those of its national symbol are articulated and left to vie for the audience's attention. Ultimately, it is left to the audience to decide which phase of the state and its heroine who symbolizes the state would accurately describe their own view of the Jacobean kingdom. The play engages its audience in the Jacobean politics of envisaging the state through the memory of Elizabeth, asking them whether they see the state as imperilled England or as pacified Britain – in other words, whether they remember Elizabeth as the imperilled heroine in need of protection or as the precursor of Jacobean peace.

Outside the theatre, the conflicting views of the state vied to win the attention of Jacobeans. James wished that his people would see the state as the united kingdom of peace and remember Elizabeth as he and his supporters reconstructed her, that is, the peace-minded queen who had laid the ground for Jacobean/British peace. However, James's expectation was dashed; his pacific stance generated unease among his people. Although James wished to bury the memory of the long-time strife that encumbered English Protestantism, that memory never seemed to fade as it was continually renewed during James's reign by events such as the failed Gunpowder Plot and the lively religious controversy that followed the implementation of the Oath of Allegiance. Jacobeans continued to see their state as besieged Protestant England and expressed dismay at James's ideal vision of peaceful Britain. Unsurprisingly, the image of Elizabeth as the precursor of Jacobean peace did not become the dominant mode of representing Elizabeth as James had wished.

At the start of this chapter, I noted the difficulty of Forman's account of *Cymbeline*. Forman's apparent disregard for the Jacobean political aspects of the play has been somewhat baffling for modern critics. However, what I have shown in this chapter is that Forman's memorandum is itself no less political than any contemporary political discourse on the British issues and Jacobean peace. Just as James's campaign for British unity and peace fell on deaf ears, the presentation of Jupiter's prophecy as well as the lengthy miraculous staging of reconciliation and peace at the end of the play apparently did not appeal to Forman. His omission of the theme of British peace was symptomatic of Jacobeans' response to James's much publicized policy of peace and unity. While he had, wilfully or not, forgotten to mention these topical elements of the play, he recorded in detail what possibly stayed in his memory or what possibly he wanted to remember by writing down – the embattlement of Innogen. While the final scene celebrates the return of Innogen, now 'tamed' and obedient, who comes to symbolize Britain's peace with Rome, it is the imperilled Innogen whom Forman had chosen to record. Forman saw Cymbeline's kingdom as 'England' – as he persistently calls it – not as Britain, and the heroine as the imperilled princess, not as the personification of British peace. Forman might have been simply drawn to erotic elements of Iachimo's intrusion into Innogen's bedchamber, yet, whatever actually attracted him in that scene, the fact that he meaningfully begins his account of the play with the plot concerning the invasion of 'England' before recording the embattlement of Innogen shows that Forman was effectively, if not knowingly, responding to the political significance of the besieged princess and thereby to the cultural undercurrent of nostalgia for the besieged Elizabethan England. I have argued in this chapter that *Cymbeline* engages its audience in the Jacobean politics of remembering Elizabeth and her England through its representation of Innogen. Indeed, Forman's seemingly apolitical text about the besieged Innogen/England was an instinctive, yet meaningfully constructed, response to the politics of Shakespeare's play.

Notes

1   G. Wilson Knight, *The Crown of Life: Essays in Interpretation of Shakespeare's Final Plays* (London: Methuen, 1948), 129–202.

2   See esp. David M. Bergeron, *Shakespeare's Romances and the Royal Family* (Lawrence: University Press of Kansas, 1985), 136–56; Emrys Jones, 'Stuart *Cymbeline*', *Essays in Criticism* 11 (1961): 84–99; Leah S. Marcus, *Puzzling Shakespeare: Local Reading and Its Discontents* (Berkeley: University of California Press, 1988), 144; Glynne Wickham, 'Riddle and Emblem: A Study in the Dramatic Structure of *Cymbeline*', in *English Renaissance Studies: Presented to Dame Helen Gardner in Honour of Her Seventieth Birthday*, ed. John Carey (Oxford: Clarendon Press, 1980), 94–113; and Frances A. Yates, *Shakespeare's Last Plays: A New Approach* (London: Routledge, 1975), 41–61.

3   For the date of *Cymbeline*, see esp. Martin Butler, introduction to *Cymbeline*, ed. Martin Butler (Cambridge: Cambridge University Press, 2005), 3–6.

4   It is understandable that Leah S. Marcus speculates from Forman's account that the potentially impressive scene of Jupiter might not have been performed in public theatres (*Puzzling*

Shakespeare, 139). Yet any discussion of omission in original performances remains speculative. The spectacle of Jupiter's descent was performable in public theatres; Thomas Heywood's mythological plays, such as *The Golden Age* (1610) and *The Silver Age* (1611), similarly featured Jupiter's spectacular descent and ascent. For the theatrical context of the staging of Jupiter, see esp. Frederick Kiefer, *Shakespeare's Visual Theatre: Staging the Personified Characters* (Cambridge: Cambridge University Press, 2003), 149–57.

5   Shakespeare uses the word 'Britain' and its variants such as 'Britain's', 'Britains' and 'British' sixty-five times throughout his plays, and forty-seven, more than two-thirds of all the uses, occur in *Cymbeline* (Marvin Spevack, *The Harvard Concordance to Shakespeare* [Hildesheim: Olms, 1973]), a fact that, together with the play's setting in ancient Britain, underlines Shakespeare's particular emphasis on British issues.

6   I quote Forman's text that has been modernized and punctuated by Butler (introduction to *Cymbeline*, 3–4).

7   So far, the play's possible links with the memory of Elizabeth have attracted little critical attention. Rowena Davies suggests that one reference to Innogen as phoenix in the play evokes Elizabeth ('"Alone th'Arabian Bird": Imogen as Elizabeth I?', *Notes and Queries* 26 [1979]: 137–40). Marcus briefly dwells on the possibility that the Queen can be read as a demonized version of Elizabeth and Innogen as her positive version (*Puzzling Shakespeare*, 128), while Butler describes the Queen as 'a distorted memory of the Elizabethan past' (introduction to *Cymbeline*, 43). Yet none of the earlier studies has examined the full extent of the ways in which the politics of negotiating the memory of Elizabeth and her reign is played out in *Cymbeline*.

8   Jodi Mikalachki, *The Legacy of Boadicea: Gender and Nation in Early Modern England* (London: Routledge, 1998), 96–114. In regard to the exclusion of the Queen, Janet Adelman's psychoanalytic approach, by way of which she dissects the play's masculine fantasy of parthenogenesis, is also insightful (*Suffocating Mothers*, 199–219).

9   Raphael Holinshed, *Holinshed's Chronicles of England, Scotland, and Ireland*, vol. 3 (London: J. Johnson, 1808), 476.

For the possible sources of *Cymbeline*, see Geoffrey Bullough, ed., *Narrative and Dramatic Sources of Shakespeare*, vol. 8 (London: Routledge; New York: Columbia University Press, 1975), 38–111.

10 See esp. Stow, *The Annales of England*, 1281.

11 For the exclusion of the Queen as a prerequisite for the final resolution of the play, see also Mikalachki, *The Legacy of Boadicea*, 97–101 and Patricia Parker, 'Romance and Empire: Anachronistic *Cymbeline*', in *Unfolded Tales: Essays on Renaissance Romance*, ed. George M. Logan and Gordon Teskey (Ithaca, NY: Cornell University Press, 1989), 189–207 (esp. 197–98).

12 For foreign policy as a royal prerogative, see, for example, Susan Doran, 'The Politics of Renaissance Europe', in *Shakespeare and Renaissance Europe*, ed. Andrew Hadfield and Paul Hammond (London: Arden Shakespeare, 2004), 21–52.

13 Adelman, *Suffocating Mothers*, 207.

14 *Bonduca*, in *The Dramatic Works in the Beaumont and Fletcher Canon*, ed. Fredson Bowers, vol. 4 (Cambridge: Cambridge University Press, 1979).

15 Aske, *Elizabetha Triumphans*, in Nichols, *Progresses of Elizabeth*, 3:458. For the comparison of Elizabeth to the historical Bonduca, see also Samantha Frénée-Hutchins, *Boudica's Odyssey in Early Modern England* (Farnham: Ashgate, 2014), 51–80 and Carolyn D. Williams, *Boudica and Her Stories: Narrative Transformations of a Warrior Queen* (Newark, NJ: University of Delaware Press, 2009), 191–94.

16 For readings of *Bonduca* in the Jacobean political context, see also Julie Crawford, 'Fletcher's *The Tragedie of Bonduca* and the Anxieties of the Masculine Government of James I', *Studies in English Literature, 1500–1900* 39, no. 2 (1999): 357–81; Mikalachki, *The Legacy of Boadicea*, 103–5; and Shepherd, *Amazons and Warrior Women*, 145–50.

17 Carroll Camden, 'The Elizabethan Imogen', *Rice Institute Pamphlets* 38 (1951): 11–12.

18 William Cobbett, *The Parliamentary History of England, from the Earliest Period to the Year 1803* (London: Longman, 1806), 1321.

19 Ann Thompson, 'Person and Office: The Case of Imogen, Princess of Britain', in *Literature and Nationalism*, ed. Vincent Newey and Ann Thompson (Liverpool: Liverpool University Press, 1991), 81.

20 See Helen Hackett, *Women and Romance Fiction in the English Renaissance* (Cambridge: Cambridge University Press, 2000), 27–31.

21 For the pervasive impact of Foxe's representation of Princess Elizabeth on Elizabethan and Jacobean discourse, ranging from historical works of Holinshed and John Speed to ballads, see esp. Freeman, 'Providence and Prescription', 27–55.

22 Georgianna Ziegler points out that 'the woman's room signifies her "self", and the man's forced or stealthy entry of this room constitutes a rape of her private space' and therefore 'though he [Iachimo] does not physically rape Imogen, we nevertheless feel that a rape has been committed in his voyeuristic intrusion on her privacy' ('My Lady's Chamber: Female Space, Female Chastity in Shakespeare', *Textual Practice* 4, no. 1 [1990]: 73, 78).

23 In addition to these dramatizations of the imperilled heroines, two of the most popular plays of the Jacobean period also feature imperilled princesses: Marina, who has to defend herself in the corrupting brothel in Shakespeare and George Wilkins's *Pericles* (1608) and Arethusa, who suffers the suit of a Spanish prince and his malicious plot to defame her, in Francis Beaumont and John Fletcher's *Philaster* (1609). Catherine Loomis also discusses several Jacobean plays which feature imperilled heroines (*The Death of Elizabeth I*, 131–33).

24 Averell, *A Meruailous Combat of Contrarieties*, C3r.

25 For the religious politics behind the popularity of the besieged Elizabeth, see also Alexandra Walsham, '"A Very Deborah?" The Myth of Elizabeth I as a Providential Monarch', in *The Myth of Elizabeth*, 143–68.

26 For the fascination of Elizabethans and Jacobeans with the popular image of the suffering Elizabeth, see, for example, Sara Mendelson, 'Popular Perceptions of Elizabeth', in *Elizabeth I: Always Her Own Free Woman*, ed. Carole Levin, Jo Eldridge Carney and Debra Barrett-Graves (Aldershot: Ashgate, 2003), 192–214.

27 For Jacobeans' deep-seated fear of the Catholic menace, see esp.
    Carol Z. Wiener, 'The Beleaguered Isle. A Study of Elizabethan
    and Early Jacobean Anti-Catholicism', *Past and Present* 51,
    no. 1 (1971): 27–62. For the revival of the popularity of
    Elizabeth as a besieged Protestant queen after the Gunpowder
    Plot, see Watkins, *Representing Elizabeth*, 25–35.

28 See, for example, Butler, ed., *Cymbeline*, 112n and
    J. M. Nosworthy, ed., *Cymbeline* (London: Arden Shakespeare,
    1955), 41n.

29 Donna B. Hamilton, *Shakespeare and the Politics of Protestant
    England* (Lexington: University Press of Kentucky, 1992), 129.
    For a similar reading of Innogen's religious significance, see Lila
    Geller, '*Cymbeline* and the Imagery of Covenant Theology',
    Studies in English Literature, 1500–1900 20, no. 2 (1980):
    241–55 (esp. 250).

30 Dekker, *The Whore of Babylon*, in *The Dramatic Works*, vol. 2.

31 See esp. Rhonda Lemke Sanford, 'A Room Not One's Own:
    Feminine Geography in *Cymbeline*', in *Playing the Globe: Genre
    and Geography in English Renaissance Drama*, ed. John Gillies
    and Virginia Mason Vaughan (Madison, WI: Fairleigh Dickinson
    University Press; London: Associated University Press, 1998),
    63–85 and Linda Woodbridge, 'Palisading the Elizabethan Body
    Politic', *Texas Studies in Literature and Language* 33, no. 3
    (1991): 327–54 (esp. 333–35). Sanford suggests a link between
    Innogen and the iconography of Elizabeth, such as the Ditchley
    portrait of Elizabeth, highlighting that both of their bodies are
    imagined as islands vulnerable to attack (64–65).

32 For the anachronistic representation of Rome as the
    contemporary Italy in *Cymbeline*, see Parker, 'Romance and
    Empire', 189–207 and Peter A. Parolin, 'Anachronistic Italy:
    Cultural Alliances and National Identity in *Cymbeline*',
    Shakespeare Studies 20 (2002): 188–215.

33 For the overview of the Oath of Allegiance of 1606 and the
    religious controversy that followed, see Conal Condren,
    *Argument and Authority in Early Modern England: The
    Presupposition of Oaths and Offices* (Cambridge: Cambridge
    University Press, 2006), 269–89 and Johann P. Sommerville,
    'Papalist Political Thought and the Controversy over the

Jacobean Oath of Allegiance', in *Catholics and the 'Protestant Nation': Religious Politics and Identity in Early Modern England*, ed. Ethan Shagan (Manchester: Manchester University Press, 2005), 162–84.

34 For polemical exchanges between Persons and Protestant polemists, see esp. Michael L. Carrafiello, *Robert Parsons and English Catholicism, 1580–1610* (Selinsgrove, PA: Susquehanna University Press; London: Associated University Press, 1998), 118–42. For a fuller account of the literary warfare that followed the Oath of Allegiance, see esp. Patterson, *King James VI and I and the Reunion of Christendom*, 75–123.

35 For the ways in which the religious controversy regarding the Oath of Allegiance features in Shakespeare's plays, see Hamilton, *Shakespeare and the Politics of Protestant England*, 128–62 and Arthur F. Kinney, *Lies like Truth: Shakespeare, Macbeth, and the Cultural Moment* (Detroit, MI: Wayne State University Press, 2001), 230–42. In particular, Hamilton focuses on the ways in which *Cymbeline* appropriates anti-Catholic rhetoric from the Oath of Allegiance controversy.

36 Robert Persons, *An Answere to the Fifth Part of Reportes* (Saint-Omer, 1606), K1v.

37 James VI and I, *Political Writings*, 91. Robert Persons, *The Iudgment of a Catholicke English-Man* (Saint-Omer, 1608), D1r–M2v. For Persons's attempt to revile Elizabeth, see also Victor Houliston, *Catholic Resistance in Elizabethan England: Robert Persons's Jesuit Polemic, 1580–1610* (Aldershot: Ashgate, 2007), 154–56; Loomis, *The Death of Elizabeth I*, 107–15; and Watkins, *Representing Elizabeth*, 21–25.

38 William Barlow, *An Answer to a Catholike English-Man* (London, 1609), K2r–K2v.

39 Barlow, *An Answer to a Catholike English-Man*, O1r.

40 *The Lady's Tragedy*, in *Thomas Middleton: The Collected Works*.

41 Julia Briggs, introduction to *The Lady's Tragedy*, in *Thomas Middleton: The Collected Works*, 837.

42 Butler, ed., *Cymbeline*, 121n. Butler also notes that Innogen's posture, 'serenely smiling and lying on a cushion as if asleep, resembles the modish taste in Jacobean funerary sculpture

for representing the dead in naturalistic attitudes' (190n), specifically associating her with a Jacobean-style marble effigy.

43 Fuller, *The Church History of Britain*, 5:258.

44 Fuller, *The Church History of Britain*, 5:258.

45 Holinshed, *Chronicles*, in Bullough, ed., *Sources*, 8:44.

46 Robert Pricket, *Vnto the Most High and Mightie Prince, His Soueraigne Lord King Iames. A Poore Subiect Sendeth, a Souldiors Resolution* (London, 1603), F3r.

47 Heather James, *Shakespeare's Troy: Drama, Politics, and the Translation of Empire* (Cambridge: Cambridge University Press, 1997), 179.

48 Brian Gibbons, *Shakespeare and Multiplicity* (Cambridge: Cambridge University Press, 1993), 23.

49 Marcus, *Puzzling Shakespeare*, 143.

50 Jonson, *Catiline His Conspiracy*, in *The Cambridge Edition*, vol. 4.

Epilogue

Although there were no simple, immediate solutions to the highly complex political issues of the period – the union of Scotland and England and relations with Spain and Catholicism – such solutions were sought and variously advocated by those who wilfully overlooked their complexity. Militant Protestants presented the revival of Elizabethan militarism as the only means to protect England from the Catholic powers, just as the Queen in *Cymbeline*, closely evoking the glorious memory of the victory over the Armada, advocates militarism as the only means to break the diplomatic deadlock with Rome. James I and his supporters, on the other hand, promoted peace and unity as the only solution to diplomatic as well as internal political issues. Despite the fact that Elizabeth I was a complex individual and her policy had been neither militant nor pacific, militant Protestants represented her as an ideal militant ruler and deployed that simplified image of Elizabeth to advance their cause, while James and the supporters of his policy deployed their own simplified version of Elizabeth as the paragon of a successful peace-minded ruler in order to justify James's political stance – something Shakespeare, in particular, I have argued, addresses in his plays. Through an examination of the ways in which the Jacobeans appropriated the representation of Elizabeth, I have argued that Shakespeare's plays effectively illuminate the complexity of the memory of Elizabeth and her reign as well as the complexity of Jacobean political issues.

While the Jacobeans struggled to appropriate the memory of Elizabeth, none was able to claim victory in the competition for representing Elizabeth. Elizabeth remained a multifaceted symbol for the Jacobeans as they continued to project their conflicting views of the past and the present onto her memory. In his plays, Shakespeare not only underlines the importance and centrality of the memory of Elizabeth to Jacobean political thinking but, through his complex representations of Macbeth's Scotland, Cleopatra, Volumnia, Cymbeline's Queen and Innogen, he also illuminates that complexity. Shakespeare's dramatic exploration of the politics of remembering Elizabeth demonstrates that the memory of Elizabeth remained a primary focus for ideological negotiation and competition during the first decade of James's reign.

When Elizabeth returned to the Jacobean stage as a character in *Henry VIII* at the end of the first decade of the Jacobean period, Shakespeare and Fletcher directly addressed the complex politics involved in representing her. As I noted in the Introduction, in the final act of the play Cranmer begins to praise Elizabeth as a terror to England's Catholic foes ('Her foes shake like a field of beaten corn, / And hang their heads with sorrow') but shifts his focus to the peaceful aspect of her reign ('In her days, every man shall ... sing / The merry songs of peace to all his neighbours'). He thus replicates the way in which James and his supporters attempted to appropriate the memory of Elizabeth:

CRANMER
   Nor shall this peace sleep with her, but as when
   The bird of wonder dies, the maiden phoenix,
   Her ashes new create another heir
   As great in admiration as herself,
   So shall she leave her blessedness to one,
   When heaven shall call her from this cloud of darkness,
   Who from the sacred ashes of her honour
   Shall star-like rise as great in fame as she was
   And so stand fixed.
                      (5.4.39–47)

Cranmer's prophetic declaration that Elizabeth will leave her legacy of peace to James – 'another heir' 'who from the sacred ashes of her honour / Shall star-like rise' – offers a stark contrast to the way in which, in Dekker's militant Protestant play *The Whore of Babylon*, James is praised as a successor to the militant Elizabeth/Titania: 'out of her ashes may / A second Phoenix rise ... his talent / May be so bonie and so large of gripe, / That it may shake all *Babilon*' (3.1.234–44).[1] Cranmer represents Elizabeth as England's 'maiden phoenix', who will metaphorically give birth to James so that her peace would not die with her. By doing so, Cranmer creates the sense of continuity between Elizabeth and James and between their foreign policies. In this regard, Cranmer's speech evokes the ways in which James and his supporters represented Elizabeth as the precursor of Jacobean peace in order to justify James's peace policy, a rhetorical and ideological strategy which also features in Shakespeare's earlier Jacobean plays. Yet the playwrights did not stop there; Cranmer goes on to problematize this political process of simplifying and appropriating the representation of Elizabeth by addressing the complexity of the memory of Elizabeth and her reign:

CRANMER
			Peace, plenty, love, truth, terror,
		That were the servants to this chosen infant,
		Shall then be his, and like a vine grow to him.
							(5.4.47–49)

Cranmer conflates 'peace' and 'terror' in one sentence, listing both of them as key elements of Elizabeth's reign. In their struggles to promote their simplified political visions, the Jacobeans attempted to attach either peace or terror to the memory of Elizabeth, yet in *Henry VIII* both elements are merged in a single account of Elizabeth. Consequently, the Elizabeth who emerges from Cranmer's speech is distinctly complex and elusive. By representing Elizabeth as a register of the complex views that Jacobeans held of the past and of the present, *Henry VIII* illuminates the complexity both of the representation of Elizabeth in the Jacobean period and of the Jacobean politics which informed that complexity.

As this brief analysis of Cranmer's speech shows, *Henry VIII* probes into the politics of the representation of Elizabeth during the first decade of James's reign, a politics which Shakespeare and his fellow playwrights had been examining throughout this period. Yet the most significant instance of the play's exploration of this theme occurs outside Cranmer's speech. We may recall that Shakespeare continuously draws our attention to a fundamental fact of the posthumous representation of Elizabeth, a fact most effectively addressed by Volumnia's total silence during her triumphal procession in *Coriolanus*. Volumnia, the mother whose son is to be brutally murdered in the next scene, remains meaningfully silent throughout the procession in which the Roman senators fashion her as a symbol of the triumph of peace over arms. Her silence, which adds a certain degree of unease to this spectacle of peace, evokes the ways in which Elizabeth was made to symbolize whatever political stance Jacobeans needed her to symbolize at any given moment, having no say in how they represented her. During the Jacobean period, Elizabeth seemed to speak to her former subjects, yet her voice was not her own.

Significantly, when Elizabeth appears on stage at the climax of *Henry VIII*, she appears as an infant who, obviously enough, cannot speak, thereby both visually and audibly enacting her inability to represent herself. The play thus reminds the audience that Elizabeth's political significance was authored by the Jacobeans themselves. Early modern staging practice would suggest that the infant Elizabeth was played by a doll.[2] In *Antony and Cleopatra*, Cleopatra had expressed her deep-seated fear that the Romans would personify her and display her in whatever way they pleased as if she were their 'puppet'. Indeed, in *Henry VIII*, the dead queen of England appears as one such puppet, a puppet which Jacobeans competed to appropriate for their own political causes.

Clearly, the sudden surge of nostalgic sentiment in 1612–13 was not the sole factor that prompted Shakespeare and Fletcher to represent Elizabeth in *Henry VIII*. In this book, through analysis of his drama, I have illustrated the ways in which Shakespeare examined the politics of representing Elizabeth during the first decade of James's reign. From this perspective, the representation of the doll Elizabeth as an intersection of Jacobeans' unresolved conflicting political views in *Henry VIII* is a fitting conclusion to his exploration of this theme. The appearance of Elizabeth as a non-speaking, non-human 'character' at the climax of *Henry VIII* was not, then, an exceptional – and certainly not the first – instance of Shakespeare's active engagement with the politics of nostalgia for Elizabeth, but its direct and logical consequence.

Notes

1 Dekker, *The Whore of Babylon*, in *The Dramatic Works*, vol. 2. For the representation of James as the phoenix born from Elizabeth's ashes, see, for example, Alan R. Young, 'The Phoenix Reborn: The Jacobean Appropriation of an Elizabethan Symbol', in *Resurrecting Elizabeth I*, 68–81.

2 For the use of props to personify infants on the early modern stage, see esp. Jennifer Higginbotham, *The Girlhood of Shakespeare's Sisters: Gender, Transgression, Adolescence* (Edinburgh: Edinburgh University Press, 2013), 104.

BIBLIOGRAPHY

Primary Works Cited

Averell, William. *A Meruailous Combat of Contrarieties*. London, 1588.

Bacon, Francis. *The Felicity of Queen Elizabeth*. London, 1651.

———. *The Works of Francis Bacon*. Edited by James Spedding, Robert Leslie Ellis and Douglas Denon Heath. Vol. 9. 1862. Cambridge: Cambridge University Press, 2011.

Barlow, William. *An Answer to a Catholike English-Man*. London, 1609.

Barnes, Barnabe. *The Diuils Charter*. London, 1607.

Beaumont, Francis, and John Fletcher. *The Dramatic Works in the Beaumont and Fletcher Canon*. Edited by Fredson Bowers. Vol. 4. Cambridge: Cambridge University Press, 1979.

Beringer, Joachim. *The Romane Conclaue*. London, 1609.

The Bible: That is, the Holy Scriptvres Conteined in the Olde and Newe Testament. London, 1587.

Bowyer, Robert. *The Parliamentary Diary of Robert Bowyer, 1606–1607*. Edited by David Harris Willson. Minneapolis: University of Minnesota Press, 1931.

Browne, William. *Britannia's Pastorals. The Second Booke*. London, 1616.

Chapman, George. *Bussy D'Ambois*. London, 1607.

Chapman, George, Ben Jonson and John Marston. *Eastward Ho*. Edited by R. W. Van Fossen. Manchester: Manchester University Press, 1979.

Chettle, Henry. *Englands Mourning Garment*. London, 1603.

Church of England. *A Psalme and Collect of Thankesgiuing*. London, 1588.

Cobbett, William. *The Parliamentary History of England, from the Earliest Period to the Year 1803*. London: Longman, 1806.

Crakanthorpe, Richard. *A Sermon at the Solemnizing of the Happie Inauguration of Our Most Gracious and Religious Soueraigne King Iames*. London, 1609.

Crashawe, William. Foreword to *Hepieíkeia*, by William Perkins, 1–9. Cambridge, 1604.

Daniel, Samuel. *A Panegyrike Congratulatorie to the Kings Maiestie*. London, 1603.

———. *The Poeticall Essayes of Sam. Danyel*. London, 1599.

———. *The Vision of the 12. Goddesses*. London, 1604.

Dekker, Thomas. *The Dramatic Works of Thomas Dekker*. Edited by Fredson Bowers. Vol. 2. Cambridge: Cambridge University Press, 1955.

———. *The Magnificent Entertainment Giuen to King Iames*. London, 1604.

———. *The Wonderfull Yeare*. London, 1603.

Deloney, Thomas. *A Ioyful New Ballad*. London, 1588.

Digges, Thomas, and Dudley Digges. *Foure Paradoxes, or Politique Discourses*. London, 1604.

Drayton, Michael. 'Rowlands Song in Praise of the Fairest Beta'. In *Englands Helicon*, edited by John Bodenham, D4r–E1r. London, 1600.

———. *The Works of Michael Drayton*. Edited by J. William Hebel. Vol. 4. Oxford: Blackwell, 1961.

Elizabeth I. *Elizabeth I: Collected Works*. Edited by Leah S. Marcus, Janel Mueller and Mary Beth Rose. Chicago: University of Chicago Press, 2000.

England and Wales. Parliament. House of Commons. *A Record of Some Worthy Proceedings in the Honourable, Wise, and Faithfull Howse of Commons in the Late Parliament*. Amsterdam, 1611.

Fenton, John. *King Iames His Welcome to London*. London, 1603.

Forset, Edward. *A Comparative Discourse of the Bodies Natural and Politique*. 1606. New York: Da Capo Press, 1973.

Fuller, Thomas. *The Church History of Britain, from the Birth of Jesus Christ until the Year M.DC.XLVIII*. Vol. 5. Oxford: Oxford University Press, 1845.

Gascoigne, George. *The Complete Works of George Gascoigne*. Edited by John W. Cunliffe. Vol. 2. New York: Greenwood Press, 1969.

Great Britain. Public Record Office. *Calendar of State Papers and Manuscripts, Relating to English Affairs, Existing in the Archives and Collections of Venice*. Edited by Rawdon Brown, George

Bentinck Lord, Horatio F. Brown and A. B. Hinds. 38 vols. London: Her Majesty's Stationery Office, 1864–1947.

Greville, Fulke. *The Prose Works of Fulke Greville, Lord Brooke*. Edited by John Gouws. Oxford: Clarendon Press, 1985.

Hakluyt, Richard. *The Principal Nauigations, Voyages, Traffiques and Discoueries of the English Nation*. London, 1599–1600.

Herbert, William. *Englands Sorrowe or, a Farewell to Essex*. London, 1606.

———. *A Prophesie of Cadwallader, Last King of the Britaines*. London, 1604.

Heywood, Thomas. *If You Know Not Me, You Know Nobody, Part I*. Edited by Madeleine Doran. London: Malone Society; Oxford: Oxford University Press, 1935.

———. *If You Know Not Me, You Know Nobody, Part II*. Edited by Madeleine Doran. London: Malone Society; Oxford: Oxford University Press, 1935.

———. *The Rape of Lucrece*. London, 1608.

———. *Troia Britanica: Or, Great Britaines Troy*. London, 1609.

Holinshed, Raphael. *Holinshed's Chronicles of England, Scotland and Ireland*. 6 vols. London: J. Johnson, 1807–8.

James VI and I. *King James VI and I: Selected Writings*. Edited by Neil Rhodes, Jennifer Richards and Joseph Marshall. Aldershot: Ashgate, 2003.

———. *Letters of King James VI & I*. Edited by G. P. V. Akrigg. Berkeley: University of California Press, 1984.

———. *Political Writings*. Edited by Johann P. Sommerville. Cambridge: Cambridge University Press, 1994.

———. *Stuart Royal Proclamations: Royal Proclamations of King James I, 1603–1625*. Edited by James F. Larkin and Paul L. Hughes. Vol. 1. Oxford: Clarendon Press, 1973.

Johnson, Robert. *Nova Britannia*. London, 1609.

Jonson, Ben. *The Cambridge Edition of the Works of Ben Jonson*. Edited by David Bevington, Martin Butler and Ian Donaldson. 7 vols. Cambridge: Cambridge University Press, 2012.

Leigh, William. *Queene Elizabeth, Paraleld in Her Princely Vertues, with Dauid, Iosua, and Hezekia*. London, 1612.

Lloyd, Lodowick. *The Tragicocomedie of Serpents*. London, 1607.

Markham, Gervase. *Honour in His Perfection*. London, 1624.

Marston, John. *The Selected Plays of John Marston*. Edited by Macdonald P. Jackson and Michael Neill. Cambridge: Cambridge University Press, 1986.

Mavericke, Radford. *Three Treatises Religiously Handled*. London, 1603.

Middleton, Thomas. *Thomas Middleton: The Collected Works*. Edited by Gary Taylor and John Lavagnino. Oxford: Oxford University Press, 2007.

Milward, John. *Iacobs Great Day of Trouble, and Deliuerance. A Sermon Preached at Pauls Crosse, the Fifth of August 1607*. London, 1610.

A Mournefull Dittie, Entituled Elizabeths Losse. London, 1603.

Mulcaster, Richard. *The Translation of Certaine Latine Verses Written uppon Her Majesties Death, Called 'A Comforting Complaint'*. London, 1603.

Niccols, Richard. *Expicedium*. London, 1603.

Nichols, John. *John Nichols's The Progresses and Public Processions of Queen Elizabeth I: A New Edition of the Early Modern Sources*. Edited by Elizabeth Goldring, Faith Eales, Elizabeth Clarke and Jayne Elisabeth Archer. 5 vols. Oxford: Oxford University Press, 2014.

———. *The Progresses, Processions, and Magnificent Festivities of King James the First, His Royal Consort, Family, and Court*. Vol. 2. London: J. B. Nichols, 1828.

Nichols, Josias. *The Plea of the Innocent*. London, 1602.

Nixon, Anthony. *Elizaes Memoriall. King Iames His Arriuall. And Romes Downefall*. London, 1603.

The Parliamentary or Constitutional History of England: From the Earliest Times, to the Restoration of King Charles II. 2nd ed. Vol. 5. London: J. and R. Tonson, 1751.

Persons, Robert. *An Answere to the Fifth Part of Reportes Lately Set Forth by Syr Edward Cooke*. Saint-Omer, 1606.

———. *The Iudgment of a Catholicke English-Man*, Saint-Omer, 1608.

Petowe, Henry. *Elizabetha Quasi Viuens*. London, 1603.

Plutarch. *The Lives of the Noble Grecians and Romaines*. Translated by Thomas North. London, 1603.

Pricket, Robert. *Honors Fame in Triumph Riding. Or, the Life and Death of the Late Honorable Earle of Essex*. London, 1604.

———. *A Souldiers Wish vnto His Soveraigne Lord King Iames*. London, 1603.

———. *Vnto the Most High and Mightie Prince, His Soueraigne Lord King Iames. A Poore Subiect Sendeth, a Souldiors Resolution*. London, 1603.

Ralegh, Walter. *The Poems of Sir Walter Ralegh: A Historical Edition*. Edited by Michael Rudick. Tempe: Arizona Center for Medieval and Renaissance Studies in conjunction with Renaissance English Text Society, 1999.

Raymonde, Henry. *The Maiden Queene*. London, 1607.

Rowley, Samuel. *When You See Me, You Know Me*. Edited by F. P. Wilson. London: Malone Society; Oxford: Oxford University Press, 1952.

Shakespeare, William. *Antony and Cleopatra*. Edited by John Wilders. London: Arden Shakespeare, 1995.

———. *The Comedy of Errors*. Edited by Kent Cartwright. London: Arden Shakespeare, 2016.

———. *Coriolanus*. Edited by Peter Holland. London: Arden Shakespeare, 2013.

———. *Cymbeline*. Edited by Valerie Wayne. London: Arden Shakespeare, 2017.

———. *Julius Caesar*. Edited by David Daniell. London: Arden Shakespeare, 1998.

———. *King Edward III*. Edited by Richard Proudfoot and Nicola Bennett. London: Arden Shakespeare, 2017.

———. *King Henry IV, Part 2*. Edited by James C. Bulman. London: Arden Shakespeare, 2016.

———. *King Henry V*. Edited by T. W. Craik. London: Arden Shakespeare, 1995.

———. *King Henry VIII*. Edited by Gordon McMullan. London: Arden Shakespeare, 2000.

———. *King Richard III*. Edited by James R. Siemon. London: Arden Shakespeare, 2009.

———. *Macbeth*. Edited by Sandra Clark and Pamela Mason. London: Arden Shakespeare, 2015.

———. *A Midsummer Night's Dream*. Edited by Sukanta Chaudhuri. London: Arden Shakespeare, 2017.

———. *Mr. William Shakespeares Comedies, Histories, and Tragedies Published According to the True Originall Copies*. London, 1623.

———. *Shakespeare's Sonnets*. Edited by Katherine Duncan-Jones. London: Arden Shakespeare, 2010.

Sidney, Mary. *The Tragedie of Antonie. Doone into English by the Countesse of Pembroke*. London, 1595.

Sorocold, Thomas. *Supplications of Saints*. London, 1612.

Speed, John. *The Theatre of the Empire of Great Britaine*. London, 1612.

Spenser, Edmund. *Colin Clouts Come Home Againe*. London, 1595.

———. *The Faerie Queene*. Edited by A. C. Hamilton. Rev. 2nd ed. Harlow: Pearson Longman, 2007.

Stow, John. *The Annales of England*. London, 1592.

Weepe with Ioy. London, 1603.

The Whole Prophesie of Scotland, England, and Somepart of France, and Denmark. London, 1603.

Secondary Works Cited

Adams, Simon. 'Spain or the Netherlands? The Dilemmas of Early Stuart Foreign Policy'. In *Before the English Civil War: Essays on Early Stuart Politics and Government*, edited by Howard Tomlinson, 79–101. London: Macmillan, 1983.

Adelman, Janet. *Suffocating Mothers: Fantasies of Maternal Origin in Shakespeare's Plays, 'Hamlet' to 'The Tempest'*. London: Routledge, 1992.

Aebischer, Pascale. 'The Properties of Whiteness: Renaissance Cleopatras from Jodelle to Shakespeare'. *Shakespeare Survey* 65 (2012): 221–38.

Alker, Sharon, and Holly Faith Nelson. '*Macbeth*, the Jacobean Scot, and the Politics of the Union'. *Studies in English Literature, 1500–1900* 47, no. 2 (2007): 379–401.

Axton, Marie. *The Queen's Two Bodies: Drama and the Elizabethan Succession*. London: Royal Historical Society, 1977.

Barkan, Leonard. *Nature's Work of Art: The Human Body as Image of the World*. New Haven, CT: Yale University Press, 1975.

Barroll, Leeds. 'The Chronology of Shakespeare's Jacobean Plays and the Dating of *Antony and Cleopatra*'. In *Essays on Shakespeare*, edited by Gordon Ross Smith, 115–62. University Park: Pennsylvania State University Press, 1965.

———. *Politics, Plague, and Shakespeare's Theater: The Stuart Years*. Ithaca, NY: Cornell University Press, 1991.

Barton, Anne. *Ben Jonson, Dramatist*. Cambridge: Cambridge University Press, 1984.

———. 'Harking Back to Elizabeth: Ben Jonson and Caroline Nostalgia'. *English Literary History* 48, no. 4 (1981): 706–31.

Bayer, Mark. *Theatre, Community, and Civic Engagement in Jacobean London*. Iowa City: University of Iowa Press, 2011.

Bergeron, David M. *Shakespeare's Romances and the Royal Family*. Lawrence: University Press of Kansas, 1985.

Bliss, Lee, ed. *Coriolanus*. By William Shakespeare. Cambridge: Cambridge University Press, 2000.

Blumenfeld-Kosinski, Renate. *Not of Woman Born: Representations of Caesarean Birth in Medieval and Renaissance Culture*. Ithaca, NY: Cornell University Press, 1990.

Box, Ian. 'Politics and Philosophy: Bacon on the Values of War and Peace'. *The Seventeenth Century* 7 (1992): 113–27.

Bradbrook, M. C. 'The Sources of *Macbeth*'. *Shakespeare Survey* 4 (1951): 35–48.

Braunmuller, A. R., ed. *Macbeth*. By William Shakespeare. Cambridge: Cambridge University Press, 2008.

Brinkley, Roberta Florence. *Arthurian Legend in the Seventeenth Century*. New York: Octagon, 1967.

Brockbank, Philip, ed. *Coriolanus*. By William Shakespeare. London: Arden Shakespeare, 1976.

Brower, Reuben A. *Hero and Saint: Shakespeare and the Graeco-Roman Heroic Tradition*. Oxford: Clarendon Press, 1971.

Brown, Keith M. 'The Vanishing Emperor: British Kingship and Its Decline'. In *Scots and Britons: Scottish Political Thought and the Union of 1603*, edited by Roger A. Mason, 58–88. Cambridge: Cambridge University Press, 1994.

Bullough, Geoffrey, ed. *Narrative and Dramatic Sources of Shakespeare*. 8 vols. London: Routledge; New York: Columbia University Press, 1957–75.

Butler, Martin, ed. *Cymbeline*. By William Shakespeare. Cambridge: Cambridge University Press, 2005.

———. *The Stuart Court Masque and Political Culture*. Cambridge: Cambridge University Press, 2008.

Camden, Carroll. 'The Elizabethan Imogen'. *Rice Institute Pamphlets* 38 (1951): 1–17.

Cantor, Paul A. *Shakespeare's Rome: Republic and Empire*. Ithaca, NY: Cornell University Press, 1976.

Carrafiello, Michael L. *Robert Parsons and English Catholicism, 1580–1610*. Selinsgrove, PA: Susquehanna University Press; London: Associated University Press, 1998.

Chamberlain, Stephanie. 'Fantasizing Infanticide: Lady Macbeth and the Murdering Mother in Early Modern England'. *College Literature* 32 (2005): 72–91.

Clare, Janet. '*Art Made Tongue-Tied by Authority*': *Elizabethan and Jacobean Dramatic Censorship*. Manchester: Manchester University Press, 1990.

Coch, Christine. '"Mother of My Contreye": Elizabeth I and Tudor Constructions of Motherhood'. *English Literary Renaissance* 26, no. 3 (1996): 423–50.

Condren, Conal. *Argument and Authority in Early Modern England: The Presupposition of Oaths and Offices*. Cambridge: Cambridge University Press, 2006.

Conklin, Willet T. 'Shakespeare, *Coriolanus*, and Essex'. *Studies in English* 11 (1932): 42–47.

Cooper, Helen. *The English Romance in Time: Transforming Motifs from Geoffrey of Monmouth to the Death of Shakespeare*. Oxford: Oxford University Press, 2004.

Craig, W. J., and R. H. Case, eds. *The Tragedy of Coriolanus*. By William Shakespeare. London: Arden Shakespeare, 1922.

Crawford, Julie. 'Fletcher's *The Tragedie of Bonduca* and the Anxieties of the Masculine Government of James I'. *Studies in English Literature, 1500–1900* 39, no. 2 (1999): 357–81.

Cressy, David. *Bonfires and Bells: National Memory and the Protestant Calendar in Elizabethan and Stuart England*. London: Weidenfeld and Nicolson, 1989.

Croft, Pauline. *King James*. Basingstoke: Palgrave Macmillan, 2003.

Curran, Kevin. *Marriage, Performance, and Politics at the Jacobean Court*. Farnham: Ashgate, 2009.

David, Richard. *Shakespeare in the Theatre*. Cambridge: Cambridge University Press, 1978.

Davies, H. Neville. 'Jacobean *Antony and Cleopatra*'. *Shakespeare Studies* 17 (1985): 123–58.

Davies, Rowena. '"Alone th'Arabian Bird": Imogen as Elizabeth I?' *Notes and Queries* 26 (1979): 137–40.

Dobin, Howard. *Merlin's Disciples: Prophecy, Poetry, and Power in Renaissance England*. Stanford, CA: Stanford University Press, 1990.

Dobson, Michael, and Nicola J. Watson. *England's Elizabeth: An Afterlife in Fame and Fantasy*. Oxford: Oxford University Press, 2002.

Doran, Susan. 'James VI and the English Succession'. In *James VI and I: Ideas, Authority, and Government*, edited by Ralph Houlbrooke, 25–42. Aldershot: Ashgate, 2006.

———. 'Polemic and Prejudice: A Scottish King for an English Throne'. In *Doubtful and Dangerous: The Question of Succession in Late Elizabethan England*, edited by Susan Doran and Paulina Kewes, 215–35. Manchester: Manchester University Press, 2016.

———. 'The Politics of Renaissance Europe'. In *Shakespeare and Renaissance Europe*, edited by Andrew Hadfield and Paul Hammond, 21–52. London: Arden Shakespeare, 2004.

Ehrenreich, Barbara, and Deirdre English. *Witches, Midwives and Nurses: A History of Women Healers*. New York: Feminist Press, 1973.

Erskine-Hill, Howard. *The Augustan Idea in English Literature*. London: Edward Arnold, 1983.

Escobedo, Andrew. 'From Britannia to England: *Cymbeline* and the Beginning of Nations'. *Shakespeare Quarterly* 59, no. 1 (2008): 60–87.

Ferguson, Arthur B. *The Chivalric Tradition in Renaissance England*. Washington: Folger Shakespeare Library, 1986.

Freeman, Thomas S. 'Providence and Prescription: The Account of Elizabeth in Foxe's "Book of Martyrs"'. In *The Myth of Elizabeth*, edited by Susan Doran and Thomas S. Freeman, 27–55. Basingstoke: Palgrave Macmillan, 2003.

Frénée-Hutchins, Samantha. *Boudica's Odyssey in Early Modern England*. Farnham: Ashgate, 2014.

Frye, Susan. *Elizabeth I: The Competition for Representation*. Oxford: Oxford University Press, 1993.

Galloway, Bruce. *The Union of England and Scotland, 1603–1608*. Edinburgh: John Donald, 1986.

Garcia, Ramona. '"Most Wicked Superstition and Idolatry": John Foxe, His Predecessors and the Development of an Anti-Catholic Polemic in the Sixteenth-Century Accounts of the Reign of Mary I'. In *John Foxe at Home and Abroad*, edited by David Loades, 79–87. Aldershot: Ashgate, 2004.

Geller, Lila. '*Cymbeline* and the Imagery of Covenant Theology'. *Studies in English Literature, 1500–1900* 20, no. 2 (1980): 241–55.

Gibbons, Brian. *Shakespeare and Multiplicity*. Cambridge: Cambridge University Press, 1993.

Goldberg, Jonathan. *James I and the Politics of Literature: Jonson, Shakespeare, Donne, and Their Contemporaries*. Baltimore, MD: Johns Hopkins University Press, 1983.

Goodman, Jennifer R. *Chivalry and Exploration, 1298–1630*. Woodbridge: Boydell Press, 1998.

Gordon, D. J. 'Rubens and the Whitehall Ceiling'. In *The Renaissance Imagination*, edited by Stephen Orgel, 24–50. Berkeley: University of California Press, 1975.

Grant, Teresa. 'History in the Making: The Case of Samuel Rowley's *When You See Me You Know Me* (1604/5)'. In *English Historical Drama, 1500–1660: Forms outside the Canon*, edited by Barbara Ravelhofer, 125–57. Basingstoke: Palgrave Macmillan, 2008.

———. '"Thus like a Nun, Not like a Princess Born": Dramatic Representations of Mary Tudor in the Early Years of the Seventeenth Century'. In *Mary Tudor: Old and New Perspectives*, edited by Susan Doran and Thomas S. Freeman, 62–77. Basingstoke: Palgrave Macmillan, 2011.

Griffin, Alice V. *Pageantry on the Shakespearean Stage*. New Haven, CT: College and University Press, 1951.

Hackett, Helen. *Shakespeare and Elizabeth: The Meeting of Two Myths*. Princeton, NJ: Princeton University Press, 2009.

———. *Women and Romance Fiction in the English Renaissance*. Cambridge: Cambridge University Press, 2000.

Hale, David George. *The Body Politic: A Political Metaphor in Renaissance English Literature*. The Hague: Mouton, 1971.

Hamilton, Donna B. *Shakespeare and the Politics of Protestant England*. Lexington: University Press of Kentucky, 1992.

Harbage, Alfred. *Annals of English Drama, 975–1700: An Analytical Record of All Plays, Extant or Lost, Chronologically Arranged and Indexed by Authors, Titles, Dramatic Companies &c*. 3rd ed. Revised by Samuel Schoenbaum and Sylvia Stoler Wagonheim. London: Routledge, 1989.

Harris, Jonathan Gil. *Foreign Bodies and the Body Politic: Discourses of Social Pathology in Early Modern England*. Cambridge: Cambridge University Press, 1998.

Hays, Michael L. *Shakespearean Tragedy as Chivalric Romance: Rethinking 'Macbeth', 'Hamlet', 'Othello', and 'King Lear'*. Woodbridge: D. S. Brewer, 2003.

Higginbotham, Jennifer. *The Girlhood of Shakespeare's Sisters: Gender, Transgression, Adolescence*. Edinburgh: Edinburgh University Press, 2013.

Holbrook, Peter. 'Jacobean Masques and the Jacobean Peace'. In *The Politics of the Stuart Court Masque*, edited by David Bevington and Peter Holbrook, 67–87. Cambridge: Cambridge University Press, 1998.

Holland, Norman. 'Macbeth as Hibernal Giant'. *Literature and Psychology* 10 (1960): 37–38.

Holloway, John. *The Story of the Night: Studies in Shakespeare's Major Tragedies*. London: Routledge, 1961.

Hope, Jonathan. *The Authorship of Shakespeare's Plays: A Socio-Linguistic Study*. Cambridge: Cambridge University Press, 1994.

Houliston, Victor. *Catholic Resistance in Elizabethan England: Robert Persons's Jesuit Polemic, 1580–1610*. Aldershot: Ashgate, 2007.

Jaech, Sharon L. Jansen. 'Political Prophecy and Macbeth's "Sweet Bodements"'. *Shakespeare Quarterly* 34, no. 3 (1983): 290–97.

James, Heather. *Shakespeare's Troy: Drama, Politics, and the Translation of Empire*. Cambridge: Cambridge University Press, 1997.

James, Mervyn. *Society, Politics and Culture: Studies in Early Modern England*. Cambridge: Cambridge University Press, 1986.

Jankowski, Theodora A. *Women in Power in the Early Modern Drama*. Urbana: University of Illinois Press, 1992.

Jones, Emrys. 'Stuart *Cymbeline*'. *Essays in Criticism* 11 (1961): 84–99.

Kahn, Coppélia. *Man's Estate: Masculine Identity in Shakespeare*. Berkeley: University of California Press, 1981.

Kantorowicz, Ernst H. *The King's Two Bodies: A Study in Mediaeval Political Theology*. Princeton, NJ: Princeton University Press, 1957.

Kerrigan, John. *Archipelagic English: Literature, History, and Politics, 1603–1707*. Oxford: Oxford University Press, 2008.
———, ed. *The Sonnets and A Lover's Complaint*. By William Shakespeare. London: Penguin Books, 1986.

Kewes, Paulina. '"A Fit Memorial for the Times to Come … ": Admonition and Topical Application in Mary Sidney's *Antonius* and Samuel Daniel's *Cleopatra*'. *Review of English Studies* 63 (2012): 243–64.

Kiefer, Frederick. *Shakespeare's Visual Theatre: Staging the Personified Characters*. Cambridge: Cambridge University Press, 2003.

King, Maureen. 'The Essex Myth in Jacobean England'. In *The Accession of James I: Historical and Cultural Consequences*, edited by Glenn Burgess, Rowland Wymer and Jason Lawrence, 177–86. Basingstoke: Palgrave Macmillan, 2006.

Kinney, Arthur F. *Lies like Truth: Shakespeare, Macbeth, and the Cultural Moment*. Detroit, MI: Wayne State University Press, 2001.

———. 'Scottish History, the Union of the Crowns and the Issue of Right Rule: Shakespeare's *Macbeth*'. In *Renaissance Culture in Context: Theory and Practice*, edited by Jean R. Brink and William F. Gentrup, 18–53. Aldershot: Scolar Press, 1993.

Knight, G. Wilson. *The Crown of Life: Essays in Interpretation of Shakespeare's Final Plays*. London: Methuen, 1948.

La Belle, Jenijoy. '"A Strange Infirmity": Lady Macbeth's Amenorrhea'. *Shakespeare Quarterly* 31, no. 3 (1980): 381–86.

Laoutaris, Chris. *Shakespearean Maternities: Crises of Conception in Early Modern England*. Edinburgh: Edinburgh University Press, 2008.

Latham, Grace. 'On Volumnia'. In *Transactions of New Shakspere Society, 1887–92*, 69–90. London: Kegan Paul, 1887.

Lee, Maurice, Jr. *James I and Henri IV: An Essay in English Foreign Policy, 1603–1610*. Urbana: University of Illinois Press, 1970.

Leggatt, Alexander. *Jacobean Public Theatre*. London: Routledge, 1992.

Levack, Brian P. *The Formation of the British State: England, Scotland, and the Union, 1603–1707*. Oxford: Clarendon Press, 1987.

Lewalski, Barbara Kiefer, *Writing Women in Jacobean England*. Cambridge, MA: Harvard University Press, 1993.

Linton, Joan Pong. *The Romance of the New World: Gender and the Literary Formations of English Colonialism*. Cambridge: Cambridge University Press, 1998.

Lockyer, Roger. *James VI and I*. London: Longman, 1998.

Loomis, Catherine. *The Death of Elizabeth I: Remembering and Reconstructing the Virgin Queen*. New York: Palgrave Macmillan, 2010.

Luckyj, Christina. *'A Moving Rhetoricke': Gender and Silence in Early Modern England*. Manchester: Manchester University Press, 2002.

———. 'Volumnia's Silence'. *Studies in English Literature, 1500–1900* 31, no. 2 (1991): 327–42.

Lyle, Emily B. 'The "Twofold Balls and Treble Scepters" in *Macbeth*'. *Shakespeare Quarterly* 28, no. 4 (1977): 516–19.

MacCallum, M. W. *Shakespeare's Roman Plays and Their Background*. London: Macmillan, 1910.

Marcus, Leah S. *Puzzling Shakespeare: Local Reading and Its Discontents*. Berkeley: University of California Press, 1988.

Margeson, John, ed. *The Conspiracy and Tragedy of Charles Duke of Byron*. By George Chapman. Manchester: Manchester University Press, 1988.

Marshall, Tristan. *Theatre and Empire: Great Britain on the London Stages under James VI and I*. Manchester: Manchester University Press, 2000.

Marx, Steven. 'Shakespeare's Pacifism'. *Renaissance Quarterly* 45, no. 1 (1992): 49–95.

McCabe, Richard. *Spenser's Monstrous Regiment: Elizabethan Ireland and the Poetics of Difference*. Oxford: Oxford University Press, 2002.

McGuire, Philip C. *Speechless Dialect: Shakespeare's Open Silences*. Berkeley: University of California Press, 1985.

McManus, Clare. *Women on the Renaissance Stage: Anna of Denmark and Female Masquing in the Stuart Court (1590–1619)*. Manchester: Manchester University Press, 2002.

Mehl, Dieter. 'The Late Queen on the Public Stage: Thomas Heywood's *If You Know Not Me You Know Nobody, Parts I and II*'. In *Queen Elizabeth I: Past and Present*, edited by Christa Jansohn, 153–71. Münster: LIT, 2004.

Mendelson, Sara. 'Popular Perceptions of Elizabeth'. In *Elizabeth I: Always Her Own Free Woman*, edited by Carole Levin, Jo Eldridge Carney and Debra Barrett-Graves, 192–214. Aldershot: Ashgate, 2003.

Mikalachki, Jodi. *The Legacy of Boadicea: Gender and Nation in Early Modern England*. London: Routledge, 1998.

Miller, Shannon. 'Topicality and Subversion in William Shakespeare's *Coriolanus*'. *Studies in English Literature, 1500–1900* 32, no. 2 (1992): 287–310.

Morris, Helen. 'Queen Elizabeth I "Shadowed" in Cleopatra'. *Huntington Library Quarterly* 32 (1969): 271–78.

Muir, Kenneth. 'The Background of *Coriolanus*'. *Shakespeare Quarterly* 10, no. 2 (1959): 137–45.

Mullaney, Steven. 'Mourning and Misogyny: *Hamlet, The Revenger's Tragedy*, and the Final Progress of Elizabeth I, 1600–1607'. *Shakespeare Quarterly* 45, no. 2 (1994): 139–62.

Munroe, Jennifer. *Gender and the Garden in Early Modern English Literature*. Aldershot: Ashgate, 2008.

Neill, Michael, ed. *The Tragedy of Anthony and Cleopatra*. By William Shakespeare. Oxford: Oxford University Press, 1994.

Norbrook, David. '*Macbeth* and the Politics of Historiography'. In *The Politics of Discourse: The Literature and History of Seventeenth-Century England*, edited by Kevin Sharpe and Steven Zwicker, 78–116. Berkeley: University of California Press, 1987.

———. *Poetry and Politics in the English Renaissance*. Rev. ed. Oxford: Oxford University Press, 2002.

Nosworthy, J. M., ed. *Cymbeline*. By William Shakespeare. London: Arden Shakespeare, 1955.

O'Dowd, Michael J., and Elliot E. Philipp. *The History of Obstetrics and Gynaecology*. London: Parthenon, 1994.

Onions, C. T. 'Animals'. In *Shakespeare's England: An Account of the Life and Manners of His Age*, edited by Sidney Lee and C. T. Onions, vol. 1, 457–99. Oxford: Clarendon Press, 1916.

Orgel, Stephen. 'Macbeth and the Antic Round'. *Shakespeare Survey* 52 (1999): 143–53.

Orlin, Cowen Lena. 'The Fictional Families of Elizabeth I'. In *Political Rhetoric, Power, and Renaissance Women*, edited by Carole Levin and Patricia A. Sullivan, 85–110. Albany: State University of New York Press, 1995.

The Oxford English Dictionary. 2nd ed. Oxford: Clarendon Press; Oxford; Oxford University Press, 1989.

Parker, Patricia. 'Romance and Empire: Anachronistic *Cymbeline*'. In *Unfolded Tales: Essays on Renaissance Romance*, edited by George M. Logan and Gordon Teskey, 189–207. Ithaca, NY: Cornell University Press, 1989.

Parker, R. B., ed. *The Tragedy of Coriolanus*. By William Shakespeare. Oxford: Clarendon Press, 1994.

Parolin, Peter A. 'Anachronistic Italy: Cultural Alliances and National Identity in *Cymbeline*'. *Shakespeare Studies* 20 (2002): 188–215.

Parry, Graham. *The Golden Age Restor'd: The Culture of the Stuart Court, 1603–42*. Manchester: Manchester University Press, 1981.

Patterson, W. B. *King James VI and I and the Reunion of Christendom*. Cambridge: Cambridge University Press, 1997.

Paul, Henry Neill. *The Royal Play of 'Macbeth': When, Why, and How It Was Written by Shakespeare*. New York: Macmillan, 1950.

Perry, Curtis. *The Making of Jacobean Culture: James I and the Renegotiation of Elizabethan Literary Practice*. Cambridge: Cambridge University Press, 1997.

Pettet, E. C. '*Coriolanus* and the Midlands Insurrection of 1607'. *Shakespeare Survey* 3 (1950): 34–42.

Richardson, Lisa. 'Elizabeth in Arcadia: Fulke Greville and John Hayward's Construction of Elizabeth, 1610–12'. In *The Myth of Elizabeth*, edited by Susan Doran and Thomas S. Freeman, 99–119. Basingstoke: Palgrave Macmillan, 2003.

Rinehart, Keith. 'Shakespeare's Cleopatra and England's Elizabeth'. *Shakespeare Quarterly* 23, no. 1 (1972): 81–86.

Ripley, John. '*Coriolanus' on Stage in England and America, 1609–1994*. Madison, WI: Fairleigh Dickinson University Press, 1998.

Rosen, William. *Shakespeare and the Craft of Tragedy*. Cambridge, MA: Harvard University Press, 1960.

Rosenberg, Marvin. *The Masks of 'Anthony and Cleopatra'*. Edited by Mary Rosenberg. Newark, NJ: University of Delaware Press, 2006.

Sanford, Rhonda Lemke. 'A Room Not One's Own: Feminine Geography in *Cymbeline*'. In *Playing the Globe: Genre and Geography in English Renaissance Drama*, edited by John Gillies and Virginia Mason Vaughan, 63–85. Madison, WI: Fairleigh Dickinson University Press; London: Associated University Press, 1998.

Schwarz, Kathryn. 'Amazon Reflections in the Jacobean Queen's Masque'. *Studies in English Literature, 1500–1900* 35, no. 2 (1995): 293–319.

Sharpe, Jim. 'Social Strain and Social Dislocation, 1585–1603'. In *The Reign of Elizabeth I: Court and Culture in the Last Decade*, edited by John Guy, 192–211. Cambridge: Cambridge University Press, 1995.

Shepherd, Simon. *Amazons and Warrior Women: Varieties of Feminism in Seventeenth-Century Drama*. Brighton: Harvester Press, 1981.

Shuger, Debora Kuller. *Habits of Thought in the English Renaissance: Religion, Politics, and the Dominant Culture*. Berkeley: University of California Press, 1990.

Simonds, Peggy Muñoz. '*Coriolanus* and the Myth of Juno and Mars'. *Mosaic* 18, no. 2 (1985): 33–50.

Smuts, R. Malcolm. *Court Culture and the Origins of a Royalist Tradition in Early Stuart England*. Philadelphia: University of Pennsylvania Press, 1987.

Sommerville, Johann P. 'Papalist Political Thought and the Controversy over the Jacobean Oath of Allegiance'. In *Catholics and the 'Protestant Nation': Religious Politics and Identity in Early Modern England*, edited by Ethan Shagan, 162–84. Manchester: Manchester University Press, 2005.

Spates, William. 'Shakespeare and the Irony of Early Modern Disease Metaphor and Metonymy'. In *Rhetorics of Bodily Disease and Health in Medieval and Early Modern England*, edited by Jennifer C. Vaught, 155–70. Farnham: Ashgate, 2010.

Spevack, Marvin. *The Harvard Concordance to Shakespeare*. Hildesheim: Olms, 1973.

Sprengnether, Madelon. 'Annihilating Intimacy in *Coriolanus*'. In *Women in the Middle Ages and the Renaissance: Literary and Historical Perspectives*, edited by Mary Beth Rose, 89–111. Syracuse, NY: Syracuse University Press, 1986.

Spurgeon, Caroline F. E. *Shakespeare's Imagery and What It Tells Us*. Cambridge: Cambridge University Press, 1935.

Stallybrass, Peter. 'Patriarchal Territories: The Body Enclosed'. In *Rewriting the Renaissance: The Discourses of Sexual Difference in Early Modern Europe*, edited by Margaret W. Ferguson, Maureen Quilligan and Nancy J. Vickers, 123–42. Chicago: University of Chicago Press, 1986.

Taylor, Rupert. *The Political Prophecy in England*. New York: Columbia University Press, 1911.

Tennenhouse, Leonard. *Power on Display: The Politics of Shakespeare's Genres*. London: Methuen, 1986.

Thomas, Keith. *Religion and the Decline of Magic*. New York: Scribner, 1971.

Thompson, Ann. 'Person and Office: The Case of Imogen, Princess of Britain'. In *Literature and Nationalism*, edited by Vincent Newey and Ann Thompson, 76–87. Liverpool: Liverpool University Press, 1991.

Vickers, Brian. *Shakespeare, Co-Author: A Historical Study of Five Collaborative Plays*. Oxford: Oxford University Press, 2004.

Walker, Julia M. 'Bones of Contention: Posthumous Images of Elizabeth and Stuart Politics'. In *Dissing Elizabeth: Negative Representations of Gloriana*, edited by Julia M. Walker, 252–76. Durham, NC: Duke University Press, 1998.

———, ed. *Dissing Elizabeth: Negative Representations of Gloriana*. Durham, NC: Duke University Press, 1998.

———. *Medusa's Mirrors: Spenser, Shakespeare, Milton, and the Metamorphosis of the Female Self*. Newark, NJ: University of Delaware Press, 1998.

———. 'Reading the Tombs of Elizabeth I'. *English Literary Renaissance* 26, no. 3 (1996): 510–30.

Walsham, Alexandra. '"A Very Deborah?" The Myth of Elizabeth I as a Providential Monarch'. In *The Myth of Elizabeth*, edited by Susan Doran and Thomas S. Freeman, 143–68. Basingstoke: Palgrave Macmillan, 2003.

Watkins, John. *Representing Elizabeth in Stuart England: Literature, History, Sovereignty*. Cambridge: Cambridge University Press, 2002.

Watson, Robert N. *Shakespeare and the Hazards of Ambition*. Cambridge, MA: Harvard University Press, 1984.

Wells, Robin Headlam. *Shakespeare on Masculinity*. Cambridge: Cambridge University Press, 2000.

Wells, Stanley, and Gary Taylor. *William Shakespeare: A Textual Companion*. Oxford: Clarendon Press, 1987.

Wickham, Glynne. 'Riddle and Emblem: A Study in the Dramatic Structure of *Cymbeline*'. In *English Renaissance Studies: Presented to Dame Helen Gardner in Honour of Her Seventieth Birthday*, edited by John Carey, 94–113. Oxford: Clarendon Press, 1980.

Wiener, Carol Z. 'The Beleaguered Isle. A Study of Elizabethan and Early Jacobean Anti-Catholicism'. *Past and Present* 51, no. 1 (1971): 27–62.

Williams, Carolyn D. *Boudica and Her Stories: Narrative Transformations of a Warrior Queen*. Newark, NJ: University of Delaware Press, 2009.

Williamson, J. W. *The Myth of the Conqueror: Prince Henry Stuart, a Study of Seventeenth Century Personation*. New York: AMS Press, 1978.

Wills, Garry. *Witches and Jesuits: Shakespeare's 'Macbeth'*. Oxford: Oxford University Press, 1996.

Wilson, Elkin Calhoun. *England's Eliza*. Cambridge, MA: Harvard University Press, 1939.

Wilson, Frank Percy. *The Plague in Shakespeare's London*. Oxford: Clarendon Press, 1927.

Woodbridge, Linda. 'Palisading the Elizabethan Body Politic'. *Texas Studies in Literature and Language* 33, no. 3 (1991): 327–54.

Woodcock, Matthew. *Fairy in 'The Faerie Queene': Renaissance Elf-Fashioning and Elizabethan Myth-Making*. Aldershot: Ashgate, 2004.

Woolf, D. R. *The Idea of History in Early Stuart England: Erudition, Ideology and 'The Light of Truth' from the Accession of James I to the Civil War*. Toronto: University of Toronto Press, 1990.

Wormald, Jenny. 'O Brave New World? The Union of England and Scotland in 1603'. In *Anglo-Scottish Relations from 1603 to 1900*, edited by T. C. Smout, 13–35. Oxford: Oxford University Press, 2005.

Wright, William Aldis, ed. *Coriolanus*. By William Shakespeare. Oxford: Clarendon Press, 1884.

Yachnin, Paul. '"Courtiers of Beauteous Freedom": *Antony and Cleopatra* in Its Time'. *Renaissance and Reformation* 15, no. 1 (1991): 1–20.

Yates, Frances A. *Astraea: The Imperial Theme in the Sixteenth Century*. London: Routledge, 1975.

———. *Shakespeare's Last Plays: A New Approach*. London: Routledge, 1975.

Young, Alan R. 'The Phoenix Reborn: The Jacobean Appropriation of an Elizabethan Symbol'. In *Resurrecting Elizabeth I in Seventeenth-Century England*, edited by Elizabeth H. Hageman and Katherine Conway, 68–81. Madison, WI: Fairleigh Dickinson University Press, 2007.

Zeeveld, W. Gordon. '*Coriolanus* and Jacobean Politics'. *Modern Language Review* 57, no. 3 (1962): 321–34.

Ziegler, Georgianna. 'My Lady's Chamber: Female Space, Female Chastity in Shakespeare'. *Textual Practice* 4, no. 1 (1990): 73–100.

———. 'A Second Phoenix: The Rebirth of Elizabeth I in Elizabeth Stuart'. In *Resurrecting Elizabeth I in Seventeenth-Century England*, edited by Elizabeth H. Hageman and Katherine Conway, 111–31. Madison, WI: Fairleigh Dickinson University Press, 2007.

INDEX